THE
LAST GENERATION

Prophecy, Current World Events, and the End Times

JIM SIMMONS

FOCAL POINT
PUBLICATIONS

---∞∞∞---

THE LAST GENERATION

JIM SIMMONS

---∞∞∞---

SECOND EDITION
Copyright © 2009 by Jim Simmons

ISBN-13: 978-0-9841680-3-3
ISBN-10: 0-9841680-3-6
Published by THE LAURUS COMPANY
Printed in the United States of America

Laurus

THE LAURUS COMPANY
P. O. BOX 2071
LAKE DALLAS, TX 75065

IN
CONJUNCTION
WITH

FOCALPOINT
PUBLICATIONS

P. O. BOX 823
DENTON, TX 76202
www.FocalPointPublications.com

Acknowledgments

In gratitude to those who contributed to the creation of this book, I would first like to thank my wife, Joanne Shipley Simmons, who supported and encouraged me in my research and writing over the last two and a half years. She was patient with me as I spent most of my nights and weekends researching, writing, and revising my previous book, *The Last Hour.* The revisions and updates became so comprehensive that my work evolved into a new book. This involved a much greater amount of research and writing than originally anticipated.

I would also like to acknowledge and thank Wayne Francis, my good friend and brother in Christ, for the charts and diagrams used in this book. His skill and ability in this area were invaluable.

My gratitude extends to my Sunday evening "life group." This group sat under my teaching most Sunday evenings for a little over nine months as I taught the material in this book. It was originally intended to last four to five months, but ended up being literally crammed into a nine-month period of time. They provided lively discussion, feedback, questions, and challenges. There are not words to thank them. I would like to acknowledge the members of this group: my wife Joanne, Jeff and Judy Fairchild, Victor and Daima Cleaver, George and Denise Elliott, Jeff and Suzanne Koroly, Isaac and Ruby Sakyi-Addo, Debra Watson, Gary and Betty Steinmetz, and Cynthia Minter Odom.

Last, but not least, I would like to thank my editors. Rebecca Ensign with Gold Leaf Press not only helped me with the initial editing and proofing, but she also helped me communicate some of the complex areas in such a way that the reader could easily understand. This proved to be a difficult task at times. Nancy E. Williams with The Laurus Company completed the task with hours of editing and rewriting, as well as designing and completing the layout. Her contributions were invaluable.

It is my prayer that God will use this book in such a way that it glorifies Jesus Christ. In doing so, my heart's desire is that the reader will become aware of the reality of the nearness of His return, and thus spread the Word and the excitement of His return to many others.

Table of Contents

FIGURES

APPENDICES

Introduction

Following the terrorists' hijacking of two commercial airliners that were piloted into the Twin Towers of the World Trade Center in New York City on September 11, 2001, our world as we knew it literally changed overnight. A cloud of uncertainty and insecurity has become the pervasive theme of our times. The 9/11 tragedy occurred just a few months after the publishing of my previous book on prophecy, *The Last Hour*.

Listening to the media reports of the attacks that day, I realized that the Bible's prophetic time clock would be accelerated by the events that had occurred. It was the beginning of the final era of biblical prophecy fulfillment for the last days. I spent the next six years doing intensive research in preparation for this book. It was time to update, revise, and expand on the prophetic events discussed in *The Last Hour*.

My purpose in writing *The Last Generation* is to give the reader a macroscopic view and a heightened realization that the time is rapidly approaching for the Rapture, the Tribulation Period, and the Second Coming of Jesus Christ. Starting with the rebirth of Israel on May 14, 1948, prophecy is unfolding right before our eyes in this generation. Jesus made reference to the "last generation" that would see the signs that precede His Second Coming. He said, "… this generation will not pass away until all these things take place" (Matthew 24:32-34).

Although there are different interpretations as to the meaning and length of a biblical generation—forty years, seventy years, etc., for the most part, the differences would not significantly affect the final conclusion. Even if one generation equaled one hundred years—from 1948 to 2048—which is a real stretch, the end time events would be close at hand. I take the plain sense interpretation, which is the average of the number of years a generation of people lives. This is usually around seventy to eighty years. As this book is being prepared for printing in 2008, the last generation is at year sixty. The reader can do the math.

I am not attempting to set a date for Christ's return. As the Bible states in Matthew 24:36: "… of that day and hour no one knows …" Most of chapter 24 is an answer to the disciples' question in verse 3: "Tell us, when will these things happen, and what will be the sign of Your coming, and the end of the age?" Jesus gave the signs that would precede His return in the first thirty-five verses of Matthew 24. We are not looking at a day, an hour, or a year, but a generation—the last generation. The focus is on a season or general time frame for His return. Since the birth of Israel on May 14, 1948, the final pieces of the prophetic puzzle have been falling into place at an unprecedented pace. With a newspaper in one hand and a Bible in the other, it is easy to see God's Word being fulfilled as current events coincide with prophecies made over 2,500 years ago.

The reader will see how scientists; ancient cultures, such as the Mayans; and other religions are in agreement that the time of the end is near. If there is an area of disagreement, it is one of interpretation and meaning as to why the time of the end is near and what that means.

The basis and the origin of this book, *The Last Generation,* have their roots in *The Last Hour*. The difference is that *The Last Generation* goes beyond being an expanded and updated version of *The Last Hour*. It has become a second book in itself.

My hope and prayer is that, once the reader has completed this book, he or she will gain a greater awareness of God's reality, a greater respect for His Word, and a renewed relationship with Jesus Christ.

Some of the "countdown toward Armageddon" events and judgments covered in this book are frightening to many people, but as Christian believers, we have great anticipation as we look forward to meeting our Lord. If the reader is not a believer in Jesus Christ, there is still time to make that choice and move from fear into hope and joyful anticipation.

Chapter One

Generation X: The Last Generation?

For nearly two thousand years, since the time of the early New Testament Church, there have been Christian believers who thought Jesus would return in their lifetime. Since He did not return as they expected, many of them began to reinterpret and distort the Bible. There were others who ridiculed and mocked those believers. The Apostle Peter predicted that this scenario would characterize the last days. He said, "… in the last days mockers will come with their mocking, following their own lusts, and saying, 'Where is the promise of His coming? For ever since the fathers fell asleep, all continues just as it was from the beginning of creation' " (2 Peter 3:3-4).

In a PowerPoint presentation, author and speaker Thomas Ice quoted a profound statement by Sir Isaac Newton in the seventeenth century: "About the time of the End, a body of men will be raised up who will turn their attention to the prophecies and insist on a literal interpretation, in the midst of much clamor and opposition."

Many of the prophecies concerning the end times were not understood prior to the last forty years. Civilization, technology, science, and the Information Age had not developed enough to understand some of the prophecies. Even Daniel in the Old Testament could not understand the great prophecies he received. In Daniel 12:8-9, he said, "As for me, I heard but could not understand; so I said, 'My Lord, what will be the outcome of these events?' And he said, 'Go your way, Daniel, for these words are concealed and sealed up until the end time.' "

It is the author's belief that this Scripture applies to this generation—

1

the *last* generation. This is the "end time" that allows for the unsealing of Daniel's prophecies, which fit perfectly with John's prophecies in the book of Revelation. This book will present solid reasons to believe that Christ will return in this generation, which began in 1948 when Israel was established as a nation. If you were born since the beginning of 1948 and barring a fatal accident or illness, you will be alive when Christ returns.

The Second Coming of Christ will happen at the end of a seven-year Tribulation Period. This will be a time of a worldwide severe judgment on this planet, such as has never been experienced since the beginning of the world (Matthew 24:21).

The Bible tells us of two worldwide judgments. The first was the universal flood in the days of Noah. The second, or final, worldwide judgment is the coming Tribulation Period. Jesus said it would be the most severe judgment since the creation of the world. It will be a traumatic time and is described in detail in Chapter One of this book. In Matthew 24:34, "these things" refers to the Tribulation Period: "… this generation will not pass away until all *these things* take place" [emphasis added].

Prior to this seven-year tribulation, Jesus will return and remove His followers from the earth in what is commonly referred to as the "Rapture." This term comes from the Latin word *rapios*, which means, literally, to be "caught up" or "snatched away." The phrase "caught up" is found in 1 Thessalonians 4:17.[1]

The true believers in Jesus Christ who are alive at this point in time will escape death. The "dead in Christ" will rise first (bodily resurrection). "Then we [true believers in Christ] who are alive and remain will be caught up together with them in the clouds to meet the Lord in the air, and so we shall always be with the Lord" (1 Thessalonians 4:16-17 [brackets by the author]). The Rapture is explained in more detail in Chapter Seven.

In Matthew 24:3, Jesus' disciples asked him specifically about a time period. When Jesus spoke about the signs of His Second Coming, the disciples asked, "Tell us, when will these things happen, and what will be the sign of Your coming, and of the end of the age?" We read in verse 34 that the generation that sees the signs Jesus names in the previous 28 verses "will not pass away until all these things take place."

What length of time constitutes a generation? Some scholars say forty years, and others say it refers to a race of people. Neither of these explanations is plausible. The forty-year period has already passed since 1948. To interpret "generation" as a "race of people" would tell us nothing about a time or season.

According to *Random House Webster's College Dictionary*, the clear meaning of "generation" is "a life cycle of an entire body of individuals born or living about the same time." The reasonable lifetime of a human being, barring any fatal accidents or illnesses, is in the range of seventy-five to eighty-five years. Whatever the time span, subtract a minimum of seven years (could be more), and this is when the Rapture is likely to occur. Looking at the numbers, we are very close to the Rapture.

It is true that Jesus said no man knows the day or hour of His return. In the same breath, however, He was giving us clues as to the season, a general time frame, of that return. Why else would He take time to answer His disciples' question by giving the signs of His return?

When the signs of the Second Coming that are described in Matthew 24 have all taken place, Jesus said in verse 33, "… recognize that He is near, right at the door." If He is "right at the door" after the judgments of the Tribulation Period, how close is He in reference to the Rapture?

No one has to go through the Tribulation Period and experience a horrible worldwide judgment. It is a choice. God spared Noah and his family from a worldwide judgment. The same God will deliver His own from the next and the worst worldwide judgment that has ever been experienced by mankind.

MIRACULOUS REBIRTH OF A NATION

Israel is the only nation to be re-established after having been destroyed for nearly two thousand years. Israel had not existed as a sovereign nation since the Babylonian conquest in 606 B.C. In the time of Christ, Jerusalem existed, but under Roman rule. Israel was declared a sovereign nation in 1948.

The Old Testament predicted Israel's final destruction. A few of these predictions include:

- Palestinian cities will resemble waste (Leviticus 26:31, 33)
- Desolation will come over the sanctuaries (Leviticus 26:31)
- Desolation will come over the land (Leviticus 26:32, 33)
- Palestine will be inhabited by enemies (Leviticus 26:32)
- People of Israel will disperse (Leviticus 26:33)
- Jews will be persecuted (Leviticus 26:33)[2]

Jesus prophesied the final destruction of Jerusalem. In response to one of the disciple's comments about the temple, "And Jesus said to him, 'Do you see these great buildings? Not one stone will be left upon another which will not be torn down' " (Mark 13:2). These predictions of Israel's destruction in both the Old Testament and the Gospels were fulfilled when the Roman army under Titus destroyed Jerusalem in A.D. 70. At present, the nation of Israel is still in the "Times of the Gentiles." To understand this, we will review how Nebuchadnezzar's prophetic dream shows Israel in its historical context. This dream covers Israel under four world empires.

FOUR WORLD EMPIRES

The four world empires covered in the second chapter of Daniel include: the Babylonian Empire, the Medo-Persian Empire, the Greek Empire, and the Roman Empire. These four world empires span history from 606 B.C. to the Second Coming of Christ.

This great span of time is referred to in Scripture as the "Times of the Gentiles." Jesus refers to this time period in Luke 21:24, "… and they will fall by the edge of the sword, and will be led captive into all the nations; and Jerusalem will be trampled under foot by the Gentiles until the times of the Gentiles are fulfilled."

The final seven years of the "times and the seasons" for Israel coincide with the final seven years of the times of the Gentiles. The termination of the final seven years of judgment is identical for Jews and Gentiles, according to Daniel 9:24-27, 38.[3]

These four world empires are shown in Daniel Chapter 2. "Daniel saw an image of four successive world empires. In order, he saw Babylon fall to the Medo-Persian Empire, which fell to the Greek Empire, which fell to the Roman Empire. The prophet saw the destruction of each of the empires in detail, except Rome. From Daniel's perspective, Rome never ceases to exist, but is still in power on the day of the Lord."[4]

The continuity of Rome is especially important to the end times. Although the Roman Empire lost its authority, it never actually fell. The preceding three world empires fell, but not Rome. The Roman Empire lost its power and authority over the next two millennia, but remnants of its culture and authority have remained.[5]

The four world empires, referred to as the "Times of the Gentiles,"

CHART 1

TIMES OF THE GENTILES FOUR WORLD EMPIRES				
EMPIRE	BODY	METAL	ANIMAL	DATE
BABYLON (Dan. 2:48)	HEAD	GOLD	LION (Dan. 7:4)	626 B.C.
MEDO-PERSIA (Dan. 8:20)	CHEST & ARMS	SILVER	BEAR (Dan. 7:5) RAM (Dan.8:3-4,20)	539 B.C.
GREECE (Dan. 8:21)	BELLY & THIGHS (Trunk)	BRONZE	LEOPARD (Dan.7:6) MALE GOAT (Dan.8:5,21)	330 B.C.
ROME (Ancient)	LEGS	IRON	BEAST (Dan. 7:7)	63 B.C.
ROME (Revived-Extended) (Future)	10 TOES	IRON & CLAY	BEAST (Dan. 7:7)	FUTURE (Under 10 Kingdoms) (10 toes)

are represented by a great image in the dream of the Babylonian king, Nebuchadnezzar. Daniel interprets the king's dream by divine revelation. This great image, found in Daniel Chapter 2, has parallel symbolism in Daniel Chapters 7 and 8 with images of ferocious animals. "Nebuchadnezzar sees Gentile dominion as man sees it: the nations in all their glory. But in Daniel Seven we will see how God sees Gentile dominion: ferocious animals devouring one another."[6]

While the fourth empire, Rome, was not destroyed or overtaken, it will be destroyed in the future. Daniel 2:45 says, "Inasmuch as you saw that a stone was cut out of the mountain without hands and that it crushed the iron, the bronze, the clay, the silver and the gold, the great God has made known to the king what will take place in the future ..." This verse shows the destruction of all the world empires, including the ten kingdoms in the revived Roman Empire. Couple this with Daniel 7:12-14: "As for the rest of the beasts, their dominion was taken away, but an extension of life was granted to them for an appointed period of time. I kept looking in the night visions, and behold, with the clouds of heaven One like a Son of Man was coming, and He came up to the Ancient of Days and was presented before Him. And to Him was given dominion, glory and a kingdom ..."

Scripture confirms that the image in Daniel or the "Times of the Gentiles" has not run its course. History confirms this as well. Missler and Eastman give the following brief overview of the history of the Roman Empire.

Around A.D. 476, the Roman Empire broke up. Each of the pieces of the empire tried for global dominion without fully succeeding. The Dutch, French, German, Spanish, and English attempted it, but never really succeeded as the Romans did.

Daniel suggested these "pieces" (Roman Empire) would recombine in the final empire. Many Bible scholars are looking for an ultimate revival of the Roman Empire.[7] Some suggest that the current moves within the European Union may be setting the stage for the final government.[8]

The image in Daniel is a picture of future things. History confirms the accuracy of Daniel's predictions. The books of Daniel and Revelation compliment each other. Daniel can be viewed as the ABC of prophecy just as Revelation may be viewed as the XYZ of prophecy.[9]

ISRAEL: GOD'S TIME PIECE

The nation of Israel serves as a pivotal nation in understanding prophecy. As previously discussed, the Old Testament prophets predicted the takeover of Israel and its scattering among the nations. They also predicted the re-gathering of Israel. "For I will take you from the nations, gather you from all the lands and bring you into your own land" (Ezekiel 36:24). For over 2,500 years, Ezekiel's prophecy was not fulfilled.

On May 14, 1948, approximately 2,500 years after Babylon captured Jerusalem, this all changed. "The Americans immediately recognized the State of Israel. The Russians also recognized the new state, not wanting to risk losing a possible client state in the region. Reluctantly, the United Nations accepted Israel's Declaration of Independence in accordance with the 1947 UN Partition Plan."[10]

The birth of the nation of Israel was also prophesied in Ezekiel 37. "Thus says the Lord GOD to these bones, 'Behold, I will cause breath to enter you that you may come to life.' ... 'Son of man, these bones are the whole house of Israel ...' " (Ezekiel 37:5, 11).

The establishment of Israel as a nation is as monumental as "bones coming to life." The rebirth of the nation of Israel is an extremely important prophetic fulfillment of these verses in Ezekiel 37 and also in Ezekiel 36: 24. This begins the countdown to the final chapter in this present era (the Church Age). We turn now to Israel, symbolized by a fig tree.

PARABLE OF THE FIG TREE

Jesus was asked by His disciples in Matthew 24:3: "… when will these things happen, and what will be the sign of Your coming, and of the end of the age?" Jesus answered their questions by first listing the signs and then giving the events that would happen in the time preceding His Second Coming. He said: "Now learn the parable from the fig tree: when its branch has already become tender and puts forth its leaves, you know that summer is near" (Matthew 24:32). What does this verse mean, and what does the fig tree symbolize? Hal Lindsey explains it as follows.

> The fig tree is a symbol for Israel today in much the same way the eagle symbolizes America or the bear is a symbol for Russia. … The Bible does refer to a fig tree some 33 times—18 times in the Old Testament alone. In context, the fig tree is always a symbol for Israel. … Just as that is a sure sign the general time of summer has arrived, so, the argument goes, is the restoration of Israel to her land a sure sign the general time of Christ's return has arrived.[11]

This verse refers to a nation—Israel, symbolized by a fig tree; this assumes that Israel is in existence, which occurred in 1948. It also refers to a time—"… when its branch has already become tender and puts forth its leaves, you know that summer is near" (Matthew 24:32).

This time reference is narrowed further by the next verse, Matthew 24:33: "so, you too, when you see all these things, recognize that He is near, right at the door."

It is then narrowed still further: "Truly I say to you, *this generation* will not pass away until all these things take place" (Matthew 24:34 [italics added]). In this passage, the word "generation" immediately follows the term "fig tree," which symbolizes Israel.

Jesus said the leaves would symbolize:

- Religious deception and occult practices
- Hot wars and Cold wars (wars and rumors of wars)
- International revolution among nations
- Ethnic conflicts
- Famines
- Earthquakes

- Plagues
- Global weather pattern changes
- Record killer storms

Like the first leaves on the fig tree, they would all come at the same time. Like birth pangs, they would all increase in frequency and intensity.[12]

The generation alive at the time of the rebirth of Israel (1948) is the same generation that will be alive at the Second Coming of Christ. The number of years in a generation is not defined, but if you were born in or since 1948, you are in that generation. If you don't die of an accident or premature illness, you will be alive at the Second Coming of Christ.

SIGNS OF END TIMES

There are a number of end time signs that the Bible lists in different references. To understand what these signs mean, they have to be seen in their context as it relates to our current time. In addition to the signs previously mentioned, these include:

- False messiahs
- Persecution of Christians
- False prophets
- People's love grows cold
- Men faint from fear
- Powers of the heavens shaken
- Falling away from sound doctrine
- Increased lawlessness
- Terrors
- Signs in the heavens
- Betrayal by relatives and friends
- Signs in the sun, moon, and stars
- Dismay among nations
- Roaring of the seas
- Sun will be darkened and moon will not give its light
- Increased travel or mobility
- Increased knowledge
- Apostasy
- Occult

- Seared-over consciences
- Forbidding marriage
- Abstaining from foods
- Murder
- Sorcery
- Immorality
- Theft[13]

This list includes things that are specific to the Tribulation Period, whereas the other signs have appeared throughout history but increase in intensity and frequency as the Tribulation Period and Second Coming draw closer in time.

The temptation in the "last days" is to say that nothing has really changed and that all continues as it always has. The Bible predicts this line of thinking. "Know this first of all, that in the last days mockers will come with their mocking, following after their own lusts, and saying, 'Where is the promise of His coming? For ever since the fathers fell asleep, all continues just as it was from the beginning of creation'" (2 Peter 3:3-4).

Some distinct differences exist between the present time and 1,500 years ago, 500 years ago, or even 50 years ago. These distinct differences, especially over the last 20 years, and to a lesser extent between 20 to 50 years ago, will show us why we are surely in the "last days."

BIRTH PANGS

Wars, famines, plagues, and earthquakes have occurred for thousands of years. Why should we believe that these are signs of the Second Coming? What is different?

The Bible uses the term "birth pangs" in at least three passages: Matthew 24:8, Mark 13:8, and 1 Thessalonians 5:3. Jesus said:

"Many will come in My name saying, 'I am He!' and will mislead many. When you hear of wars and rumors of wars, do not be frightened; those things must take place; but that is not yet the end. For nation will rise up against nation, and kingdom against kingdom; there will be earthquakes in various places; there will also be famines. These things are merely the beginning of *birth pangs*." (Mark 13:6-8 [emphasis added])

Jesus compared the time sequence between His first and second coming to the gestation period a woman goes through before she gives birth. A closer look at the meaning of "birth pangs" is helpful to understanding Mark Chapter 13.

In the first trimester of pregnancy following the female's egg being fertilized, cell division begins to occur. Biological processes are occurring on a microscopic level in the early days following conception.

By the second trimester, the mother feels the first movement of the fetus. During this time period, the fetus is growing rapidly.

"Toward the middle of the last trimester (32-40 weeks of gestation), the mother starts to feel false labor pangs, called Braxton-Hicks contractions. However, 'the end is not yet ... All these are the beginnings of sorrows.' These false contractions are a warning sign that a birth is on the way, but a significant period of time is still left."[14]

When the mother begins to feel false labor pains, it is a sign that the actual birth is not far off. If she is wise, she will prepare in advance for the actual delivery.

Early birth pangs are similar to false labor pains. When true labor begins, the frequency and intensity of the contractions accelerate until the actual delivery.[15]

This analogy could be expanded by comparing the frequency and acceleration of the false labor pains to the years preceding the seven-year Tribulation Period. The Tribulation Period (70th week in Daniel), which lasts for seven years, will be a horrible time of judgment on the whole world. It is consummated by the Second Coming of our Lord Jesus Christ. There will be great joy for true believers in Jesus Christ as there is great joy for a mother when a child is born and her period of labor is completed. We turn now to the "signs" spoken of by Jesus.

EARTHQUAKES

Earthquakes have always been with us, but not as frequent or severe as they are currently. Over the last thirty years, earthquakes have been on a steady incline. (See the graph following.)

The graph measures earthquakes that are greater than 6.0 on the Richter scale. This is considered "significant" by the National Earthquake Information Center.[16]

As one of the signs that precede the return of Christ, earthquakes, by themselves, do not tell us much. However, when the number of major earthquakes (6.0+) increase steadily for three decades in a row (1975-2005), this is significant.[17] Prior to the 1970s, the increase in significant earthquakes had remained fairly constant with slight variations from decade to decade.

CHART 2

**Number of Significant Worldwide Earthquakes
Greater than 6.0 on the Richter Scale
[covers the past 30 years (in 10 year intervals)]**

Number of Earthquakes per Decade		Average Number of Earthquakes Annually	
1,800		180	
1,700		170	*167
1,600		160	159.6
1,500		150	
1,400		140	
1,300		130	129.5
1,200		120	
1,100		110	113.3
1,000		100	

1975-1985	1985-1995	1995-2005	2005-06 (1 Year)

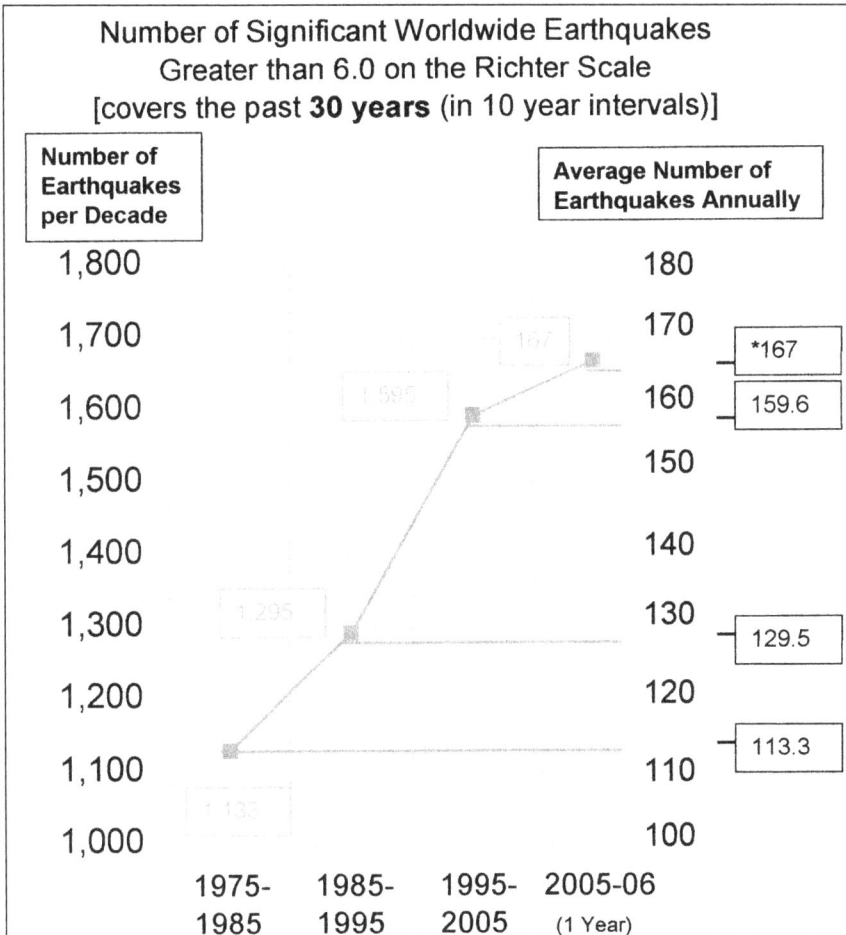

*Note continual progression of average annual earthquakes, with 2005-2006 being the highest

- Located by the US Geological Survey National Earthquake Information Center (NEIC)
- The magnitude range is from 6.0 (considered significant) to 9.9 (average of 1 or less per year)
- Catalog used: PDE [http://earthquake.usgs.gov/]

"Skeptics argue that the increase in the frequency of earthquakes is simply due to our improved ability to measure earthquakes worldwide. However, when this objection is carefully examined, it does not stand up. Since the 1960s the number of seismographs has been sufficient to detect any earthquake greater than 5.0 on the Richter scale worldwide."[18]

CLIMATE CHANGES

"There will be signs in sun and moon and stars, and on the earth dismay among nations, in perplexity at the roaring of the sea and the waves, men fainting from fear and the expectation of the things which are coming upon the world; for the powers of the heavens will be shaken. " (Luke 21:25-26). [In addition, see Matthew 24:7, 29; Daniel 12:4.]

We are going to touch on a few signs that are related to climate changes and cosmic events. Some can be backed up with data. One cannot be supported by data.

GLOBAL WARMING

Prior to 2007, global warming appeared to be indisputable. There was a sufficient amount of data to back up a coming global warming crisis. Since 2007, we have had a general cooling trend. This has not stopped certain politicians, like Al Gore, from staying on the global warming bandwagon. The scientific facts clearly show that we are not experiencing a global warming.

Dr. David Legates, with the Center for Climate Research at the University of Delaware stated: "Climate is not a constant. We go through periods where it is much warmer and much cooler, and periods where it is wetter and dryer. The sun is the key ingredient to climate. 99% of the energy on the earth that goes into the climate comes from the sun."[19] Over the last 2000-plus years the earth has experienced heating and cooling trends.

Dr. Willie Soon, astrophysicist at the Harvard-Smithsonian Center for Astrophysics, agreed with Legates research. He made the following statement: "The sun is the main driver and supplier of energy, and is the true external driver of the climate system."[20]

"Both scientists [Legates and Soon] emphasized global warming is a natural change, even though some politicians argue differently."[21]

According to Legates, some of the policy makers [politicians] will actually ask scientists to change their findings so they will match the findings of the policy makers. He also says that "many scientists actually amend their official documents for the legislators."[22] According to Soon, there is a clear scientific consensus on this issue.[23]

THE REAL CONCERN

The real concern isn't really global warming; it is solar activity, especially starting around 2011. The sun goes through eleven-year cycles. Currently [2009], we are on the minimal side of the cycle in regards to solar activity. The maximum side (at the beginning of a cycle) will begin in 2011, which may coincide with the Mayan 2012 calender.[24] This may account for the cooling trend since 2007. The prior years through 2006 were very hot. This is not currently the case.

The beginning of the next cycle in 2011 could disrupt many aspects of life that societies take for granted, i.e., communication and navigation systems (including GPS) and satellites (including weather) could be damaged beyond repair for many years. The consequences of a solar storm could affect commerce, transportation, agriculture, food stocks, water supplies, human health, national security, and life in general.[25]

There is a lack of media coverage given to solar storms. This is probably due to the fact that they are a less controversial subject than climate change [global warming] and yet they could bring greater consequences than climate change.[26]

The scientific data does not point to global warming from pollution. There is a better explanation for global warming than air pollution. Two Harvard researchers state: "… the sun is increasing in brightness and radiance. Changes in the sun can account for major climate changes on earth for the past 300 years, including part of the recent surge of global warming," claims Sallie Baliunas, an astronomer at the Harvard-Smithsonian Center for Astrophysics (CfA).[27]

BOTTOM LINE

Global warming appears to be cyclical. It is also influenced more by solar changes, i.e. sun spots, solar storms, and eleven-year cycles. Does pollution play a part? Does carbon dioxide play a part? It appears they do play a part, but the sun's activity and cycles play the major part. Consider the possibility of a correlation or connection between the year 2011, the beginning of the next solar cycle, and the Mayan year of 2012. This is given by the Mayan calendar as the end of the 5th cycle, or last cycle, of the Mayan calendar. They were advanced in their calendrick calculations. According to the Mayans, the year 2012 is the year of a catastrophic end of an age. Could this bear any connection to the end times, i.e., this being the last generation? In accordance with Luke 21:25-26, there will be signs in the sun, moon, and stars prior to the Lord's return. Maybe we should be more concerned about the signs in the sun than air pollution. It is the sun that has the power to cause catastrophic weather patterns as described in Luke 21:25-26. Global warming is not the issue. Solar activity and the signs of the end times are the real issues.

EARTHQUAKES

Since the 1970s, note the rise of earthquakes (Chart 2), the rise in violent crimes in the U.S. (Chart 3), and the increase in the growth of knowledge (Chart 8). The last thirty-five years have shown exponential increases in all of these areas.

POLE REVERSALS

Movement toward the end times is showing up in a number of different ways, including catastrophes and potential catastrophes. Added to other alarming signs, consider the potential of the movement of the earth toward a pole reversal. Over earth's history, there have been a number of magnetic pole reversals.[28]

The North Pole (True North) is not the same as the magnetic north (the direction the compass needle points). The magnetic north pole is situated in Canada, about 11 degrees from the True North Pole.[29]

S.K. Runcorn, a geologist at the University of Cambridge, published an article in *Scientific American* about the earth's magnetic field and its relation to the earth's rotation. He "appears to be envisaging a complete 180-degree flip of the poles ..."[30] A magnetic field reversal would have devastating consequences for all of civilization and life.

There is evidence that the earth's poles are already moving. The Magnetic North Pole moved ten feet from 1900 to 1960 (a rate of two-and-a-half inches a year). From 1900 to 1968 it had moved twenty feet. In other words, it moved ten feet from 1960-1968 (a rate of four inches a year). In other words, it took sixty years (1900-1960) to move ten feet. In a mere eight-year period of time (1960-1968), it moved ten more feet. If these observations are correct, we have a geometrical acceleration of the rate of motion.[31] Scientists expect the next reversal of the earth's magnetic poles to occur around A.D. 2030.[32]

If a pole reversal occurs during the last generation (this generation), could it possibly coincide with the Second Coming of Christ near the end of the Great Tribulation (last three-and-one-half years)? Would it possibly be the fulfillment of Luke 21:25-26? Jesus prophesied about the last days in the following passage. He stated in verse 25: "There will be signs in the sun and moon and stars, and on the earth dismay among nations, in perplexity at the roaring of the seas and waves."

WARS AND RUMORS OF WARS

Wars have existed since the beginning of mankind. There have been many wars, including two world wars. What is different today? The answer lies in *frequency* and *intensity*, like the analogy of the mother in labor. Now, we add a third difference, *potential*.

> The 20th century has been labeled by many the century of war and the bloodiest century of all history. At no time during this century has there been peace. At any one time in the 1990s, there have been as many as 70 wars and regional conflicts being waged around the world. In recent years, there have been more wars and devastation by wars, with several technologies now providing even greater opportunities for mass destruction.[33]

The frequency of wars has increased, as well as the intensity and the devastation that has resulted from these wars. When Jesus made this prophecy in Matthew 24:7, He indicated two groups that were in conflict. "For nation will rise against nation, and kingdom against kingdom ..." Hal Lindsey expounds on the interpretation of this verse.

> What is rendered "nation shall rise against nation" in context is generally adequate to convey the meaning intended. But a closer examination shows the Greek word translated "nation" is *ethnos*—the word from which we get

the word 'ethnic.' The word means 'a race, or tribe'—not an inconsistent definition for our modern understanding of ethnicity."[34]

Ethnic conflict is worldwide. We are continually bombarded by news of ethnic conflicts. Some examples of ethnic unrest include the former Yugoslavia, with the tension between Serbs, Muslims, and Croats. As a result of that conflict, we have the new term, "ethnic cleansing," in place of "genocide,"[35] which is more politically correct, as if relabeling something that is wrong will somehow make it okay.

There are problems relating to ethnicity in Pakistan, Bangladesh, Sri Lanka, India, Algeria, and France. At one point in 1995, it was reported that there were some 46 ethnic wars raging around the world."[36]

Riding on the heels of ethnicity is terrorism. When terrorism is combined with the nuclear potential that is present worldwide, we have an unpredictable monster on our hands. If one did not believe in God and His promises to those who put their faith in Jesus Christ, the reality of the world's status would be terrifying.

Concerning our present world status, Missler and Eastman make the following statement:

Currently, more than a dozen countries possess nuclear weapons, more than two dozen countries are building intercontinental ballistic missiles, and more than sixty countries have the technology to build a surface skimming cruise missile. And, they are all mad at each other. The cloud of imminent nuclear attack hangs over all foreign policy negotiations. The nightmare of a virtual wipe out of major civilizations remains only thirty minutes away. The unthinkable lurks behind every major strategic decision. The threat of nuclear terrorism is of great concern to the U.S. State Department. By smuggling a device just smaller than a footlocker into the United States, terrorists could demolish a city the size of Los Angeles.[37]

In the future, there will be a World War III, and the final battle will occur at Armageddon (Revelation 16:12-21). This will happen at the end of the Tribulation Period. Jesus will return before mankind completely destroys itself. This is the Second Coming of Christ (Revelation 19).

Billy Graham made the following statement concerning mankind's dilemma and man's solution.

Pope John Paul II has stated, "Our future on this planet, exposed as it is to nuclear annihilation, depends on one single factor: humanity must make a moral 'about-face.'" But the question that confronts us is, how can this happen? Technologically, man has far exceeded his moral ability to control the results of his technology. Man himself must be changed.[38]

Billy Graham goes on to say that the change is possible through a spiritual renewal. The Bible teaches that man must undergo a spiritual rebirth (John 3:3).

INCREASE IN IMMORALITY AND VIOLENCE

If you have been slowly desensitized by it, you may not have noticed it. Over the 40-year period from 1960 to 2000, the number of violent crimes committed in the U.S. increased per capita (per 100,000 inhabitants) from an average of 214.06 per year from 1960 to 1969 to an average of 672.8 per year from 1990-1999 (see Chart 3).[39] In the 30 years from 1965 to the mid-1990s, illegitimate births have increased by 419 percent. Divorce rates have tripled. The number of children living in single-parent homes has tripled. The teen suicide rate has increased 200 percent.[40]

The increase in immorality and violence is obvious. What was acceptable in our culture in the 1990s and early 2000s was not acceptable in the 1960s. Movies, television, and morality in general have declined drastically, while immorality and violence have snowballed from 1960 to 2005. The numbers tell us that there is a very real problem in our society. Things are not improving; they are deteriorating rapidly.

Over this forty-five year time span, from 1960 to 2005, there has been a considerable increase in violent crimes. The numbers, as seen in Chart 3, illustrate the rapid increase of violent crime in the U.S.

Each decade following 1960 to 1969 shows a definite increase in violent crime. The exception to this is the decline that began in the 1990s. This does not reflect an improvement in the moral fiber of the U.S. This decrease has more to do with population shifts and age groups. Consider the following explanation for this decline.

The crime rate (violent and nonviolent) in the latter part of the decade of the 1990s, decreased nationwide. "Nationally, the reasons given for the drop aren't too flattering to baby boomers. The nation's longest and steepest crime rise ... came as baby boomers reached the crime

CHART 3

VIOLENT CRIMES IN THE U.S.
1960 – 2005

Years	Total Number Over 10 Years	Average Annual Number Over 10 years	Rate per 100,000 Inhabitants Over 10 Years	Average Annual Number per 100,000 Inhabitants Over 10 Years
1970-1979 (10 years)	4,134,930	413,493	2,140.6	214.06
1970-1979 (10 years)	9,607,930	960,793	4,517.2	451.72
1980-1989 (10 years)	14,073,292	1,407,329.2	5,940.01	594.01
1990-1999 (10 years)	17,531,214	1,753,121.4	6,728.9	672.89

Years	Total Number Over 6 Years	Average Annual Number Over 6 years	Rate per 100,000 Inhabitants Over 6 Years	Average Annual Number per 100,000 Inhabitants Over 6 Years
2000-2005* (6 years)	8,423,102	842,310.2	2,913.6	485.6

Crime in the U.S. 2005   PROVIDED BY THE DEPARTMENT OF JUSTICE - FEDERAL BUREAU OF INVESTIGATION

Note the following points:

- 2004-2005 Rate of Crime increased by 1.3%. The actual number of violent crimes increased by 2.3%
- All Violent Crime Rates increased in 2005 with the exception of the rate for "forcible rape."
- The murder rate was 5.6 offenses per 100,000 inhabitants, a 2.4% increase over 2004.

*Note that all these numbers are based on 6 years, not 10 years.

Also, the murders and non-negligent manslaughters that occurred as a result of September 11, 2001, are not included in this table.[41]

prone ages of fifteen to twenty-five. The rate began to decline several years ago as people born right after World War II grew older and wiser" (*Denton Record Chronicle*, May 28, 2000, p. 1A).

There are a number of possible reasons for this reduction in the crime rate. One is a shift in population and the crime prone years. It would be erroneous to conclude that this reported drop in crime is a result of an increase in morality and godliness.

We live in an immoral and violent time, but this is only the beginning of "birth-pangs." Immorality and violence will peak during the Tribulation Period (Revelation 9:21). On the average, crime continued to rise world-wide in the 1990s, as it had in the 1980s. Violent crimes account for around 10 to 15 percent of all reported crimes. Countries reporting crime statistics to the "United Nations Survey of Crime Trends" and "Operations of Criminal Justice Systems" have been able to adapt their definitions of traditional crime categories to fit the United Nations definitions.

In all countries, police-recorded crime figures give an incomplete figure of crime experienced by the population. For example, Arab countries generally report very low crime rates for all types of crime, regardless of actual rates.[42] In other words, violent crime figures have increased worldwide despite the under-reporting by some countries. The increase in violent crime is found worldwide, as well as in the U.S.

In one generation, we have undergone a cultural deterioration. "We have gone from 'Ozzie and Harriet' to Ozzie Osborne, from 'Donna Reed' and 'Leave it to Beaver' to Marilyn Manson in one generation."[43]

Several years ago, Billy Graham said, "If God doesn't judge America soon, He would have to apologize to Sodom and Gomorrah."[44] Immorality is on the increase worldwide, not just in America.

PERSECUTION OF CHRISTIANS

To the average American, the persecution of Christians may seem like a thing of the past, perhaps occurring only in early Christianity or in the Middle Ages. This is just not the case. There is worldwide persecution of Christians happening now. This is another one of the signs preceding the return of the Lord (Matthew 24:9).

Christians are already the most persecuted religious group in the world today, according to the international human rights group Freedom House.

Eleven countries now practice systematic persecution of Christians, says Nina Shea, author of *In the Lion's Den*. ... These eleven nations — and others that practice a more random brand of persecution — are dominated by one of two belief systems, communism or militant Islam.[45]

There are many examples of Christian persecution worldwide. International Christian Concern cites the following two examples of this.

1) There were two Christians who were arrested in Pakistan in 1998 on charges of blasphemy. The blasphemy involved an attempt to buy ice cream from a Muslim ice cream vendor. A report was filed by the vendor that slanderous remarks were made against Mohammed and Islam. According to Pakistan's Penal Code, if convicted they face mandatory execution.[46]

2) A thirteen-year-old daughter of a Christian Egyptian family was raped and kidnapped in March 1998 and forced by a terrorist group to convert to Islam. Later, the girl was released, but when she returned home, her family was attacked by the terrorists and were murdered by crushing their heads with stones and slitting open their bellies.[47]

Most Christians in America are not aware of the plight of our brothers and sisters in other countries. People who have studied Christian persecution over the ages tell us that a larger number of Christians have been martyred in the twentieth century than the combined total of the past nineteen centuries.[48]

FUTURE PREDICTIONS FROM A HUMAN PERSPECTIVE

This chapter has reviewed biblical prophecies and several signs that precede the Second Coming of Christ. These signs have included:

- The uniqueness of Israel and the re-establishment of the nation of Israel
- Numerous signs of the end times
- A review of the history and current status of earthquakes
- Weather changes
- Wars and rumors of wars

- Increase in immorality and violence
- Persecution of Christians

Our focus has been on the geometric increase in both number and intensity. The re-establishment of Israel is a hallmark of the times, especially when considered in light of the other signs.

"Ironically, it is not just Bible prophecy students who see the world moving toward a climax. Lots of others agree — from Indian Shamans to secular scientists."[49] Any astute person who honestly looks at human history and the current state of our world would be hard pressed to be optimistic about the future of mankind.

There are already enough nuclear-tipped missiles on standby and ready to launch to destroy civilization. "Dr. W. H. Pickering of Cal Tech confirmed this when he warned, 'in half an hour the East and West could destroy civilization.'"[50]

"In fact, if the Book of Revelation had never been written, some astute twentieth-century person might well predict these very catastrophes within this generation. And, of course, many who don't believe the Book of Revelation, or who are unfamiliar with it, are doing just that."[51]

We live in a high-tech society with the nuclear capacity to destroy mankind. The world is a powder keg. If you ignore what the Bible says, if you are an atheist and, therefore, do not believe in the validity of prophetic fulfillment, the outlook for mankind is dismal.

"In the computer age, the most likely way for the world to be destroyed, most experts agree, is by accident. That's where we come in; we're the computer professionals. We cause accidents."[52]

A computer accident that destroys the world is a very real possibility. With the existence of an arsenal of nuclear weapons, the increase in terrorist activities, and the moral decline of mankind, the possibility of a computer accident brings us to the edge of Armageddon.

Dr. George Wald, Nobel Prize-winning scientist, Harvard University, made the following statement: "I think human life is threatened as never before in the history of this planet. Not just by one peril, but by many perils that are all working together and coming to a head at about the same time ... I am one of the scientists who finds it hard to see how the human race is to bring itself much past the year 2000."[53]

Since 9/11 the outlook for our civilization, and our planet, has become extremely precarious. Oceans had protected the U.S. mainland from foreign invaders from 1865 to September 11, 2001 (9/11). "We were granted protection from nuclear war and atomic accident after 1945, and the peaceful collapse of our main enemy in the Cold War."[54]

After 9/11 the enemy moved inside our borders. Our enemy doesn't wear a uniform or combat boots. He could be a college professor, a flight instructor, or even our next-door neighbor. There is no foolproof way to identify a terrorist outside of a system of complete control, and that is currently in the process of developing (see Chapter Eight for further discussion).

Following World War II, a group of physicists founded the *Bulletin of the Atomic Scientists*. The logo on the cover of each issue is a clock, similar to the clock on the cover of this book. The proximity of the hands relative to midnight indicates how precarious the world situation is, or is thought to be by the *Bulletin's* editorial board. Every few years the minute hand is shifted, either forward or backward. These adjustments stretch from 1947 to the present day. It tracks the crisis level in international relations.[55] "In the early 1990s, the *Bulletin's* clock was put back to seventeen minutes to midnight. But it has been creeping forward again since then; in 2002 it was seven minutes to midnight."[56] The Doomsday Clock may not be a perfect metaphor, but it does give you an idea of our current nuclear risk according to a group of scientists.

The Doomsday Clock only reflects "the level of threat posed by nuclear weapons and other changing factors in international security."[57] The clock, as of June 27, 2005, stood at seven minutes before midnight.[58] The Doomsday Clock, as of January 17, 2007, has moved two minutes closer to midnight. It is now set at five minutes to midnight. (See the website: http://en.wikipedia.org/wiki/Doomsday_Clock) The most current setting moved two minutes due to the most immediate hazard we face, namely the thousands of nuclear armed weapons aimed at Russia and the U.S. "Growing concerns of a 'second nuclear age' marked by grave threats, including ambitions in Iran and North Korea, unsecured nuclear materials in Russia and elsewhere, the continuing launch-ready status of 2,000 of the 25,000 nuclear weapons held by the U.S. and Russia, escalating terrorism and new pressure from climate change for expanded civilian nuclear power that could increase proliferation risks." ["Doomsday Clock Reset," *Common Dreams Headlines*, January 17, 2007, accessed at the website: www.commondreams.org/headlines07/0117-06.htm]

If all of the worldwide risks were factored in, one wonders how much closer to midnight we really are. Midnight would represent Armageddon (the final all-out world war), which the Bible tells us will happen in the latter part of the Tribulation Period.

In conclusion, we must look at Bible prophecy next to current events. If we view the world from God's perspective and the human perspective, the evidence points to this generation as the last generation.

This chapter reviewed Israel's place in history in relation to the four world empires and its rebirth as a nation. The "parable of the fig tree" was interpreted in light of the "last generation." The signs preceding the Second Coming of Christ were covered as viewed from a progressive or exponential standpoint.

This chapter outlines reasons to believe that we are currently living in the last generation. The establishment of the nation of Israel is a pivotal point in history as it relates to biblical prophecy. This hallmark in history, combined with signs of the end times and the future predictions of scientists, presents a strong case that the time of Christ's return is near. According to Matthew 24:33, "… He is near, right at the door."

This brings us to our next chapter, which presents worldviews from man's perspective and from God's perspective. The purpose of the next chapter is to help the reader realize the importance of a reference point, a standard, for developing a worldview. Another way of stating it: When climbing the ladder of success, it is crucial to determine that your ladder is leaning against the right building. If not, you would be engaged in an exercise of futility, which could have devastating consequences for yourself and possibly other people, as we will show. We will look at some ways famous people have determined a false reference point (or anchor) and what the consequences were.

NOTES:

Chapter Two

Worldviews from a
Human and Divine Perspective

T he last generation began in 1948, the year Israel was re-established as a nation. The previous chapter focused on this and the end time signs that would occur during the time of this final generation.

The current chapter focuses on worldviews primarily from a human perspective and how that contrasts with God's perspective. A man's belief system is extremely potent. We will see how the human mind is a battle-field in the supernatural realm.

The purpose of this chapter is threefold. The first is to help the reader understand the importance of establishing a point of reference, or standard, that is an objective, absolute truth, with an ultimate goal of enabling the reader to clearly recognize what comes from God and what comes from Satan, the "father of lies" (John 8:44). The second purpose is to help the reader realize the importance of one's belief system. The final purpose is to show how our changing worldviews have prophetic significance.

TRUTH OR LIES

Time magazine interviewed a terrorist suicide bomber in training. The following are a few of the statements made by Marwan Abu Ubeida (a pseudonym): "First, I will ask Allah to bless my mission with a high rate of casualties among the Americans. ... The most important thing is that

he (Allah) should let me kill many Americans. ... I admit I am a terrorist. [The *Koran*] says it is the duty of Muslims to bring terror to the
enemy, so being a terrorist makes me a good Muslim. ... The only person
who matters is Allah, and the only question he will ask me is 'How many
infidels did you kill?' "[1] *Infidels*, according to Muslims, are defined as
"people who are not Muslims, especially Jews and Christians."

In the same month as the preceding *Time* magazine article, *The
Dallas Morning News* reported the explosions of terrorist's bombs in
London on July 7, 2005. It stated:

> Four bombs exploded in the heart of London on Thursday morning, killing
> at least 37 people, injuring up to 700, and stranding millions when the city's
> vast rail, subway, and bus transportation ground to a halt. Authorities call it
> the deadliest terrorist attack in Britain's history.[2]

A couple of days later the death toll had climbed to fifty. The innocent people who died would be considered infidels. Are a person's beliefs
really important? The bombings speak for themselves.

The suicide bomber who was interviewed is one of many who believe
this way. The consequences of this false belief system have resulted in the
loss of many innocent lives. This man's ladder of success is leaning against
the wrong tower (a lie). He believes that, following his suicide mission,
Allah will be waiting for him at the top with open arms. Once he blows himself up, taking innocent lives with him, the mask of Allah will be removed,
and he will find himself facing Satan, who previously had been disguised as
Allah. "... Satan disguises himself as an angel of light" (2 Corinthians
11:14). We are told that "... the god of this world [Satan] has blinded the
minds of the unbelieving ..." (2 Corinthians 4:4 [brackets by author]).

A world-famous question over the last two thousand years is, "What
is truth?" In the sentencing of Jesus under Pilate, Jesus said, "... Every
one who is of the truth hears my voice" (John 18:37). In response, Pilate
said, "What is truth?" (John 18:38). It is popular to talk about reality as
if it varies among individuals. A common phrase often heard is, "That
may be your reality, but it's not mine." What does this mean?

We know there is a *subjective* reality, which is unique to the individual. This is the way he sees the world as determined by his upbringing,
the environment, and his individual genetic makeup.

What we are looking for is an *objective* reality, one that stands apart from human nature and personal experiences. There is a Truth that stands apart from personal experience, genetic makeup, and personality. It is eternal, unchanging, absolute, and is not dependent on circumstances or opinions.

The issue is between absolute truth as opposed to relativism. An unchanging point of reference is an absolute by which all other beliefs are measured. This is in contrast to relativism, which is only another word for anarchy. Without a point of reference, truth itself becomes elusive.[3]

Not long ago a survey was made among Canadian young people. The majority acknowledged that what they longed for most was to find someone they could believe in.[4] This reflects a person's need to find a truth to believe, as reflected in a person, "someone to believe in." Jesus fits that need.

According to the Scriptures, the enemy of our souls is Satan, the father of all lies. "He will do anything to keep us from coming to the truth because it is the most valuable thing in the world and leads us to the source of all truth, to God Himself."[5] **The only way truth can exist is through the existence of an objective standard. That unchanging, objective, and absolute standard is God.**[6]

LOOKING FOR TRUTH IN ALL THE WRONG PLACES

Just like the well-known country and western song that began, "Looking for love in all the wrong places," man has searched for truth literally in all the wrong places. The following sections will give a general overview of how and where man has searched.

MIND BENDERS

Great thinkers and philosophers have shaped man's thinking. As a result, mankind is conditioned by the thoughts and ideas of influential people of the past who thought in terms contrary to biblical principles.

Oftentimes, thought patterns and ideas contrary to God's Word are very subtle. In most cases, the deception is woven in with the truth.

To understand mankind's hostility toward God today, we must understand different worldviews and how they have changed over time. Philosophers have shaped our worldviews dramatically, especially over the last 300 years. Erasing God from the picture didn't happen overnight. It happened in stages.

Prior to the 1700s, there was a classical philosophy that was based on cause/effect and logic. According to classical philosophy, values were absolute.[7]

This shift in worldviews was, in reality, a shift in points of reference. This shift is a movement from an objective standard, which is absolute and separate from one's personality and experience, to a self-reference point, or personal reality. Instead of dependence on God as the reference point, the focus is now on man as his own god. Another term for this is *humanism*.

CHART 4

Three-Century Slide Toward Relativism and Beyond[8]

FIVE STAGES OF DEVELOPMENT OF MEGA IDEAS		MAJOR THINKERS AND WRITERS
1.	Western man declares Autonomy and emancipates himself from revelation and God.	1651-1859	T. Hobbs, Voltaire, T. Paine, J. Rousseau, Kant, Hegel, Emerson
2.	Man declares himself to be an evolving progressing mind. Naturalism reigns supreme.	1859-1900	Darwin, Huxley, K. Marx, F. Engels, Nietzsche
3.	God is dead. Science will save us. Reason is cut loose from God.	1900-1946	Freud, Adler, B. Russell, Jung, J. Dewey, A. Maslow, F. Pearls
4.	Man asserts all truth and morals are relative and meaningless. Intuition is cut loose from God.	1947-1999	Existentialists (Heidegger J.P. Sartre, A. Camus), B.F. Skinner, R. Dawkins, F. Crick.
5.	Relativism is almost complete. New Age optimism and anti-rationalism, and postmodern globalism.	2000-last days	Humanistic psychologists Carl Rogers, Ram Dass, Eastern gurus, T. Merton, M. Fox, World Council of Churches, The Jesus Seminar, Process Theologians

Chart 4 on the previous page is an extremely condensed form of a downhill movement away from God, the objective absolute standard. This downhill decline in worldviews (belief systems) underlies the decline in morality, which is indicative of the last days. Paul states, "... in the last days difficult times will come. For men will be lovers of self, lovers of money, boastful, arrogant ... disobedient to parents ... unholy, unloving ... without self-control ... lovers of pleasure rather than lovers of God ..." (2 Timothy 3:1-4).

"If we accept the history of our evolution, then one fact stands out clearly: Namely, that we have arisen essentially as primate predators."[9] Man, according to Darwin, evolved and was not created.

"Hegel introduced the philosophical basis for man to see no necessity for a Creator God to whom man was responsible. The impact of this thought bomb is that, since man had no special beginning, he has no special purpose or destiny. This thinking leads many to sink into amoral behavior, disorientation, and despair."[10]

LINE OF DESPAIR

Once man's changing worldview had crossed this line of despair (see Chart 5: *Changing World View*), the downhill slide accelerated. Prior to the three-century chart, before 1651, man's reference point was an external absolute moral law or standard. This reference point was God and His truth as recorded in His Word, the Bible. This reference point was moved in the seventeenth and eighteenth centuries from God (external, absolute) to man (internal moral law) with experience being man's ultimate guide, as illustrated by Kant.

When this movement was made, the door was open to relativism, with no moral law and no absolutes, as illustrated by Hegel. It was at this point in time that mankind's worldview shifted from hope and purpose to despair and meaninglessness. It was a critical time in history. Relativism was gaining supremacy in man's thinking. Once man had been influenced away from God, Satan became more prominent on the world stage. The prophetic puzzle began rapidly to fall into place.

As a result of this reference point shift from God to man, a Pandora's box was opened on worldviews. For example, the Utopian View grew out of the Enlightenment. This is the view that humans are intrinsically good and, under the right social conditions, their good nature will emerge.

Western intellectuals rejected biblical creation and chose to believe the theory that nature is our creator and the human race arose out of primordial slime to the apex of evolution.[11] The logical conclusion of this view is that we are the product of our environment. Ignorance, poverty, or bad social conditions have created our problems. The solution for an ideal society is to create a better environment. "Given the right conditions, human perfectibility has no limits."[12]

According to this worldview, the reasons we have crime include: poverty, racism, or a dysfunctional childhood. The only explanation never offered is "sin." It is sin that unleashes the capacity for raw evil. It is sin that blinds us to anything beyond our own selfish desires.[13] Which worldview—Christian or Utopian—meets the test of reality? The enlightened worldview has proven irrational and unbelievable.[14] (This is further discussed later in this chapter under "Man's Nature: An Understanding of the Problem.")

Another result of this perceptual shift occurs after the line of despair is crossed. This is the Doctrine of Meaninglessness, which was expressed through the philosophical movement of Existentialism, especially in the twentieth century. From 1947 to 1999, some of the major thinkers who expressed this doctrine included: Heidegger, Sartre, B.F. Skinner, and Camus, to name a few. The teachings of some of these great philosophers and thinkers have influenced society toward meaninglessness and despair. Kierkegaard, an existentialist, "foresaw the basis of our nihilistic thinking over a century ago. ... Kierkegaard himself saw the route out of this terrifying despair within the pages of the Gospels. He saw Christ as providing the only hope in the world."[15]

When the reality of good and evil is disbelieved, the options left are: a hopeless and meaningless world, defiant hedonism, or a new kind of mysticism enters the picture. The end result of these options is an open door to the pursuit of evil.[16] This is diametrically opposed to the Gospels. Jesus said in John 10:10, "I came that they may have life, and have it abundantly." In other words, a life full of meaning and purpose.

The final mega idea over the last three centuries is Relativism. The battleground is centered in the mind. Ephesians 6:12 states: "For our struggle is not against flesh and blood, but against the rulers, against the powers, against the world forces of this darkness, against the spiritual forces of wickedness in the heavenly places." Relativism takes on different forms. One of those forms is language. Tal Brooke, author of *One*

World, states: "When the language of value relativism replaces clear statements about good and evil, it becomes that much harder to back out of the trap. Good is mocked at, and people become trapped."[16] The relativism of values deletes absolute truths and renders moralities impotent.

The farther society moves from an absolute standard of truth, the more relative everything becomes. If everything is considered relative, each person must find his own meaning "by looking within himself or hearkening to 'channeled' messages."[17]

The slide to relativism is the result of attempts by philosophers to arrive at a certainty about what the mind can know. These attempts can be compared to a chess game. "One can imagine what it would be like to play chess with an immortal being whose I.Q. is half a million, who has been around for millennia (like Satan). The best human player would be trapped in no time, perhaps wondering what their own names were!"[18]

NEW THEOLOGY / NEW WORLD / NEW AGE

There was an incredible bridge of consciousness that was built between the straight society of the 1950s, with its decency and traditional values, to the psychedelic, explosive era of the 1960s, with no limits. This paradigm shift takes us toward the New World and the New Age.[19] Spirituality and theology in this day and time have little in common with the era of the 1950s.

According to pollster George Barna, spirituality is on the increase. It is not, however, leading toward a Christian nation but "a syncretistic, spiritually diverse society."[20] Religion is being perceived in a new way, as "a personalized, customized form of faith views which meet personal needs, minimize rules and absolutes, and ... bear little resemblance to the 'pure' form of any of the world's religions."[21]

Many U.S. seminaries (not all) are producing theologians who are so removed from the fundamentals of the faith that one would be hard pressed to see a connection between what the Bible says—the true reference point—and what they believe and preach. These are theologians of a New Paradigm. In lay terms, one might wonder what planet they came from. Scholars now say, "We are in an era of unprecedented 'paradigm shifts.' In other words, people's models of the world, or mental frameworks, are changing drastically."[22]

The decline in Christianity is unprecedented. Western civilization

today is predominantly pagan. Seventy-five years ago, "despite inconsistencies, it was still predominantly Christian."[23] One of the ways
liberalism attacks orthodox (biblical) Christianity is through negating
the miracles of the Bible and attacking its inspiration. For example,
Bishop Spong, an Episcopalian minister and author of *Why Christianity
Must Die*, states: "We must stop reasserting those words of antiquity." He
claims that we need to, instead, "refashion the symbols by which
Christianity is to be understood in our time."[24] Spong systematically
reinterprets, or spiritualizes, biblical Christianity. This includes doing
away with the literal interpretations of God, worship, Easter, Christmas,
the virgin birth, the resurrection, the deity of Christ, the great commission, confession, and forgiveness.[25]

Spong spiritualizes each of the above doctrines. One wonders where
these new interpretations originated. On what authority are the new interpretations based? The answer is clear. He is his own authority. After all, we
are all "God-bearers" or a "life force." What standard is used to validate his
interpretation? If the standard is "self," why is his interpretation more valid
than someone else's interpretation who uses "self" as the standard?

The Christian church, at least in the Western world, has become so
anemic that it has laid itself open to pagan and pantheistic heresies.[26] Sin
and evil are often very subtle. "Evil does not come only in the garb of a
masked murderer. In its most cunning and destructive form, it comes as
an idea dressed in sophisticated attire, rationalized by these prophets of
the wind."[27]

Western civilization, in a religious sense and despite inconsistencies,
presents us with a real paradox. On one hand, many of the "Christian"
seminaries are producing ministers who are denying the supernatural
events of the Bible, i.e., the virgin birth, the resurrection, miraculous
healings, etc. On the other hand, our society, especially the younger
generation, is more open to the supernatural, i.e., psychic experiences,
telepathy, channeling, psychic surgery, and movies about the supernatural (excluding Christian movies, with rare exceptions).

There is a movement toward spirituality and the supernatural, as
long as it doesn't include true Christianity and the God of the Bible. This
movement is laying the groundwork for the end times. The Antichrist
and the False prophet will exhibit supernatural power during the seven-
year Tribulation Period. Revelation 13:2-4 states: "… And the dragon
[Satan] gave him [the Antichrist] his power and his throne and great

authority. … And the whole earth was amazed and followed after the beast [Antichrist]; and they worshiped the dragon [Satan] because he gave his authority to the beast …" [brackets by author].

CHANGING WORLD VIEW

This shift or evolving worldview is one of despair starting with Hegel. Once we have disconnected from absolutes, we have disconnected from God, our Creator. We have lost our reference point. Francis Schaeffer, well-known Christian author, states the following: "Finite man in the external universe, being finite, has no sufficient reference point if he begins absolutely and autonomous from himself and thus needs certain knowledge. God gives us this in the Scriptures. With this in mind, the scientist can understand, in their ultimate relationships, the truths that he is looking at."[28]

MAN'S NATURE: AN UNDERSTANDING OF THE PROBLEM

In order to find a solution to a problem, it is essential to identify the problem accurately. We have touched on a few philosophical views of our world. This approach to man's nature has originated from a human standpoint and not a divine one.

The development of psychological theories originated from one or more philosophical schools of thoughts, primarily in the nineteenth century. This search for truth using man as the reference point has proven futile.

Man was created completely free, with moral choices. Once he sinned, the whole creation fell. Human nature became morally distorted, and we inherited a natural inclination to do wrong. This is known as "original sin."[29] We are born to rebel. People do not like this concept and find it unpalatable. Modern thinkers have dismissed the idea of sin as repressive and unenlightened. This is why it is essential to have a true reference point, and that can only be God's Word.

According to the Bible, man is born with a sinful nature. Psalm 51:5 says, "Behold, I was brought forth in iniquity, and in sin my mother conceived me." Carl Rogers, a twentieth-century existentialist and humanist, believed, and taught, that man is innately good, and that if all goes well in man's life, his potential and his "real self" will be actualized. According

CHART 5

Changing World View
Philosophy

Classical Philosophy
(Absolutes, cause and effect)

↓

Kant
(Trust in experience based on
obedience to moral law within)

↓

*Line of Despair _____ **Hegel**
(No absolutes,
no morals, only relativity)

↓

Kierkegaard
(No reasoning, irrationality, existentialism)

↙   ↘

Secular Existentialism   **Christian Existentialism**
(no purpose, no meaning)   (leap of faith, not rational)

*Chart based on information from Francis Schaeffer, *The God Who Is There* (Downers Grove, Ill.: InterVarsity Press, 1968) p. 21

to Doctors Minirth and Meier, well-known Christian psychiatrists and authors, man is not basically good, as Carl Rogers believed. The Bible claims that no human is sinless and that man can never satisfy God by attempting to establish his own righteousness (Romans 7:14-25; 10:1-4).[30]

If our worldview originates from the premise that man has a sinful nature, we then have a point of reference—God's truth—on which to build. Building a school of thought, whether it is in the area of philosophy, psychology, or science, has a better chance of staying on track when the reference point is divine rather than human.

According to the French philosopher Blaise Pascal (1623-1662), every man has a "God-shaped vacuum" inside. People innately search for meaning in their life. "According to logotherapy, the striving to find a meaning in one's life is the primary motivational force in man. That is why I speak of a will to meaning in contrast to the pleasure principle (or, as we could also term it, the will to pleasure)."[31]

In psychotherapy, man needs to be understood in three dimensions: body, soul, and spirit. It is of vital importance to understand man in a holistic way. He is a physical, psychological, and spiritual being. All three of these dimensions are interrelated.[32] The problem with some of the schools of psychology is that they address the physical and the psychological but ignore the spiritual side. Psychological counseling is beginning to add the spiritual dimension. "Spiritual" does not necessarily mean the God of the Bible or, for that matter, even a "higher power."

When psychotherapy fails to address the spiritual side of man, the therapy process becomes less effective. Finding meaning in life gives hope to the individual. According to Viktor Frankl, the psychiatrist who developed "logotherapy," "*Logos* is a Greek word that denotes *meaning*!"[33] From a biblical-Christian viewpoint we could apply this to John 1:1 and 1:14: "In the beginning was the Word [meaning], and the Word [meaning] was with God, and the Word [meaning] was God ... And the Word [meaning] became flesh, and dwelt among us ..." [brackets by author].

We now have two reference points. First, understanding the basic nature of man as sinful. This means that man is flawed, and it is irrational to use himself as a reference point in understanding the meaning of life. Second, through Jesus Christ we have meaning and purpose in life. Apart from Jesus Christ we are lost. Jesus said, "... I am the way, and the truth, and the life; no one comes to the Father but through Me" (John 14:6).

TWO KINGDOMS / TWO FOUNDATIONS

We have discussed man's thinking process as expressed through philosophers, psychologists, and scientists. The reason for this extended discussion on man's worldview is to understand where it originates.

"In eternity past, there was only one will, God's will. There was no evil whatsoever, only harmony, holiness, and righteousness. When the second will entered the universe, generated by the heart of Lucifer, rebellion broke out. Time, as we know it, began with two wills in existence."[34]

Lucifer, otherwise known as Satan, is an extremely powerful force in rebellion against God. He has also led man into rebellion, starting with Adam and Eve. **One of Satan's strategies is to influence the mind.** When he controls a man's thought process and worldview, he is gaining control of the person's mind and the lives he influences. Satan's aim is to control man's thoughts, promote a lie, and oppose God's truth. Once a person's thoughts are controlled, Satan can control that person's behavior.[35] A few biblical examples of Satan putting thoughts into a person's mind include: David (1 Chronicles 21:1); Judas (John 13:2); and Ananias (Acts 5:3).

Satan deceives each individual to believe that all of his thoughts are his own. In many cases the unbeliever, or non-Christian, does not believe in Satan. He therefore believes he is the originator of his own thoughts, as in the examples of the previously mentioned philosophers. For believers in Jesus Christ, the Bible sheds light on our struggles that appear to be human conflict. "For our struggle is not against flesh and blood, but against the rulers, against the powers, against the world forces of this darkness, against the spiritual forces of wickedness in the heavenly places" (Ephesians 6:12).

Satan works undercover and is a liar. In reference to Satan, Jesus said, "… He was a murderer from the beginning, and does not stand in the truth because there is no truth in him. Whenever he speaks a lie, he speaks from his own nature, for he is a liar and the father of lies" (John 8:44).

Satan lies to us and influences our thoughts. "Satan is the ruler of this world and the whole world is in his power (John 12:31; 1 John 5:19)."[36] When Adam and Eve sinned, they gave up their authority and rulership over God's creation to Satan and subjected themselves to his authority and rulership.

Neil Anderson describes the transfer of authority and rulership in his book, *Bondage Breaker*. Using the Bible as his source, he makes the following three points:

1. We were all born spiritually dead and subject to Satan or "the prince of the power of the air" (Ephesians 2:2).
2. When we accept Christ as our Savior, we are transferred from the kingdom of darkness to the kingdom of God's Son (Colossians 1:13).
3. Our citizenship was transferred from earth to heaven (Philippians 3:20), and from Satan to Christ as our ruler.[37]

Satan is the ruler of this world, but he has limitations in accordance with God's will. He can do nothing without God's permission (Job 1:6-12). God actively restrains Satan (Job 1:12; 2:6).

Satan has a hierarchy of fallen angels who work to carry out his purpose. We see this in Ephesians 6:12, as quoted above. A specific example of this is seen in Daniel 10:12-13, where an angel was sent to deliver a message to Daniel. The angel Gabriel told Daniel about an encounter with the prince of the kingdom of Persia (fallen angel). Michael the archangel (good angel, see Jude 1:9) helped Gabriel, who told Daniel: "... and I have come in response to your words. But the prince of the kingdom of Persia was withstanding me for twenty-one days; then behold, Michael, one of the chief princes, came to help me, for I had been left there with the kings of Persia" (Daniel 10:12-13).

There are two common errors in belief concerning Satan. One is disbelief in him, denying his existence by believing there is only one supernatural power in the universe, which is in harmony with many New Age beliefs, or, as in the case of atheism, believing in nothing spiritual. The other error is to have an unhealthy interest in the demonic, elevating Satan as an equal with God. Satan would love man to believe either error. They are both lies.

Satan uses a two-prong attack on mankind. Minirth and Meier describe Satan's tactics in this two-prong attack. *He desires to keep the nonbeliever in spiritual darkness* (John 3:19-21). *He wants to destroy the mental health of Christians* (Ephesians 6:11-16; 1 Peter 5:8-9). *He does this through deceiving people with false beliefs* (1 Timothy 4:1-3). *He can influence our thinking* (Matthew 16:21-23), *and he can hinder the spread of the gospel* (1 Thessalonians 2:2, 14-16).[38]

Mankind has a choice to build on one of two foundations. According to the gospel of Matthew, Jesus said, "... everyone who hears these words of Mine and acts on them, may be compared to a wise man who built his house on the rock. And the rain fell, and the floods came, and the winds blew and slammed against that house; and yet it did not fall, for it had been founded on the rock" (Matthew 7:24-25). What we believe is extremely important. If we build a belief system on the Word of God, we have a guide for this present life, as well as eternity.

In regard to the second foundation, Jesus said, "Everyone who hears these words of Mine and does not act on them, will be like a foolish man who built his house on the sand. The rain fell, and the floods came, and the winds blew, and slammed against that house; and it fell—and great was its fall" (Matthew 7:26-27). Mankind's alternative is to ignore God's Word and build a belief system on what the philosophers had to say using themselves as a reference point.

We are faced with a choice of two reference points to discern truth. Do we choose God's way or Satan's way (usually disguised as man's way)? Do we have an external thermometer based on God's truth or an internal thermometer based on our own subjective nature?

FLYING BY INSTRUMENTS

Without an objective standard or reference point, our emotions, feelings, and human reasoning guide us. We are literally "flying by the seat of our pants." Our own self-confidence, developed through our human abilities, can actually hinder us from trusting God's instrument—the Word of God.[39] Hal Lindsey went flying with a friend of his named Hal Henkle, a former commander of the Strategic Air Command. While in flight, Lindsey took over the controls.

As they were climbing they flew through heavy clouds and rain. Lindsey had never flown by instruments, although he was familiar with them. The following story was communicated in Hal Lindsey's book, *Faith for Earth's Final Hour*, about a personal flying experience he encountered. To use his words, he related the following experience:

> The turbulence was strong and I got the distinct feeling we were banking to the left. But the artificial horizon, which shows whether the plane is banking or level, clearly indicated that we were climbing straight and true. For the first time I could remember, my senses of equilibrium and balance were

deceiving me. I felt as if we were going down, and kept fighting the urge to pull back on the controls, which would have caused the plane to stall. Then I felt as if the plane was banking again, only this time to the right. Each time, my senses and the instruments were in conflict. It took all my strength of will and concentration to keep from reacting to the false signals my physical senses were giving me. I realized that believing the flight instruments in spite of my feelings meant life or death.[40]

He goes on to recall a taped conversation between an air controller and a pilot who was in severe trouble. Due to the bad weather and being low on fuel, the pilot had to let down through a heavy overcast to land.

The pilot had never flown by instruments before. Within a few minutes, the pilot was screaming that his aircraft was out of control. The air controller kept telling him to let go of the controls and the plane, which was upside down, would right itself. "But the pilot, who had many hours of flying by visual regulations, could not stop following his feelings instead of the aircrafts instruments. Minutes later he was killed as his plane crashed, completely out of control."[41]

"The balance mechanism in the inner ear also causes him to antici-pate and correct movements. But these feelings can be completely deceived and confused without the natural horizon as a reference point."[42]

WHERE IS YOUR THERMOMETER?

According to the *American Heritage Dictionary of the English Language*, "cold blooded," in a zoological sense, is "having a bodily tem-perature that varies with the external environment." In other words a cold-blooded animal's body (such as a lobster) conforms to the external temperature. You can slowly increase the temperature of the water until it boils and the lobster dies. The cold-blooded animal cannot determine the temperature until it is too late.

In the same manner, a person who determines truth or establishes a worldview based on his own subjective nature is like the man who builds his house on the sand. The thermometer inside himself rises and falls with the culture and opinions of other people. According to the New Age move-ment, there is no one right religion. Every person defines his own truth.[43]

If the individual defines truth, and each person has a different truth, what is truth? In the Gospel of John, when Jesus was being tried before

Pilate, He said, "'... I have come into the world, to testify to the truth. Everyone who is of the truth hears My voice.' Pilate said to Him, 'What is truth?' ..." (John 18:37-38). From Pilate's frame of reference—himself— he came to the only conclusion possible. From his reference point, truth was subjective, not absolute.

Having an internal thermometer (standard) or subjective measure- ment of truth is essentially the philosophy of humanism. Humanism is a system that puts man in the center. He begins with himself and tries to rationally build a belief system to find knowledge, meaning, and value. He uses himself as his integration point.[44]

It is impossible for a person to determine truth and meaning in life when left to his own reasoning ability. Man's basic nature is flawed by sin, which distorts his ability to reason, in regards to spiritual truths, apart from God's truth. According to the Book of Proverbs, we are directed to: "Trust in the Lord with all your [our] heart, and do not lean on your [our] own understanding. In all your [our] ways acknowledge Him, and He will make your [our] paths straight" (Proverbs 3:5-6 [brackets by author]).

God tells us in His word not to trust our own reasoning apart from Him. If we choose to take the humanist approach, it will lead to death. "There is a way which seems right to a man, but its end is the way of death" (Proverbs 16:25).[45]

If we rely on an external thermometer, a standard outside of self, we have a standard that is independent of our sinful nature and subjectivity. In contrast to our earlier analogy of a cold-blooded animal, we now have a warm-blooded animal. A warm-blooded animal cannot be slowly boiled without its awareness.

Human beings, as warm-blooded creatures, are aware by their five senses if they find themselves in a boiling pot. They can, however, be boiled mentally and have their consciences desensitized slowly and com- pletely without their awareness. Even true believers who have a relation- ship with Christ can become desensitized to immoral behavior when they get away from the standard and the convicting power of God's Word.

Man's external thermometer consists of a standard outside of him- self. It is God's truth as revealed in the Bible and confirmed through experience. God's standard is an objective standard.

As we mentioned earlier, Satan is the god of this world but is bound by the limitations God imposes on him. He works through our culture and media to deceive and turn mankind away from God. "Not only is man lost, incomplete, and depraved, but he is under constant attack by a most powerful enemy—Satan. Satan is more powerful, clever, and shrewd than most people realize."[46]

Our culture and media are, for the most part, determined by human beings with a basic sin nature who are heavily influenced by Satan. The culture and media influence the population at large. It is a downward cyclical spiral that feeds on itself. Remember, Proverbs 14:12 says, "There is a way which seems right to a man, but its end is the way of death."

Satan's influence + man's sinful nature → influences media → distorts reality for the mass population → forms our culture → influences our worldview (belief system).

Concerning the New Age movement, authors Missler and Eastman state: "The prophets of the New Age claim that we are rapidly headed for a new understanding of our place in the universe and that sin, the notion that we have missed the mark in the eyes of God, is an archaic belief which will have no place in the coming new age."[47] We are in this New Age presently. To mention the Judeo-Christian worldview with its concept of "sin" is considered archaic and primitive.

CONTRASTING WORLDVIEWS / BELIEF SYSTEMS

God's Way
- Foundation is the Bible (2 Timothy 3:16)
- Man's nature is sinful (Psalm 51:5; Romans 7:14-25)
- Salvation is through a relationship with Jesus Christ alone (John 14:6)
- Results are: love, joy, peace, patience, kindness, goodness, faithfulness, gentleness, and self control (Galatians 5:22-23), eternal salvation (John 3:16, Romans 6:23)

Satan's Way
- Based on man's thinking apart from God (Proverbs 14:12; Psalm 14:1)
- Man's nature is good or neutral (Philosophers, psychologists, scientists)
- Salvation through many different ways or religions (Matthew 7:13)
- Results are immorality, impurity, sensuality, idolatry, sorcery, enmities, strife, jealously, outbursts of anger, disputes, dissensions, factions, envying, drunkenness, and carousing (Galatians 5:19-21), eternal damnation (Matthew 25:41, 46; Luke 16:23-31; Revelation 20:15)

We have covered two worldviews, kingdoms, and foundations. **Reality is a worldview that is dualistic. This dualism is not one of equality. It consists of good and evil, God and Satan, but they are not equal opposites.** God is the Creator. Satan was originally created as a good angel named Lucifer. He was a beautiful, powerful angel who rebelled against God his Creator (Ezekiel 28:14-17).

To understand prophecy, we must comprehend the importance of our worldview and the foundation of that view. What roles do faith and reason play in the development of our worldview?

FAITH AND REASON

Faith and reason sound like contradictory terms. The word "faith" often implies stupidity or ignorance. "Probably the best way to describe this concept of modern theology is to say that it is faith in faith, rather than faith directed to an object which is actually there."[48] For Christianity, faith is based upon an object. It is not a subjective, mystical experience.

True Christian faith should not be based on an existential experience. The philosopher Kierkegaard erroneously believed faith should be based on an existential experience, where one finds truth through a "leap of faith." Reason, based on God's Word, is disregarded.

The Christian faith is built on historical facts. There is sufficient evidence to believe in biblical revelation, as we will see in the next chapter.

Francis Schaeffer equates the word "grace" with faith, and the word "nature" with rational ability or reason. If we presuppose that the humanist (using himself as a point of reference) seeks truth in a rational way, he will be led to meaninglessness and despair (nature's outcome). The nonrational approach (grace) leads to meaning.

According to Schaeffer, this tension between nature (reason) and grace (faith) was necessary to find a meaning for the two together. Philosophers have tried to unite the two based on human reasoning. Schaeffer believed that the answer to solving this struggle can only be found in the "full biblical system." It is because these philosophers have looked for a rationalistic and humanistic answer that they failed.[49]

Reason alone, from a human reference point, cannot help man to find real meaning and purpose in life but only despair. Schaeffer's "line of despair" started with Hegel when he threw out absolutes and the need for a Creator. Kierkegaard threw out reason for experience or a "leap of faith."

These men struggled to blend faith and reason to find meaning in life. Coming from a self-reference or humanistic viewpoint in their thinking, they had to sacrifice one to save the other.

The Bible teaches both concepts. Proverbs 3:5 says, "Trust in the Lord with all your heart, and do not lean on your own understanding." This, along with many other Scriptures, says "faith" is the answer, not reason. Isaiah 1:18 says, "'Come now, and let us reason together,' says the Lord." Here, the Scripture says reason is important. Consider the following statement from the manual used in a well-known 12-step program.

> We couldn't duck the issue. Some of us had already walked over the Bridge of Reason toward the desired shore of faith. The outlines and the promise of the New Land had brought luster to tired eyes and fresh courage to flagging spirits. Friendly hands had stretched out in welcome. We were grateful that reason had brought us so far. But somehow we couldn't quite step ashore. ... without knowing it, had we not been brought to where we stood by a certain kind of faith? [50]

Using reason, based on God's Word, as our reference point, we can begin our study of the defense of the Christian faith. The problem is that reason alone will not lead us, by itself, all the way to truth and salvation. God requires faith. Reason will bring us to the line for the infinite or salvation, but faith is needed to cross the line from finite (reason) to infinite (faith).

Infinite (faith)
Man can only cross this line by faith built on reason —

Finite (reason)

God comes to our level through biblical revelation to reason with us. Based on this biblical revelation, we take a step of faith and meet God at the Cross of Jesus Christ. God allows us to connect with the infinite (Himself) but does not allow us to understand His thoughts or His ways. Isaiah 55:8-9 says, " 'For My thoughts are not your thoughts, nor are your ways My ways,' declares the Lord. 'For as the heavens are higher than the earth, so are My ways higher than your ways and My thoughts than your thoughts.'" This is the tension point; we reach God through faith built on reason and historical evidence. He reaches us through His Word and His Son, Jesus Christ.

REASON + FAITH → Confirms Reliability of Bible → Reveals TRUTH and SALVATION

The recurring theme throughout this chapter is the need for a reference point that is absolute, objective, and embodies truth. We briefly traced man's worldview over the last three centuries and the outcome when his reference point is centered in himself. This has resulted in a downhill slide away from God and His Truth. Jesus made the following statement in the gospel of John: "I am the way, and the truth, and the life …" (John 14:6).

This brings us to the current worldview, which is characterized by relativism and anti-rationalism. This worldview opens the door to an increasing demonic influence and lays the groundwork for the last days and our current generation (the last generation). This chapter concludes with a discussion of faith and reason.

The next chapter will present evidence that the Bible is God's Word. It will tell of Old Testament prophecies and their fulfillments. We will see solid evidence as to why the Bible and Jesus Christ are legitimate reference points. This chapter discussed the need for a legitimate reference point or standard. The next chapter demonstrates what that reference point is and why it is valid.

Chapter Three

Will the Real Prophet Stand Up?

T he previous chapter covered worldviews from God's perspective and from man's perspective. Although it briefly covered changing worldview trends over the last three centuries, the primary purpose of the chapter was to emphasize the need to find a reference point or standard. We saw the move away from God, when man looked to himself to determine truth. Once God and His Word become our anchor, we can measure the world's knowledge against His Word.

This chapter will help the reader to understand Bible prophecy. It will also show reasons why we can trust the biblical prophets, along with ways to test their reliability and authority. In addition to biblical prophecy, we will look at some additional sources of evidence that will validate the Bible and Christianity as authoritative and reliable and will serve as our Anchor for Truth as a Reference Point.

MODERN DAY BELIEFS ABOUT THE FUTURE

The future fascinates us. What does the future hold? What does God say about the future? What does the Bible say about the future?

With the new millennium, people have various opinions about what the future holds. In spite of terrorist activities and the threat of biological and/or chemical weapons, Americans on the whole remain positive, as shown in the following newspaper article.

Still, four out of five people in a poll by the Pew Research Center for the People and the Press say they are hopeful about life in the new millennium. That hopeful outlook is fueled by their faith in science and technology, modern medicine and higher education.

Previous polls also have shown American optimism is based largely on the roaring economy. "I think optimistically about the future because I don't want to think negatively," said Janice Royce of Anchorage, Alaska. ... "The economy is great. Politics will always be politics, but I like the direction the country is going in." [1]

Other statistics give a more pessimistic outlook. Approximately two out of three people expect a major terrorist attack on this country through biological or chemical warfare. They also fear a worldwide threat through an energy crisis and environmental problems.[2]

Two-thirds of the people polled expected a major terrorist attack in this country. They were right.

That quote was published in my previous book, *The Last Hour*, in 2001. Since that poll was taken, our country suffered the attacks of 9/11, and terrorism has become a major threat to our country and to others. The new Department of Homeland Security that was formed post 9/11 indicates the level of concern of our leaders in government.

The problem lies in the fact that terrorism cannot be defeated. It can only be slowed through intelligence and defensive measures. **The only way to stop terrorism is for a government or a person to gain absolute authority and control.** This can only happen at the expense of our freedom, and it will happen in the end times when the Antichrist gains worldwide control (see Revelation 13:16-18). Our faith is essential for the days that are ahead of us. That faith needs to be in a solid anchor, God's Word and His Son, Jesus Christ. Hopefully, this chapter will help the reader to increase his faith.

The Pew Research Center for the People and the Press conducted a poll about expectations beyond year 2000. The question was asked, "If life is going to be better in this country, how big of a role do you think each of the following will play?" There were three major areas that Americans believed would cause things to improve. Eighty-nine percent put their faith in science and technology, eighty-five percent in medical advances, and seventy-nine percent in schools and universities.

Historically, neither science, nor medicine, nor education has prevented wars or eliminated poverty, prejudice, or crime. These are not the answers because the real problems are not addressed, only the "presenting" problems. The heart of the problem is man's basic nature, which was discussed in Chapter Two.

WHY STUDY PROPHECY?

Understanding the future is one reason to study prophecy. Other reasons include the following:

1. Through the study of prophecy, we see that God has ultimate control over world events.

2. Many books in the Bible are devoted to prophecy, so God must believe it is important. If it is important to God, it should be important to us.

3. Prophecy helps confirm the Bible's authority. For example, there are prophecies in the Old Testament that are fulfilled in the New Testament, such as Isaiah 7:14 that is fulfilled in Matthew 1:22-23. When we read prophecies about the future, such as the Rapture, Tribulation, and Antichrist, we know that God is working through events in accordance with His will.

4. The study of prophecy brings assurance to the true believer in Jesus Christ. Since God was faithful to fulfill past prophecies, we can trust Him to fulfill future prophecies. No matter how bad things look, we know that God has a plan, and He will see it through as prophesied.

5. The study of prophecy produces a holy life. New Testament references to the Second Coming of Christ usually include an exhortation to godliness (Titus 2:12-14).[3]

The study of prophecy helps confirm the reliability of the Bible, the foundation stone of Christianity. The Bible, the origin of the Christian message, is under attack on numerous fronts. It is important to understand the nature of these attacks and have the knowledge necessary to defend the Christian message, as well as to build one's faith. As we will see, Christianity is an intelligent faith.

CURRENT CHALLENGES TO CHRISTIANITY

The Christian message is challenged today on two battlefronts. The first is the Historicity and Nature of Jesus. The second is the Reliability and Authority of Scripture.[4] The nature of each of the following examples will fit into one or both of these categories.

In the previous chapter we discussed worldviews, or man's opinion apart from God. The ideas of the great philosophers and thinkers did not arise from intellect alone. They reflected one's whole personality, their hopes, fears, longings, and regrets. A person's reasoning reflects his personality, and he is subject to an intellectual pressure to find a rationale for it. As human beings, we all have a sinful nature. This nature, in what the Reformers call "total depravity," distorts our ability to reason apart from biblical truth.[5]

When attempting to use one's reasoning to determine the nature of truth or reality, it is important to understand that man's reasoning originates from a sinful nature. Apart from God's help, it is impossible for a man to reason his way to truth, and because of this disadvantage, it is impossible to be objective. Before sin entered the world, man had the ability to reason objectively in a state of innocence. Our sinful nature has distorted that ability. The attacks on Christianity and the Bible originate from man's inability to reason as a result of his sinful nature.

A major area of challenge to Christianity falls under the broad category of "Liberalism." One example of an attack on the authority of Scripture comes from Rudolph Bultman, a New Testament liberal theologian. He believed the Gospel material was mythological and antiquated and could not be taken literally.[6]

This criticism can easily be disputed. Myths, legends, and folklore develop as a gradual process over many generations. Bultman makes an assumption that the time of the gospels, when Jesus lived, and the first recorded manuscripts involved between 130 to 150 years, or two generations. Bultman's assumptions are not based on factual evidence. William Albright, who was one of the world's foremost biblical archaeologists, writes: "We can already say emphatically that there is no longer any solid basis for dating any book of the New Testament after about A.D. 80."[7]

The time period for the historical records of Jesus did not allow enough time for mythology to corrupt it, especially in light of the eyewitnesses who had personal knowledge of Him. Legend has never developed that fast anywhere in history.[8] The Gospels were not hearsay. The writers were either eyewitnesses of Jesus or obtained information directly from an eyewitness, such as the Gospel of Luke.

Another attack against the content of the Scriptures concerns the Personhood of God. God is redefined as a "What" instead of a "Who." This redefinition of God "becomes the guide to the ultimate spiritual life."[9] God moves from External Personality (Who) to the Internal (based on our perceptions) or one's experience of God.[10] Bishop Spong, author of *Why Christianity Must Change or Die*, is basically saying that the Bible is wrong, and he then proceeds to change it. Our defense is an abundance of evidence for biblical reliability. This will be covered briefly in the following sections of this chapter.

Christianity is a Relationship Religion, not a system of ideas. Spong also attacks the heart of Christianity. He challenges the belief that Jesus is God's "only Son." He states that no other religious system in the world offers a point of connection with God, which he believes makes God look very un-godlike. He states: "This arrogant claim also denies our own modern-day experience."[11]

His own argument serves as a rebuttal to his claims. If no other system offers this point of connection with God, then Christianity is unique, and its claim of being the only way to connect with God is further confirmation of the uniqueness of Jesus: "… I am the way, and the truth, and the life; no one comes to the Father but through Me" (John 14:6).

It is interesting to take note of Spong's reference point. It was personal experience. When he says, "our own modern-day experience," who is the "our" he is talking about? It has not been part of my experience or the experience of millions of other Christians. He is depending on his own personal experience. He lets his experience dictate his theology. His emphasis on experience undercuts his objectivity and leads him away from the truth. According to Proverbs 14:12: "There is a way which seems right to a man, but its end is the way of death." What "seems right" is the outcome of using self as one's reference point. What seems right to Bishop Spong will not necessarily seem right to other people. This is the danger of using self as a reference point. There is no objective standard to discern truth. Everyone's truth is different.

Bishop Spong is a Protestant minister who viciously attacks the Bible, Christianity, and the supernatural. He served as a perfect example of a person with a sin nature who chose to use himself as a reference point in order to determine or seek truth. His end product led him to totally discredit God and His Word as a reference point. Professing to be wise (knowing the truth), he stumbled over it (Truth). Bishop Spong does not stand alone. He is just one example of liberalism permeating our seminaries and turning out other ministers like Spong.

In addition to liberalism, which is a direct attack on Christianity, we have the infiltration of the New Age Movement. This movement is a mixture of Eastern and Western religions combined with philosophy, metaphysical sciences, and psychic phenomena. It includes many different beliefs, thus, making it hard to define.

Al Gore, former vice president and presidential candidate, expresses some of the New Age thinking in his book, *Earth in the Balance*. According to *Christianity Today*, he "blasts Western civilizations as 'deeply dysfunctional.' In his prescription for change, Gore draws on Islamic, Hindu, Sikh, and Bahai texts, along with Native American prayers to the Great Spirit. He waxes nostalgic about 'a single earth goddess' who benevolently reigned in the hearts of prehistoric humans."[12]

Gore's idea for progressive change involves a melting pot of world religions mixed in with paganism. "Mother Earth" is a common expression that originates from a single "earth goddess" named Gaia. A number of New Age books speak of the planet Earth as a female goddess. This is a pagan belief, which encompasses pantheism, an Eastern belief that the Earth is God. The *Creation* has become the *Creator*.

Many New Age books express a concept known as the evolution of consciousness for mankind. The implication is a rise toward godhood. The ultimate temptation in the Garden of Eden, made by the Serpent (Satan), was the promise that "your eyes will be opened, and you will be like God" (Genesis 3:5). The promise was to raise Eve's consciousness to become like God.

As a result of the ultimate revelation of the perfect man, Jesus Christ, it is not necessary to wait for the "evolution" of a new man or culture.[13] According to C.S. Lewis, "It has happened already. In Christ a new kind of man appeared: and the new kind of life that began in Him is to be put in us."[14] This higher consciousness was in Jesus Christ, Who was God manifested in human form. The Holy Spirit indwells the true Christian, which gives him a God consciousness. This is a far cry from the New Age concept of the evolution of man's consciousness.

It seems the New Age Movement includes a Heinz 57 variety of world religions, including paganism and Eastern religions. Because the New Age Movement has so many tentacles, it intertwines its beliefs into Christianity. If a Christian is not grounded in the Scriptures, he will find himself blending New Age beliefs into Christianity, resulting in a distortion of the gospel.

In Paul's letter to the Galatians, he cautioned them to be careful not to distort the gospel. He said: "I am amazed that you are so quickly deserting Him who called you by the grace of Christ, for a different gospel; which is really not another; only there are some who are disturbing you and want to distort the gospel of Christ. But even though we, or an angel from heaven, should preach to you a gospel contrary to what we have preached to you, he is to be accursed" (Galatians 1:6-8).

This admonition could certainly apply to Christianity in our day with regards to the New Age Movement. Note how emphatic Paul was when he said, "… even though … an angel from heaven, should preach to you a gospel contrary to what we have preached to you, he is to be accursed." The emphasis here is theology (God's Word) over experience, even if it is a supernatural manifestation (an angel).

One of the central attacks on Christianity is the attempt to discredit the reliability of the Bible, specifically the New Testament. F. C. Baur, a German critic, assumed that most of the New Testament was written late in the second century. He concluded that this would have been so long after the days of Christ that it could not be accurate and the writings came from myth and legend.

The evidence shows this is not the case. There are existing manuscripts confirming that our current copies of the Bible are accurate. Three archaeological discoveries that confirmed the accuracy of the New Testament manuscripts include: the John Ryland Manuscript, A.D. 130; the Chester Beatty Papyri, A.D. 155; and the Bodmer Papyri, A.D. 155. These manuscripts bridged the gap between the time of Christ and existing manuscripts from a later date.[15] For further resources, go to footnote 16 on page 288.[16]

As mentioned earlier, according to William Albright, there is no evidence for dating the New Testament after A.D. 80. More recently, evangelical scholars affirm that the Book of Revelation was written in A.D. 95 or 96 (*The Bible Knowledge Commentary, New Testament*, by John Walvoord and Roy Zuck, S.P. Publications, 1983, p. 925).

When we consider ancient manuscripts, like the Dead Sea Scrolls

discovered in 1947, we look at two measures in determining their reliability as true copies of the original manuscript. The first measure is the
time interval between the original and the extant copy, the first copy of
the original. The second measure is the number of copies produced and
whether they confirm the extant copy.[17]

No one questions the authenticity of the works produced by such
authors as Caesar and Aristotle, yet they question the authenticity of the
Bible. Chart 6, shown on the following page, compares famous authors and
works with the New Testament, using the same criteria for authenticity.

In reviewing the table, the shortest time span between the original
manuscript and the earliest copy, apart from the New Testament, is
Homer's *Iliad* at 500 years. The greatest number of copies, apart from the
New Testament, is 643 from the same source. The other manuscripts had
time spans ranging from 750 years to 1,600 years, with a range of copies
from 1 to 200.

Contrasting these numbers with the New Testament, the time span
between the original manuscripts of the New Testament to the earliest
copy is only 25 years, with over 24,000 copies.

"The application of the bibliographical test to the New Testament
assures us that it has more manuscript authority than any piece of literature from antiquity."[18] In reference to the Dead Sea Scrolls, consider
the following facts:

1. Since 1947 (one year before Israel became a nation) and the discovery of the Dead Sea Scrolls, the textual reliability of the Old
   Testament has become more universally recognized. It therefore
   became much easier to defend the reliability of the Bible.
2. The oldest manuscript prior to 1947 was from the late 900s (10th
   century A.D.), which was a copy of a copy.[19]
3. Although the biblical scrolls are copies of copies, there was a 95%
   agreement that the differences were mainly slips of the pen and
   spelling deviations. The biblical scrolls reflect a text 1,500 years
   earlier than the Masoretic Text, which was used as a base text for
   our English translation of the Old Testament.[20]
4. As of 2002 (45 years after the discovery of the scrolls) only 20% of
   the 500 scrolls had been published. Following 2002, rapid progress
   was made. As of 2006, all of the Dead Sea Scroll texts had been
   published in the "Discoveries of the Judean Desert (DJD) series."[22]

CHART 6

COMPARISON TABLE OF AUTHORS AND MANUSCRIPTS[21]

AUTHOR	WHEN WRITTEN	EARLIEST COPY	TIME SPAN	NO. OF COPIES
Caesar	100-44 B.C.	900 A.D.	1,000 yrs.	10
Livy	59 B.C. - A.D.17			20
Plato (Tetralogies)	427-347 B.C.	900 A.D.	1,200 yrs.	7
Tacitus (Annals)	100 A.D.	1100 A.D.	1,000 yrs.	20 (-)
also minor works	100 A.D.	1000 A.D.	900 yrs.	1
Pliny the Younger (History)	61-113 A.D.	850 A.D.	750 yrs.	7
Thucydides (History)	460-400 B.C.	900 A.D.	1,300 yrs.	8
Suetonius (De Vita Caesarum)	75-160 A.D.	950 A.D.	800 yrs.	8
Herodotus (History)	480-425 B.C.	900 A.D.	1,300 yrs.	8
Horace			900 yrs.	
Sophocles	496-406 B.C.	1000 A.D.	1,400 yrs.	193
Lucretius	Died 55 or 53 B.C.		1,100 yrs.	2
Catullus	54 B.C.	1550 A.D.	1,600 yrs.	3
Euripides	480-406 B.C.	1100 A.D.	1,500 yrs.	9
Demosthenes	383-322 B.C.	1100 A.D.	1,300 yrs.	200 *
Aristotle	384-322 B.C.	1100 A.D.	1,400 yrs.	49 +
Aristophanes	450-385 B.C.	900 A.D.	1,200 yrs.	10

*All from one copy.   +Of any one work

WORK	WHEN WRITTEN	EARLIEST COPY	TIME SPAN	NO. OF COPIES
Homer (Iliad)	900 B.C.	400 B.C.	500 yrs.	643
NEW TESTAMENT	40-100 A.D.	125 A.D.	25 yrs.	Over 24,000

5. By 1991, a public relations campaign, led by *Biblical Archaeology Review* magazine, demanded a release of the unpublished scrolls to the academic world.[23]

The evidence gathered from these manuscripts is voluminous, and only about twenty percent of them have been disclosed to us. One wonders how much more confirmation of biblical reliability will become available once the remaining seventy-five to eighty percent are published. The rigid tests for manuscript reliability show that no manuscript of antiquity even comes close to the validity and reliability of the Bible.

One of the challenges to Christianity concerns the three-hour darkness that occurred between the hours of noon and three o'clock p.m. when Christ was on the cross. Bishop Spong denies that darkness covered the earth at the time of Jesus' death. He does this by claiming that computers can go back and "preclude the possibility of an eclipse in Palestine anywhere near that time."[24]

The problem with Spong's assertion is in his premise. He assumes that the only cause for darkness at that time of the day would be due to a solar eclipse. His statement does not take into consideration the possibility of a supernatural occurrence. He takes the philosophical assumption of Naturalism.

In fact, secular historical sources claim darkness occurred but excused it as a supernatural occurrence by claiming it was a solar eclipse. There is evidence of a period of darkness in secular sources. Dr. Gary Habermas, author of *The Historical Jesus*, writes about a historian named Thallus. In A.D. 52, Thallus "wrote a history of the eastern Mediterranean world since the Trojan War. Although Thallus' work has been lost, it was quoted by Julian Africanus in about A.D. 221, and it made reference to the darkness that the gospels had written about!"[24] In the third book of his histories, Thallus attempted to explain away the darkness as an eclipse of the sun. Thallus verifies the darkness but speculates on the cause. "Africanus then argues that it couldn't have been an eclipse, given when the crucifixion occurred."[25]

Scholar Paul Maier makes reference to the darkness in a footnote from his book, *Pontius Pilate*, written in 1968. He states: "This phenomenon, evidently, was visible in Rome, Athens, and other Mediterranean cities. According to Tertullian ... it was a 'cosmic' or 'world event' ..."[26]

There is an abundance of evidence to support Christianity and dispute the numerous challenges it has faced. Although the Bible cannot be proven scientifically, it is oftentimes confirmed by scientific findings. The following section will review the methods used to prove the Bible.

WHAT ABOUT SCIENCE?

Can the Bible be proven scientifically? The answer is "no," but we are really asking the wrong question. The fact that George Washington lived cannot be proven scientifically, but no one doubts the fact that he once lived.

Scientific proof is based on showing that a fact is repeatable and observable and is done in a controlled environment. Observations are made, data is accumulated, and a hypothesis is empirically verified.[27]

Historical events cannot be proven scientifically since there is no way to repeat the event in a controlled environment.[28] For example, if a person says they went to the store yesterday at a certain time, this event cannot be scientifically proven. It can be proven beyond a reasonable doubt.

In order to verify historical events, we use the legal-historical method. This method shows that something can be proven beyond a reasonable doubt. This means there is no reasonable basis for a reasonable person to doubt the fact or event. It depends on three types of evidence: oral testimony, written testimony, and exhibits (such as a gun, bullet, notebook).[29]

You cannot scientifically prove that George Washington lived or that Jesus was raised from the dead. According to the legal-historical method, we do have eyewitness accounts (oral testimony), written testimony (the Bible), and exhibits (Dead Sea Scrolls).

The New Testament was recorded by men who were eyewitnesses to the actual events of the life of Christ or to the eyewitnesses of others who witnessed the events in the life of Christ.[30] A detailed account of the events in the life of Christ was written down, "having investigated everything carefully" and "in consecutive order" (Luke 1:1-3).

Luke detailed the time and geography as "in the fifteenth year of the reign of Tiberius Caesar, when Pontius Pilate was governor of Judea, and Herod was tetrarch of Galilee, and his brother Philip was tetrarch of the region of Ituraea ..." (Luke 3:1). The Gospel of Luke, primarily Chapters 1 through 3, gives a detailed account of the time and place when Christ was born.

The material presented in this book on the reliability of the Bible and Christianity barely presents the tip of the iceberg. There are volumes of additional material. Christianity is not a blind, ignorant belief, but an intelligent faith. The weight of the evidence is far beyond a reasonable doubt. Once all of the evidence is considered using the legal-historical method, it would take more blind faith to deny the truth of Christianity, the Bible, and the Resurrection than to believe. As we will see in the next section, prophecy is further evidence of the Bible's reliability.

BIBLICAL RELIABILITY

The reliability of the Bible as the infallible Word of God is the essential foundation stone for the Christian message. Strong evidence is essential in order to "give an account for the hope that is in you, yet with gentleness and reverence" (1 Peter 3:15). The Bible tells us to always be ready to defend our faith.

There are numerous books on apologetics—the branch of theology that is concerned with defending or proving the truth of Christian doctrines. One defense is the uniqueness of the Bible. Josh McDowell, a well-known Christian author in the area of apologetics, discussed in his book, *Evidence that Demands a Verdict*, some of the characteristics that establish the Bible's uniqueness. He stated that the Bible was written by 40 authors from every walk of life over a period of 1,500 years, covering 40 generations. The authors included fishermen, poets, kings, peasants, statesmen, and scholars. Furthermore, the Bible was written from different places: a wilderness, a dungeon, a palace, a prison, and the isle of Patmos. It was written at different times, times of war and peace. It was written from three continents: Asia, Africa, Europe; and in three languages: Hebrew, Aramaic, Greek.[31]

McDowell not only discusses the Bible's uniqueness, but also provides a comprehensive defense of the Christian faith. He acknowledges that the above points cannot prove that the Bible is the Word of God, but "to me it proves that it is unique ('different from all others; having no like or equal'). A professor remarked to me: 'If you are an intelligent person, you will read the one book [Bible] that has drawn more attention than any other if you are searching for the truth' " [brackets by author].

The Bible can be defended in the following ways: archeologically, historically, prophetically, and philosophically. One example is the historical evidence of a great worldwide flood. A biologist and dean of science said, "There are more than 500 accounts of vast primordial floods from cultures all over the world. Some scientists think the stories have a factual basis. Scientists agree that major extinctions of animals occurred about 11,500 years ago. Palmer reports that North America lost three-fourths of its large animals; devastation was even worse in other parts of the globe ..."[32]

Prophecy is one of the major ways the Bible is unique and is set apart from other religious books. Only the God of the Bible has the ability to foretell the future with 100% accuracy through His prophets. No other "god" or supernatural force has that ability.

The Bible is the only volume ever produced by an individual or group of individuals that contains many prophecies relating to Israel, to certain cities, to all people worldwide, and to the coming of the Messiah. In the ancient world, many devices were used to determine the future through divination. In all Greek and Latin literature, we cannot find a specific prophecy of a great historical event to come in the future, nor is there a prophecy of a Savior to arise in the human race.[33]

PROPHET OR FRAUD?

If prophecy sets the Bible apart from all other manuscripts as infallible, what sets the prophet apart from a fraud, a psychic, or a fortune-teller? There has to be a way to distinguish the true prophet of God from all others. One way to begin is to examine what God said to Moses.

"I will raise up a prophet from among their countrymen like you [Moses], and I will put My words in his mouth, and he shall speak to them all that I command him. It shall come about that whoever will not listen to My words which he shall speak in My name, I Myself will require it of him. But the prophet who speaks a word presumptuously in My name which I have not commanded him to speak, or which he speaks in the name of other gods, that prophet shall die." You may say in your heart, "How will we know the word which the LORD has not spoken?" When a prophet speaks in the name of the LORD, if the thing does not come about or come true, that is the thing which the LORD has not spoken The prophet has spoken it presumptuously; you shall not be afraid of him. (Deuteronomy 18:18-22 [brackets by author])

"This teaches us that the true prophet had to predict some things that would take place in his lifetime so that his authenticity could be verified."[34] From this we can make the following observations:

1. If a prophet speaks something that does not come true, he has spoken "presumptuously." What he has spoken is not from God, and he is not to be feared.
2. If a prophet speaks a word presumptuously in "My name" (God's name) which God has not commanded him to speak, or it is "in the name of other gods, that prophet shall die."

The test of a true prophet of God is very simple. It leaves no room for error or guessing. He has to have a 100% success rate, or he dies.

There have been many so-called "prophets" throughout history and in our day. Many have written books, or books were written about them, carrying on their "prophetic" messages. Some of the more famous individuals who have declared themselves "prophets" include: Jean Dixon, Edgar Cayce, Nostradamus, Mayan Calendar interpreters, Hopi Indian prophets, New Age prophets, palm readers, astrologers, Tarot card readers, and channelers. None have an accuracy rating comparable to the prophets of the Bible. In biblical times, these so-called "prophets" needed to have a 100% accuracy record. If not, they were cast out as false prophets, had their writings burned, or were stoned to death.[35]

Notice that the so-called "prophets" listed above would be classified as secular, non-Christian men and women. Mature Christians know that these "prophets" do not speak for God, so they are not as much of a threat for deception in the Church. The real danger is from those who are within the Church who claim to be speaking as "prophets of the Lord" and are not. In Deuteronomy 18:15, Moses told the people, "The Lord your God will raise up for you a prophet like me from among you, from your countrymen, you shall listen to him." This was referring to the prophet coming from among the people of God. Paul writes to the church in Corinth:

> But I am afraid that, as the serpent deceived Eve by his craftiness, your minds will be led astray from the simplicity and purity of devotion to Christ. For if one comes and preaches another Jesus whom we have not preached, or you receive a different spirit which you have not received, or a different gospel which you have not accepted, you bear this beautifully. (2 Cor. 11:3-4)
> For such men are false apostles [or false ministers], deceitful workers, dis-

guising themselves as apostles* [or false ministers] of Christ. No wonder, for even Satan disguises himself as an angel of light. Therefore it is not surprising if his servants also disguise themselves as servants of righteousness, whose end will be according to their deeds. (2 Cor. 11:13-15 [brackets by author]) *The Bible Knowledge Commentary, p. 635, defines apostle as "one sent as an authoritative delegate."

For you endure it if a man assumes control of your souls and makes slaves of you, or devours [your substance, spends your money] and preys upon you, or deceives and takes advantage of you, or is arrogant and puts on airs, or strikes you in the face. (2 Cor. 11:20 AMP)

How does the Christian protect himself and his family from these disguised ministers of unrighteousness? It is critical that Christians study the Word of God and learn to discern the true from the false. Is the "prophet" appealing to the lust of the flesh or the pride of life, with great swelling words? Is he promising you the "prophet's reward" for giving to his ministry, or trying to instill fear for not giving? This author would say that it is time to close your ears, and to close the door behind you as you leave. The true prophet of the Lord will be speaking the heart of the Lord. He will speak of denying self, taking up one's cross, and following Jesus faithfully. His demeanor will often be humble and serious, his heart broken, and His words will often be called "hard sayings" (John 6:60). It is important to remember that persons with the gift of prophecy are not held to the same criteria as the prophets.

One of God's requirements for a prophet is 100% accuracy. Even though a prophet may have a good track record of predicting events accurately, although not 100%, the word still may not be from God.

"Deuteronomy 18 claims that what does not become fulfilled is not true prophecy. It should be remembered that this is a negative criterion. Thus, what does become fulfilled is still not necessarily from God. When a false prophet makes a fulfilled prediction, this may be a test of God's people. Deuteronomy 13:1-3, deals theologically with and strikes a clear and ringing blow; if the prophet uses other gods removed from the true God (v. 2), then he is obviously not of Yahweh."[36]

We know that there are no "other gods." In Paul's letter to the

Corinthians, he makes it clear that idols, or other gods, are really demons disguised as gods. (See 1 Corinthians 10:19-20.)

Besides 100% accuracy, there are two questions to consider about a true prophet. Is he merely guessing—a fraud? Or is he prophesying from another "god" or supernatural being—demonic?

The criteria to test the prophet are clearly identified in the Bible. The messages we have received through New Age psychics or the occult cannot be 100% supported by empirical evidence. When they are accurate, it is either guesswork, or they are fed information from a demonic being.

God dwells in eternity outside of the confines of time, according to Isaiah 57:15. "But how does He authenticate His message to us? How does He assure us that the message really comes from Him and is not a fraud or a contrivance? One way is to demonstrate that the message has its source from outside our time domain. God declares, 'I alone know the end from the beginning' (Isaiah 46:10). His message includes history written in advance. We call this 'prophecy.' "[37]

Many biblical prophecies were written several hundred years before Christ and were fulfilled both in the Old Testament, as well as during the time of Jesus.

OLD TESTAMENT PROPHECIES

Some of the Old Testament prophecies that were fulfilled in history include:

1. Destruction of the City of Tyre. Ezekiel 26:3, 4, 7, 8, 12, 14, 21 (592-570 B.C.)
2. Destruction of Sidon. Ezekiel 28:22-23 (542-570 B.C.)
3. Destruction of Samaria. Hosea 13:16 (748-690 B.C.); Micah 1:6 (738-690 B.C.)
4. Destruction of Gaza — Ashkelon. Amos 1:8 (775-750 B.C.); Jeremiah 47:5 (626-586 B.C.); Zephaniah 2:4, 6, 7 (640-621 B.C.)
5. Destruction of Moab — Ammon. Ezekiel 25:3-4 (592-570 B.C.); Jeremiah 48:47 (626-586 B.C.), 49:6
6. Destruction of Petra and Edom. Isaiah 34:6, 7, 10, 13-15 (783-704 B.C.); Jeremiah 49:17-18 (626-586 B.C.); Ezekiel 25:13-14 (592-570 B.C.); Ezekiel 35:5-7
7. Destruction of Thebes and Memphis. Ezekiel 30:13-15 (592-570

B.C.)
8. Destruction of Nineveh. Nahum 1:8, 10; 2:6; 3:10, 13, 19 (661-before 612 B.C.)

These are just a few examples of prophecies made several hundred years before Christ that were fulfilled in history.[38] In addition to these, Josh McDowell lists four more Old Testament prophecies and their fulfillment in his book, *Evidence that Demands a Verdict*.

One obvious truth that stands out in the study of prophecy is God's direct influence throughout history. The prophets could not control the fulfillment. They made no claim from their own authority. They were the prophets, and God was responsible for the fulfillment of the judgments.[39]

God is a merciful and patient God, but He is also a just God. He has prophesied judgment on cities and nations, and these prophecies were fulfilled. He prophesied a great judgment over the whole earth (Matthew 24:3-44; Mark 13:3-32; Luke 21:25-33; 1 Thessalonians 5:2-3; 2 Thessalonians 2:2-12; Revelation 6-19), which will be fulfilled.

ALEXANDER THE GREAT: AN IMPORTANT FIGURE IN PROPHETIC HISTORY

Daniel prophesied four great world empires. The first world empire was the Babylonian Empire, followed by the Medo-Persian Empire, then the Greek Empire, followed by the Roman Empire. Alexander the Great ushered in the Greek empire. Prior to the rise of Alexander, Greece was divided into five tribes who spoke different dialects. They were too busy fighting each other to become a great empire.

Alexander, a genius tutored by Aristotle, was fathered by a warrior king from the tribal state of Macedonia. His father disliked his mother who was devoutly occultic. The survival of Alexander's mother depended upon Alexander's success. She taught Alexander that he was much more than a mere man. The driving force in his life was a result of his own vision of personal greatness.[40]

Alexander learned battle tactics from his father, later killed by an assassin, which thrust the eighteen-year-old Alexander into a mighty leadership role. He ingeniously devised new battle strategies and quickly learned how to keep his enemy off balance. He conquered all the other Greek tribes and united them into one nation. He also developed one common language. "Since they spoke in five dialects, Alexander, knowing that exact communication was essential in battle, fused together the best of the dialects and made one common language. ... This dialect was named *Koine Greek*, which means 'Common Greek.' Alexander commanded all the tribes to learn 'common language.' "[41]

Within two years, Alexander had Greece united and ready for conquest. Through clever psychological and military training, he had the Greek army capture Persia, the second world empire, in 331 B.C.

Following the downfall of the Persian Empire, Alexander employed an unusual tactic. Instead of making the Persians slaves, he made friends with them. He required them to learn the Greek language and to embrace the Greek culture. **Providentially, God accomplished His purpose through Alexander by making Koine Greek the universal language.**[42]

GREEK: A PROVIDENTIAL LANGUAGE

The original manuscript of the New Testament was written in Koine Greek, a creation of Alexander the Great. During the time of Christ, the Roman Empire was in power, but the universal language was Koine Greek.

The Old Testament was written in Hebrew and was later translated into Greek. The Greek translation, completed in 165 B.C., was known as the Septuagint, or LXX, for the Seventy Translators. To understand why this translation took place, we have to return to the scene of Alexander's conquests.

Hal Lindsey, a well-known author in the area of prophecy, relates the historical account of the translation of the Septuagint. During the time of Alexander's conquest, he made his move to conquer Jerusalem. A Jewish High Priest met with Alexander and explained how his life and career were prophesied in the second, seventh, and eighth chapters of Daniel. As a result, Alexander spared Jerusalem and took many of the royal family of Judah to become administrators over his kingdoms. These Hellenized Jews needed a Greek translation of their Hebrew Bible. As a result, we have the Septuagint.[43]

God used Alexander the Great, from a pagan background, to create a language; his encounter with a Jewish High Priest resulted in a Greek translation of the Hebrew Bible. The Bible was now available to the Gentile world. "Thus, long before his birth, there were now available for the Gentile world the prophecies of the Messiah's coming as a humble servant who would provide a way to God for all peoples."[44]

Our God has sovereign control over people, events, and history. He transcends time and space to have control over everything. What a great and awesome God we have!

JUDGMENT ON ISRAEL

The Jewish people are, in themselves, evidence of the inspiration of the Bible.

> When Frederick the Great asked a preacher one time for a proof of the inspiration of the Bible, the preacher replied, "The Jew, your majesty." The emblem of the Jewish nation is a bush burning unconsumed.

Why did God preserve this nation? It is because He had a great plan for them. Here are several reasons:

1. The Jewish race was raised up to teach that there is only one God. In the days of Abraham, the world was given over to idolatry and paganism. The Jews have been the teachers of monotheism (one God) to the nations.
2. This nation was raised up to be the writers and preservers of the Scriptures (Romans 3:1, 2).
3. This nation was preserved so that God could give the world a Savior through them (Jesus was a Jew).[45]

The nation of Israel has remained a nation against all the odds. It was conquered and destroyed in 606 B.C. by Babylon. Although the captives of Israel were allowed to return to their land and rebuild Jerusalem, it did not become a sovereign nation until May 14, 1948.

The Old Testament predicted the destruction of Israel and the scattering of the Jews among the nations. Because of Israel's idolatry and disobedience, they were judged. Consider the following Old Testament prophecy:

> I will lay waste your cities as well and will make your sanctuaries desolate, and I will not smell your soothing aromas. I will make the land desolate so that your enemies who settle in it will be appalled over it. You, however, I will scatter among the nations and will draw out a sword after you, as your

land becomes desolate and your cities become waste. (Leviticus 26:31-33)

This prophecy was fulfilled starting with the Babylonian captivity. The final destruction of the rebuilt Jerusalem, which was still not an established sovereign nation, occurred in A.D. 70 by the Roman army led by Titus. There are Old Testament and New Testament prophecies made by Jesus concerning the destruction of Jerusalem and the Temple. The following Old Testament prophecies are examples of these predictions.

The Destruction of the Temple: "... and the Lord, whom you seek, will suddenly come to His Temple ..." (Malachi 3:1). This verse along with four others (Psalm 118:26; Daniel 9:26; Zechariah 11:13; Haggai 2:7-9) demands that the Messiah come while the Temple of Jerusalem is still standing. This is of great significance when we realize that the temple was destroyed in A.D. 70 and has not since been rebuilt![46]

When Jesus, the Messiah, came the first time, the Temple was standing. When He comes back the second time, the Temple will also be standing. Orthodox Jews are currently making plans to rebuild it. It will be in place prior to the Second Coming.

The following prediction in the book of Daniel lays out the chronology and timing of both the crucifixion and the destruction of Jerusalem and the Temple. This remarkable prophecy is often referred to as "Daniel's Seventy Weeks."

"Then after the sixty-two weeks the Messiah will be cut off and have nothing, and the people of the prince who is to come will destroy the city and sanctuary ..." (Daniel 9:26)

This is a remarkable statement! Chronologically:

1. Messiah comes (assumed)
2. Messiah cut off (dies)
3. Destruction of city (Jerusalem) and sanctuary (the Temple)

The city and the Temple were destroyed by Titus and his army in A.D. 70; therefore, either the Messiah has already come or this prophecy was a lie.[47]

In the New Testament, Jesus prophesied the destruction of the Temple approximately forty years before it happened. He said in Matthew 24:2: "Do you not see all these things? Truly I say to you, not one stone here will be left upon another, which will not be torn down." In Luke, He made the same prophecy and gave the reason for the destruction of the temple: the Jews' rejection of the Messiah. "For the days will come upon you when your enemies will throw up a barricade against you, and surround you and hem you in on every side, and they will level you to the ground and your children within you, and they will not leave in you one stone upon another, because you did not recognize the time of your visitation" (Luke 19:43-44).

FULFILLMENT OF THE JUDGMENT OF ISRAEL

These Old and New Testament prophecies were literally fulfilled when Jerusalem was taken in A.D. 70. When Jesus was crucified, the Jews said, "His blood shall be on us and on our children" (Matthew 27:25). In A.D. 70, under Titus, a Roman army of 100,000 destroyed both the Temple and the city. The city was defended by ninety towers, and the siege lasted four months. Famine was within the city, and mothers killed and ate their babies (Deuteronomy 28:52-53). Many fled from the city but were caught and crucified. The Romans swarmed around the Temple.

Titus commanded his soldiers to spare the Temple; yet, one soldier threw a blazing torch through a doorway, and the Temple was burned, leaving nothing but the rock upon which it stood. "On this rock today is an Islamic shrine called the 'Dome of the Rock.' Josephus said 1,000,000 perished and 97,000 were taken captive. So God scattered His people because they dishonored His name (Ezekiel 36:17-21), and they crucified His Son. Has God forgotten His people? No! (Romans 11:1-2, 25-26). He has temporarily set them aside."[48]

After over two thousand years of persecution and dispersion among the Gentile nations, Israel was reborn. God will restart the Jewish time clock as shown in Daniel's prophecy of seventy weeks.

DANIEL'S SEVENTY WEEKS: A PHENOMENAL PROPHECY

The seventy-week prophecy found in Daniel 9:24-27 is probably one of the most important prophecies in history. This prophecy is specific concerning God's dealing with the Jewish nation.

Hal Lindsey, author of *Planet Earth: The Final Chapter*, refers to Daniel's seventy-week prophecy as a view of Jewish history from Daniel's day until the return of Jesus Christ. Lindsey explains the Jewish measurement of time. In the same way the Greeks use *decade* for a period of ten years, the Hebrews use *shabua,* or *week*, for a period of seven years. Seventy of those "weeks" would represent a period of 490 years. This is a seventy-week (or 490-year) prophecy concerning the Jews and the Holy City, Jerusalem.[49]

The historical background helps us understand Daniel's seventy-week prophecy. The Babylonians captured and deported Daniel as a teenager. While in captivity and reading the prophecies of Jeremiah, Daniel understood that the seventy-year captivity was about to end. He then committed himself to prayer. During this prayer, the angel Gabriel gave him the most remarkable prophecy in the Bible, the seventy-week prophecy.[50]

The seventy-week prophecy (70 x 7 = 490 years) in Daniel was in regard to the Jewish nation. "Seventy weeks have been decreed for your people [Jewish people] and your holy city ...

[1] to finish the transgression,
[2] to make an end of sin,
[3] to make atonement for iniquity,
[4] to bring in everlasting righteousness,
[5] to seal up vision and prophecy,
[6] and to anoint the most holy place"[51]
     (Daniel 9:24 [brackets by author]).

The six promised blessings are related to the two works of the Messiah: His death and His reign. "The first three have special reference to the sacrifice of the Messiah, which anticipate the establishment of His reign."[52]

The seventy "sevens" are divided into three categories of prophecy. The first category is seven weeks of seven (forty-nine years), then sixty-two weeks of seven (four hundred thirty-four years), and the final week of seven (seven years). The entire prophecy period covers 490 years.

How do we calculate a year? When determining the length of the years, we rely on the 360-day year in Scripture. The calendar year used in the Scriptures must be determined from the Scriptures themselves.

1. Historically: Compare Genesis 7:11 with Genesis 8:4, and the two of

these with Genesis 7:24 and Genesis 8:3.

2. Prophetically: Many Scriptures refer to the great tribulation under various terms, but all have the common denominator of a 360-day year.[53]

There are several decrees that had to do with the restoration of the Jews from the Babylon captivity. "However, in all these, permission was granted for the rebuilding of the Temple, and nothing was said about the rebuilding of the city."[54] These decrees did not fit the necessary requirements of the passage. "When we turn to the decree of Artaxerxes, made in his twentieth year and recorded in Nehemiah 2:1-8, for the first time permission is granted to rebuild the city of Jerusalem. This, then, becomes the beginning of the prophetic time appointed by God in this prophecy."[55]

How do we determine the date of this decree of Artaxerxes? According to Nehemiah 2:1 this decree was made "in the month of Nisan, in the twentieth year of King Artaxerxes ..." "There is no date specified, so according to the Jewish custom, the date is understood as the first day of the month, which would be Nisan 1, 444 B.C. March 5, 444 B.C. is our corresponding calendar date."[56]

The first sixty-nine weeks terminated when Christ presented Himself to Israel as the Messiah. The time calculation is precise. From the edict to rebuild Jerusalem to the coming of the Messiah is 483 years (69 x 7). Each year is a Jewish prophetic year of 360 days or a total of 173,880 days.

This time period is equal to 476 solar years. Each solar year has 365 days. H. Hoehner describes the calculations as follows. "By multiplying 476 by 365.24219879 or by 365 days, 5 hours, 48 minutes, 45.975 seconds (there are 365.25 days in a year), one comes to 173,855 days, 6 hours, 52 minutes, 44 seconds, or 173,855 days. This leaves only 25 days to March 5 (of 444 B.C.); one comes to March 30 (or A.D. 33), which was Nisan 10 in A.D. 33. This is the triumphal entry of Jesus into Jerusalem."[57] The sixty-nine weeks cover the period of time between 444 B.C. and A.D. 33.

Chart 7 on the next page is a representation of Daniel's seventy-week prophecy. (See endnote 58 for sources of more charts regarding this prophecy.)

Daniel's prophecy has taken us through 483 years, or sixty-nine weeks, of the prophecy. The destruction of the city (Jerusalem) and the

CHART 7

Daniel's Seventy Weeks [58]
(Daniel 9:24-27)

539 BC	March 5, 444 BC	March 30, AD 33		

	7+62 Weeks (483 Years)	◄ Mystery: ► Church Age	¹/2 Week 3¹/2 Years	¹/2 Week 3¹/2 Years
	Weeks: 69	Messiah Cut Off Apr. 3, A.D. 33	1 Week (7 Years)	
	Years: 69x7=483			
	Days: 360x483= 173,880	X City and Sanctuary Destroyed Aug. 6, A.D. 70	Daniel 9:27	

| Daniel's Vision | Decree to Restore & Build Jerusalem under Artaxerxes | Messiah The Prince (Triumphal Entry) Luke 19:28-40 | The Coming Prince | Messiah Returns |

sanctuary (Temple) was prophesied to occur after the crucifixion of Christ. "… Messiah will be cut off [crucified] and have nothing, and the people [Romans] of the prince to come [Antichrist] will destroy the city [Jerusalem] and the sanctuary [Temple]. And its end will come with a flood; even to the end and there will be war; desolations are determined" (Daniel 9:26 [brackets by author]).

The destruction of Jerusalem and the temple was by the Romans, under the leadership of Titus as predicted by Daniel 9:26 and by Jesus in Matthew 24:2, Mark 13:2, and Luke 21:24. This prophecy was literally fulfilled. Sixty-nine weeks of the seventy weeks have been fulfilled.

This brings us to the final week or seven years in this prophecy. There is a great time interval between the sixty-ninth and seventieth week. This interval has lasted for over 1,975 years and includes the present Church Age (nearly 2,000 years). This is a mystery in the Old Testament. It is alluded to, but not clarified until the New Testament.

MYSTERY OF THE CHURCH AGE

To understand biblical prophecy one must understand that Israel and the Church are on different time clocks. "It seems that the Lord deals with Israel and the Church mutually exclusively. A chess clock, with its two interlocked representations, is an illustrative example; one clock is stopped while the other is running."[59]

The Church Age is a mystery hidden in the Old Testament. Paul said, "To me, the very least of all saints, this grace was given, to preach to the Gentiles the unfathomable riches of Christ, and to bring to light what is the administration of the mystery which for ages has been hidden in God who creates all things; so that the manifold wisdom of God might now be made known through the church to the rulers and the authorities in the heavenly places" (Ephesians 3:8-10).

The Church Age can be viewed as a parenthesis in God's plan for Israel. This does not imply that God decided at the last minute to set Israel aside. It was a mystery alluded to in the Old Testament and revealed in the New Testament.

The Messiah is referred to in Isaiah 53 "… like a lamb that is led to slaughter …" (v. 7), and as Someone who would die for our sins. "… He himself bore the sin of many, and interceded for the transgressors" (v. 12). He was also referred to as a Mighty King. "For a child will be born to us, a Son will be given to us; and the government will rest on His shoulders; and His name will be called Wonderful Counselor, Mighty God, Eternal Father, Prince of Peace" (Isaiah 9:6). In this one verse we have the birth of Christ prophesied in line one and His reign in line two. An unspoken time gap exists between the first line and the second line, which says, "the government will rest on His shoulders." The events of line two do not happen until the Second Coming of Christ when He ushers in the thousand-year millennial kingdom where Christ will reign (Revelation 20:6).

The Messiah was described in the Old Testament as a "Suffering Servant" or "Lamb," and also as King or "Mighty God" and "Prince of Peace." These two roles of Jesus the Messiah are similar to seeing two mountains from a distance with an unseen valley between them. The unseen valley is the Church Age, a truth hidden in the Old Testament and revealed in the New Testament.[60]

God works differently with Israel than He does with His Church. This difference is an important piece of the puzzle that helps us interpret and unlock the prophetic puzzle. It actually illuminates prophecy, especially in light of our current world status.

The seventieth week in Daniel, or the final seven years, is referred to as the Tribulation Period. It is a time of judgment upon the world. This final period of time, when Israel's clock starts ticking again, begins with a seven-year covenant, or treaty, between the Antichrist and the nation of Israel (Daniel 9:26-27). In verse 26, "the prince to come" refers to the future Antichrist. Verse 27 says, "And he will make a firm covenant with the many for one week ..." The "many" refers to Israel, as shown in verse 24. "Seventy weeks have been decreed for your people ..." Daniel's people refers to the nation of Israel. The "prince to come" cannot refer to "Messiah, the Prince" because it refers to the future, and the "prince who is to come" is associated with evil "abominations."

JESUS CHRIST: THE FULFILLMENT OF THE OLD TESTAMENT PROPHETS

The literal fulfillment of the Old Testament prophecies demonstrates the accuracy and reliability of the Bible. "The fact of fulfilled prophecy is found in the Bible alone; hence, it presents proof of divine inspiration that is positive, conclusive, and overwhelming. Here is the argument in brief: no man, unaided by divine inspiration, foreknows the future, for it is an impenetrable wall, a true 'iron curtain' to all mankind. Only an almighty and all-knowing God can infallibly predict the future."[61]

Jesus Christ was the Messiah that Israel longed for but did not accept. In Corinthians, Paul said, "... but we preach Christ crucified, to Jews a stumbling block ..." (1 Corinthians 1:23). The Jews were looking for a mighty king to rule over them. Remember the mountain peaks? They rejected Jesus as a "lamb" to die for their sins. They were looking for the second mountain peak, which will be revealed in the future.

Israel rejected Jesus as their Messiah. As a result, they were temporarily set aside, but not rejected. "I say then, God has not rejected His people, has He? May it never be! ..." (Romans 11:1). The Lord will again deal with the nation of Israel in Daniel's seventieth week, the Tribulation Period.

The Old Testament contains many predictions of the Messiah that only Jesus could fulfill, and these prophecies were fulfilled in the Gospels. More than 400 years passed between the Messianic predictions of the Old Testament and their fulfillment in the Gospels. Many of the predictions were much older than 400 years. Predictions from Moses (1500 B.C.) to Malachi (400 B.C.) cover over 1,100 years. During that time, a succession of prophets and predictions testified to the coming Messiah.[62]

When looking at fulfilled prophecy, it is inconceivable how anyone could not believe in the reliability of the Bible as the inspired Word of God. The fulfillment of specific, detailed prophecies validates the Bible and sets it apart from all other faiths. Many other world religions try to build their claims upon miracles that cannot be proven. There is no other religion in the history of the world that has ventured to frame prophecies and has shown their fulfillment.

CHANCE FULFILLMENT?

The probabilities of coincidence or chance fulfillment of these prophecies are minute.

"Suppose," says Dr. Olinthus Gregory, "that there were only 50 prophecies in the Old Testament (instead of 333) concerning the first advent of Christ, giving details of the coming messiah, and all meet in the person of Jesus ... the probability of chance fulfillment as calculated by mathematicians, according to the theory of probabilities, is less than one in 1,125,000,000,000,000. Now add only two more elements to these 50 prophecies, and fix the time and the place at which they must happen and the immense improbability that they will take place by chance exceeds all the powers of numbers to express (or the mind of man to grasp)."[63]

BRIEF SUMMARY OF THE OLD TESTAMENT PROPHECIES FULFILLED IN CHRIST

1. He was to come from the tribe of Judah (Genesis 49:10);
   Fulfillment: Matthew 1:3, Hebrews 7:14.
2. He was to be born of a virgin (Isaiah 7:14);
   Fulfillment: Matthew 1:18-23.
3. He was to be born in Bethlehem (Micah 5:2);
   Fulfillment: Matthew 2:1; Luke 2:5-6.
4. He must come at a specific time in history (Daniel 9:24-26);
   Fulfillment: Luke 2:1.
5. He must be preceded by a forerunner (Isaiah 40:3);
   Fulfillment: Luke 1:17 and Matthew 3:1-3.
6. His ministry was to begin in Galilee (Isaiah 9:12);
   Fulfillment: Matthew 4:12, 16-23.
7. His ministry was to be characterized by miracles (Isaiah 35:5-6);
   Fulfillment: Matthew 11:4-6; John 11:47.
8. He was to be sold out for 30 pieces of silver (Zechariah 11:12);
   Fulfillment: Matthew 26:31-56.
9. His hands and feet were to be pierced (Psalm 22:16);
   Fulfillment: John 19:18, 37; John 20:25.
10. He was to be buried with the rich in His death (Isaiah 53:9);
    Fulfillment: Matthew 27:57-60.

These ten prophecies and their fulfillment in Christ barely scratch the surface of over 300 Old Testament prophecies. Just using these ten prophecies, the odds against any man fulfilling these prophecies are astronomical. As we saw in Daniel 9:24-27 (seventy-week prophecy), the Messiah not only had to fulfill all of the other prophecies, He had to fulfill them at a specific time in history.

There can be no question that Jesus Christ was the Messiah who was crucified to pay the penalty for our sins. The accuracy and precision of those Old Testament prophecies could not have come from anyone other than God Himself.[64]

This chapter has covered evidence that validates the Bible and Christianity as our reference point or standard. We also presented current challenges to Christianity and provided a defense or answer to each challenge. We covered evidence of the Bible's reliability, including verification of a miraculous event, and the confirmation provided by the discovery of the Dead Sea Scrolls. We also clarified the distinction between the scientific method and the legal-historical method as ways of proving the reliability of the occurrence of a past event.

We saw how prophecy fulfillment is one of the ways of confirming the Bible's reliability. We covered how a true prophet is determined, the fulfillment of some of the Old Testament prophecies, and then briefly covered the Church Age and the amazing seventy-week prophecy found in the book of Daniel. We established the foundation and the reliability of prophecy, along with the extreme improbability of chance fulfillment. In the next chapter, we will look at prophecy as it unfolds in the last days.

NOTES:

---⊗⊗⊗---

Chapter Four

The Emerging Final Empire

═══════════════════════════════════════

T he previous chapter focused on prophecy fulfillment and reasons to trust the authority and reliability of the Bible. This chapter will focus on the development of the final empire. We will first lay the biblical prophetic foundation that characterizes this empire and then review its historical-political development. This will enable us to see how it all ties in to the last generation.

This chapter involves historical details. Historical events will help the reader see the prophetic picture more clearly. By examining the trees more closely (historical detail) the forest will be viewed with a clearer perspective (the prophetic picture).

OVERVIEW OF FOUR EMPIRES

Chapter One briefly covered the final four world empires, known as the "Times of the Gentiles" (see Chart 1, Chapter One). In order to cover this time span from a telescopic view, we must first examine the historical events chronologically. This will help us see the larger prophetic picture. In other words, first we examine the biblical foundation for the whole puzzle, and then we take a more detailed look at the pieces of the puzzle to see how they fit together.

THE BACKGROUND

Under the leadership of Nebuchadnezzar, Babylon defeated the Assyrians in 609 B.C. Following this victory, the Babylonians went on to defeat Egypt in 605 B.C. in the Battle of Carchemish. Nebuchadnezzar expanded his territorial conquests southward into Syria and Palestine. After learning of the death of his father, Nabopolassar, he returned to Babylon in August 605 B.C. to receive the crown.[1] He then returned to Palestine and proceeded to attack Jerusalem in September 605 B.C., taking Daniel and his companions as captives to Babylon.[2] It is in this setting that the Book of Daniel was written. "According to the contents of the Book of Daniel, it was written in the sixth century [B.C.] by Daniel who lived during its events"[3] [brackets by author]. Daniel lived during the time of the Babylonian Empire and part of the following Medo-Persian Empire (Empire number two).

The Babylonian captivity of Judah lasted seventy years (605-536 B.C.) and was prophesied in Jeremiah 25:11-12. According to 2 Chronicles 36:20-21 and Leviticus 26:33-35, the Lord had commanded that the Israelites allow the land to rest every seventh year. The seventh year was known as the "Sabbath year."

To paraphrase, the Lord said that, one way or another, the land would be given its Sabbath year of rest, and, if violated, it would be made up. The prediction of the seventy-year captivity by Jeremiah 25:11-12 was to make up for the number of times the Sabbath year was violated, which obviously was seventy. The land was allowed to rest by a concentrated seventy-year Sabbath, while the Israelites were punished for breaking this law. Jeremiah prophesied from about 627 to 586 B.C.[4]

Daniel lived through the seventy-year Babylonian captivity, which ended three years into the Medo-Persian Empire that was under Cyrus and began in 539 B.C. We know that Daniel was still alive in the third year of Cyrus, that is, until 536 B.C.[5]

When we consider that Jeremiah predicted the seventy-year captivity prior to Daniel's time and it was then fulfilled in Daniel's time, we have every reason to believe that Daniel's prophecies will also be fulfilled in their appointed time. Our God does exactly what He says He will do; His timing, His mercy, and His justice do prevail.

This is the background and setting of Daniel and his prophecies.

THE SETTING

King Nebuchadnezzar had a dream and was troubled by it to the extent that it was interfering with his sleep.

> Now in the second year of the reign of Nebuchadnezzar, Nebuchadnezzar had dreams; and his spirit was troubled and his sleep left him. Then the king gave orders to call in the magicians, the conjurers, the sorcerers and the Chaldeans to tell the king his dreams. So they came in and stood before the king. The king said to them, "I had a dream and my spirit is anxious to understand the dream." (Daniel 2:1-3)

Nebuchadnezzar's dream was most likely a recurring dream. The use of the plural "dreams" would seem to indicate a recurrence of the same dream, and Daniel interprets only one dream.[6] It is also confirmed with the singular use of the word in the king's statement in verse three, "I had a dream ..."

Nebuchadnezzar was aware that his "wise men" could meet together and make up an interpretation to appease the king, so he required that they first tell him the dream. If they had the ability to tell him what he had dreamed, then their interpretation of his dream would be valid. When the "wise men" tried to reason with the king, he said to them, "... My word is final: If you don't tell me the dream and its interpretation, you will be torn limb from limb, and your houses will be made a garbage dump" (Daniel 2:5 HCSB).

They responded that no man could interpret the dream except "the gods." In the king's anger, he decreed that all the "wise men" in Babylon be executed (v. 12). This decree included all people who professed to be able to reveal the future, which included Daniel and his three companions.[7]

Daniel asked for more time from the king and said he would then reveal the interpretation (v. 16). Daniel and his friends prayed for "mercy concerning this mystery" (v. 18). God revealed the dream in a vision at night and Daniel praised God for His answer (vs. 19-23).

Daniel then approached the king and said, "This mystery has been revealed to me, not because I have more wisdom than anyone living, but in order that the interpretation might be made known to the king ..." (Daniel 2:30 HCSB). It is important to note that Daniel did not take the credit for knowing the dream and its interpretation. The king's dream and its interpretation originated from God.

Daniel tells the king two important points. First, no man can interpret the dream, only God. Second, God is revealing "what will happen in the last days" (v. 28). The dream and its interpretation originated from God, and it is prophetic of what will happen in the "last days."

THE DREAM

Nebuchadnezzar's dream and its interpretation are found in Daniel Chapters 2, 7, and 8. The following overview is based on these three chapters. The king's dream involved a colossal image, or statue of a man. Each part of the statue represents one of the final four successive empires before Christ returns at the end of the seven-year Tribulation Period. The first three empires will be covered briefly. The fourth empire will be the primary focus of this chapter since it deals with the "last days." The dates and rulers of the empires are drawn from the Bible and historical literature.

The head of the image, composed of gold, represents the first empire, Babylon. While the Babylonian Empire began in 626 B.C., King Nebuchadnezzar's rule began around 606 B.C. The chest and arms, composed of silver, represented the second empire, Medo-Persia, under the rule of Cyrus, which began around 539 B.C. The belly and thighs, composed of bronze, represented the third empire, Greece, under the rule of Alexander the Great. After Alexander's death, four generals followed his reign. The Greek empire began around 332 B.C. The legs, composed of iron, represented the fourth and final empire, the Roman Empire, which began between 63 B.C. and 68 B.C.

Daniel Chapter 7 records that, late in his life, Daniel had a dream "with visions in his mind." Daniel's dream concerned the same empires that had been represented by the image in Nebuchadnezzar's dream except that, in Daniel's dream, the empires were symbolized by animals. Nebuchadnezzar's dream (Daniel 2) represents the empires from man's point of view, and Daniel's dream (Daniel 7) represents the empires from God's point of view. Each of the empires in Daniel's dream is symbolized by an animal that illustrates characteristics of that particular empire. Daniel Chapters 7 and 8 parallel Chapter 2, but with more details.

Taken together, these three chapters give a more complete picture of the time period covered by the image in Daniel 2. Each of the animals symbolizes characteristics of that particular empire. The first three empires name identifiable animals, with certain variations to them. The animal characterizing the fourth, or final, empire is different. It is described as "dreadful and terrifying and extremely strong, and it had large iron teeth. It devoured and crushed, and trampled down the remainder with its feet; it was different from all the beasts before it, and it had ten horns" (Daniel 7:7). [Refer to Chart 1 on page 5.]

The Roman Empire appears to be extended in the sense that the composition changes within the same empire. The composition of the legs is iron, but the feet and toes are made of iron and clay. **It also has ten toes that represent ten kings, kingdoms, or regions that rule simultaneously.**[8] **This has never occurred historically and is, therefore, a future event.** The composition change from iron in the legs to iron and clay in the feet, alludes to a similarity (iron) but an altered version of the empire (iron and clay). This is an historical reference to the deterioration of the Roman Empire. It also applies to a future empire that will be similar in some ways to the Roman Empire, perhaps a revived form of it.

The iron and clay represent a weakness in the empire. Iron suggests strength and clay suggests weakness. Iron and clay will not adhere to one another. "The Roman Empire was characterized by division (it was a divided kingdom) and deterioration (it was partially strong and partially brittle). Though Rome succeeded in conquering the territories that came under its influence, it could never unite the peoples to form a united empire. In that sense, the people were a mixture and were not united."[9]

THE IMAGE AND THE FINAL EMPIRE

In Nebuchadnezzar's dream image, any future events that have not yet happened seem to be tied primarily to the ten toes, representing ten kingdoms that will rule simultaneously. The kingdom of God will rule immediately following the final empire (Roman or a revised version of it), putting an abrupt end to that empire.

Following the ten toes (kings), a kingdom will be established that will never be destroyed. "In the days of those kings [the ten kings represented by the ten toes in the preceding two verses] the God of heaven will set up a kingdom which will never be destroyed, and that kingdom will not be left for another people; it will crush and put an end to all these kingdoms, but it will itself endure forever" (Daniel 2:44 [brackets by author]). Daniel interpreted how this would happen in verses 34 and 35:

"… a stone was cut out without hands, and it struck the statue on its feet of iron and clay and crushed them … so that not a trace of them was found. But the stone that struck the statue became a great mountain and filled the whole earth."

"In Scripture a 'rock' [and a 'stone'] often refers to Jesus Christ, Israel's Messiah (e.g., Psalm 118:22; Isaiah 8:14; 28:16; 1 Peter 2:6-8) [and] … a mountain is often a symbol for a kingdom."[10] When Christ comes back the second time, He comes at the end of the Tribulation Period that "… He may strike down the nations, and He will rule them with a rod of iron …" (Revelation 19:15).

This is a future event. There are not currently ten kings ruling the earth, although there are ten member states (countries) in the European Union (EU) that are the core countries by way of authority and voting privileges. We know that the ten kingdoms originate out of what was considered the Roman Empire area, what now is the European Union. This may be an extension of the ten original member states of the EU. Also, Christ (the "Stone") has not made His triumphant appearance, i.e., the Second Coming (the stone crushing the image), and God has not established His kingdom (the great mountain that fills the earth), which will be everlasting. These are future occurrences.

The Roman Empire was characterized by division, which is symbolized by the two legs of iron. It was divided into the Western and the Eastern Roman Empire. Rome served as the capital of the Western Empire. Constantinople served as the capital of the Eastern Empire. The Western Roman Empire ended around A.D. 476, but the Eastern Roman Empire did not end until A.D. 1453. Usually, when one speaks of the Roman Empire, it is in reference to the Western Roman Empire. The Western Empire was never conquered by another country or empire and did not really "fall." It literally broke up into pieces, and a patchwork of independent kingdoms emerged.[11] The kingdoms did not merge into another empire. "Instead, individual nations emerged out of the old Roman Empire. Some of these nations, and others stemming from them, have continued to the present day."[12] This is the fourth and final empire.

The culture and influence of the Roman Empire has continued through the years. The re-combining of the pieces of this empire will comprise the ten toes of the image, which represent the ten kings (or rulers). The fourth empire does not end until the Second Coming of Christ at the end of the Tribulation Period.

The book of Daniel is an integral part of biblical prophecy. It is an important key to understanding the book of Revelation. Daniel is sometimes considered the ABC of prophecy, while the book of Revelation is considered the XYZ of prophecy. The credibility of the book of Daniel has been attacked. Considering its importance, it would make sense that Satan would attack its credibility.

As early as the third century, Porphyry (A.D. 233-305) was a student of Neoplatonic philosopher Philostratus, a scholar of comparative religions. Porphyry wrote a powerful pagan work against some Christian doctrinal and historical claims, such as the book of Daniel. (See note 15.)

The period of time that spans the four empires of the image in Daniel Chapter 2 is referred to as the "Times of the Gentiles." In Luke 21, Jesus tells of the Tribulation Period and some of the signs that precede His Second Coming. He then makes reference to the "times of the Gentiles" in verse 24: "… and they [the Jews] will fall by the edge of the sword, and will be led captive into all the nations; and Jerusalem will be trampled under foot by the Gentiles until the times of the Gentiles are fulfilled" [brackets by author]. When Jesus returns the second time, at the end of the Tribulation Period, it will be during the time of the Revived Roman Empire. This will be a world empire, which appears to be emerging under the name of the "European Union." Jesus will return as Conqueror and Judge. He came the first time as a Lamb, but will return the second time as the "… Lion that is from the tribe of Judah …" (Revelation 5:5).

THE FOURTH EMPIRE: MORE TO COME?

The fourth, and final, empire has not completed its course. In summary, there are at least five reasons for this belief:

1. According to Daniel Chapter 2, God Himself will crush the final empire when Christ returns at the end of the Tribulation Period. He cannot crush an empire that is not in existence.
2. The "Times of the Gentiles" takes in the time span of the whole image in Daniel, which covers the time span from the Babylonian Empire to the end of the Tribulation Period when Christ returns to set up His Kingdom. It is at that point in time that the fourth empire is conquered "… and that kingdom will not be left for

another people ..." (Daniel 2:44).

3. The material of the feet and toes is iron and clay (not just iron). This variation may indicate a deteriorating Roman Empire. A modified version of the Roman Empire (the ten toes-kings) is future.

4. The ten toes in Daniel 2:42 represent ten kings who rule simultaneously; they parallel the ten horns and ten kings in Daniel 7:24. This has never occurred in the history of the Roman Empire. It is a future event.

5. The fourth kingdom "... will devour the whole earth and tread it down and crush it" (Daniel 7:23). This has not yet occurred. It is a future event.

As mentioned earlier, Daniel Chapters 7 and 8 expand the image in Daniel Chapter 2, giving a more comprehensive picture of this four-empire time frame. The emphasis, for our purpose, is on the fourth or final empire. The "beast with ten horns" in Daniel 7:7, 19-20 correspond to the legs, feet, and toes in Daniel 2:40-43.

THE ELEVENTH HORN
THE ULTIMATE DICTATOR OF HORRORS

Daniel Chapter 7 adds an additional horn. The toes and horns represent kings; this additional horn is described in Daniel 7:7-8 and 20-21. It states in part: "... that horn which had eyes and a mouth uttering great boasts and which was larger in appearance than its associates. I kept looking, and that horn was waging war with the saints and overpowering them ..." This description fits the ruthlessness of the final One World Dictator, the Antichrist (Revelation 13:4-7).

BIBLICAL DESCRIPTIONS OF THE ANTICHRIST

Antichrist is referred to in the Bible as the "man of lawlessness," "the son of destruction," the "antichrist," and "the beast." His character is described in the Bible.

[He] who opposes and exalts himself above every so-called god or object of worship, so that he takes his seat in the temple of God, displaying himself as being God ... whose coming is in accord with the activity of Satan, with all power and signs and false wonders (2 Thessalonians 2:3-4, 9) ... he speaks in blasphemies against God (Revelation 13:6) ... he makes war with the saints [true believers] (Revelation 13:6) ... he will make a firm covenant with the many [Jews] for one week [seven years], but in the middle of the week [after three and one half years], he will put a stop to sacrifice and grain offerings; and on the wing of abominations will come one who makes desolate ... (Daniel 9:27). [brackets and parentheses by author]

Note the specific discrimination against the Christians—he "makes war with the saints" (Revelation 13:7)—and against the Jews. He takes his seat in the temple of God (2 Thessalonians 2:4). He breaks his seven-year covenant with the Jews by stopping their sacrifices in the temple and makes desolate to a complete destruction. In the beginning, he gains their trust, but then turns against them (Daniel 9:27).

THE ROMAN EMPIRE: PART OF THE PROPHETIC PUZZLE

The Roman Empire, together with its revived form, corresponds to the fourth empire in Daniel's image as the final empire. According to the book of Daniel, it was the last human-ruled empire. The following empire is ruled by Christ Himself, the "Stone" [capitalization by author as reference to future Messiah] that "was cut out of the mountain without hands" (Daniel 2:45). This is an empire ruled supernaturally by the King of kings and Lord of lords. This must refer to a future event. Let's look at some things we know about the Roman Empire.

The Roman Empire had spread throughout Europe by A.D. 200[13] and was a highly sophisticated, technologically powerful, and economically efficient civilization. This empire had a universal language and currency. It had a single government and a consistent set of written laws. The empire was highly organized and durable around a system of roads that in many places remain to this day.[14]

The Roman Empire was divided under Emperor Diocletian in A.D. 284. The two iron legs of the image portrayed in Daniel Chapter 2 represent this division. In A.D. 312, Constantine moved the capital to Constantinople (named after Constantine) in the Eastern Roman Empire. Rome became known as the religious capital of the empire, and Constantinople was known as the political capital.

Geographically, the Roman Empire covered most of Europe, the Middle Eastern countries, and much of North Africa. These are the approximate areas that are currently covered by the European Union. Maps of the Roman Empire in the first 200 years A.D. (in Jesus' day) are comparable to today's maps of the EU. The EU is expanding and will soon cover a much larger area than the Roman Empire. According to Daniel 7:23, the fourth beast "... will devour the whole earth and tread it down and crush it." The "beast" is a reference to the one world government under the rule of the Antichrist—an expanded or revived Roman Empire.

The religious beliefs of the Roman Empire were primarily pagan and included a pantheon of gods and beliefs. It was in Jesus' day that the Roman Empire was in power. Following the resurrection and ascension of Jesus was the day of Pentecost, the official beginning of the early Christian Church. Christianity spread rapidly. The persecution of Christians began under Nero in A.D. 64. Christians were crucified and burned alive, being used as human torches. This was particularly true from the very early church until A.D. 311. The Emperor Diocletian also had a reputation for persecution of Christians.

Galerius, while under Diocletian, continued to persecute Christians. Diocletian eventually retired in A.D. 305 after a prolonged illness.[15] Galerius then became emperor. In time, he "grew ill and needing all the divine help he could get, issued the famous 'Edict of Toleration' for Christians in 311." (See note 16.) This allowed Christians to practice their faith legally.[16] Eventually, Christianity was established as the state religion under the Emperor Constantine in A.D. 330. Constantine "supposedly" converted to Christianity, but continued his pagan practices. Christianity was the state religion, but there also existed a tolerant attitude toward different religions, cults, and paganism. Christianity, as the state religion, was mixed with paganism and the Babylonian mystery religions, resulting in a paganized Christianity. The details of this will be discussed in more detail in a later chapter.

Christianity, under Constantine, was a prototype of the One World Religion. This tolerant attitude, often referred to as "unity in diversity," is tolerant of all religions and cults, with the exception of Christianity and Judaism. This intolerance will manifest itself to the extreme during the Tribulation Period when Christians will be martyred, and the Antichrist will turn against the Jews by breaking his covenant with them. Hitler's mass slaughter of millions of Jews will look like child's play when compared to the millions or hundreds of millions slaughtered by the Antichrist. Hitler was a prototype of the Antichrist, the coming world dictator.

The Roman Empire was considered a world empire in the time when it existed. It was multicultural with a single currency and a single government. The European Union (EU) is also multicultural with a single government and a single currency known as the "euro." Not presently a dictatorship, the EU is operating more like the United States federal government. Both have member states—countries within the EU and state governments in the United States. The single government that is currently ruling the EU will gain in power and momentum and will eventually become a worldwide dictatorship. It will be the central power base for the whole earth. This is much larger than the "known earth" in the Roman Empire days.

The worldwide dictator coming out of the EU is the Antichrist, who is referred to in Daniel 7:20-21 as the "other horn" that arises after the ten horns. This horn has "eyes and a mouth" and utters "great boasts." He is described as "waging war with the saints," the born-again Christians. We know that the Antichrist will come from the geographical area that comprised the Roman Empire, out of the ten horns (Daniel 7:7-8, 20-21). The ten horns represent ten kings in Daniel 7:24. These parallel the ten toes in Daniel 2:41-43 that correspond to the fourth empire, the Roman Empire. The EU currently includes a large area that was in the Roman Empire.

The three pillars of the final One World Empire include:

1. One World Government
2. One World Economy
3. One World Religion

The following section reads like a history lesson on the development of the final empire. This is not a comprehensive list of all the developments that took place. The value of the chronological sequence of these events is connected to their prophetic significance as they relate to the last generation. **A prophetic puzzle is falling into place in the same way a jigsaw puzzle is pieced together—very slowly in the early stages, but near the end, it is completed quickly.** In this case, God is putting it together, and He has chosen to do it rapidly near the end.

HISTORICAL DEVELOPMENT OF THE FINAL EMPIRE

There were three significant events that instigated the uniting of the European countries. The first event was World War I that lasted from 1914 until 1918. The second event was World War II that lasted from 1939 until 1945. The third event was the development and use of the atomic bomb in 1945.

Both world wars involved the European countries. With the exception of Japan and the United States, all the other countries shared borders. Neighboring European countries were at war with each other. Europe was at war with neighboring countries during both world wars, with no ocean to provide a buffer or protection.

Once the atomic bomb was used, the world entered a new age, an age characterized by insecurity. To counter this threat, Europe and the rest of the world began taking measures to unite. The push toward a one world government had picked up momentum.

THE UNITED NATIONS (1945)

On April 25, 1945, the United Nations Conference (UN) drafted a charter in San Francisco. The designated purpose of the UN was to provide peace, security, and cooperation. The international headquarters for the UN is in New York. All recognized independent countries are members. The exceptions are: China (Taiwan), Western Sahara, Palestine, and the Holy See (permanent observer state).

The UN presently consists of 192 countries, or member states. It is interesting to note that this number has greatly multiplied between 1947 and 1991 as a result of divisions into hostile camps within the countries (ethnic divisions).[17]

The drafting of the charter for the UN on April 25, 1945, occurred just prior to the dropping of the atomic bombs on Hiroshima and Nagasaki on August 6th and 9th of 1945. By October 24, 1945, the UN was officially established.

The Atomic Age was both beneficial, providing nuclear energy, and destructive, bringing the threat of nuclear weapons. It began an age of insecurity and initiated the start of an international nuclear arms race. The advent of the atomic bomb and the nuclear arms race clarified the judgments found in the Book of Revelation.

GENERAL AGREEMENT ON TRADES AND TARIFFS (GATT) (1947): ROOTS OF THE WORLD TRADE ORGANIZATION (WTO) (1995)

Following the establishment of the United Nations, the General Agreement on Trades and Tariffs (GATT) was established in 1947. This evolved into the World Trade Organization (WTO) by 1995, establishing the roots of the global economy.

The World Trade Organization gives equal weight to all countries in their votes. This means that the vote of the United States would count the same as that of a small third world country. At the present time, the authority for overseeing GATT rests in the hands of a few men. Any authority given to a few men could be given to one man as an oversight lord. This is significant in the development of a one-world economy, one of the three pillars of a one-world empire, as outlined by Hal Lindsey in his televised *International Intelligence Briefing*, July 27, 2005.

THE WORLD FEDERALIST MOVEMENT (1947)

The World Federalist Movement (WFM) was established in August 1947. It actually originated prior to 1947 in informal groups. The first formal conference was in 1947. The purpose of the WFM was to form a cohesive and effective group. This purpose was changed in 1954. From 1947 to 1948, it grew from 300 participants to 150,000 members and included nineteen nationalities. By 1951, the groundwork was laid for the "World Associations of Parliamentarians for World Government." In 1954, the first formal statement of purpose was established. Their overall purpose was to establish a World Government.[18] This involves a global economy and a world government, two of the three pillars in the forming of the Final Empire.

THE UNIVERSAL DECLARATION OF HUMAN RIGHTS (1947)

In December 1947, the Universal Declaration of Human Rights (UDHR) was enacted. According to Article 29 of the UDHR, humans have the rights and freedoms granted unless "exercised contrary to the purposes and principles of the United Nations."[19] The implications of this article are sweeping. It is saying that the government gives us our rights, and those rights are therefore limited to the purposes of the UN.

The *United States Constitution*, on the other hand, says our rights are God given, which limits the government. The UDHR empowers the UN, which does not acknowledge a Creator.[20] This is a significant piece of legislation. It is a philosophical worldview shift from a God-centered point of reference to a government-centered point of reference.

1948: A PIVOTAL YEAR

The year 1948 was a pivotal year. It is the year that Israel was established as a nation (May 14, 1948), and it is the start of the last generation. The year of 1948 began the countdown of events of the final generation before Christ returns. The final stretch begins with the birth of Israel and the final empire and concludes with the Second Coming of Christ following the Tribulation Period. The following three political events led up to May 14, 1948.

CONGRESS OF EUROPE (1948)

Following WWII, the Congress of Europe met in 1948 in Hague, Holland. They adopted seven resolutions on political union. The relevance of this event can be seen in resolution #7, which reads, "The creation of a United Europe must be regarded as an essential step towards the creation of a united world."[21] Obviously, a one world government was in the planning from 1948, the year that the last generation began the countdown to the Second Coming of Christ.

THE BENELUX TREATY (1948)

The second political event was the signing of the Benelux Treaty in 1948. This treaty was the result of the joining together of the three Benelux countries as a customs union. These three countries are Belgium, The Netherlands, and Luxembourg. As a result of two world wars in less than half of a century, plus the advent of the atomic bomb, the Benelux countries were formed for economic purposes.[22] The Benelux Alliance became the nucleus for the modern super state of Europe,[23] which evolved into the European Union.

THE BRUSSELS TREATY (MARCH 17, 1948)

The final event preceding the establishment of Israel as a nation was the Brussels Treaty, signed on March 17, 1948. This treaty added Britain and France to the three Benelux countries. The Brussels Treaty was also a precursor to the NATO agreement in the following year.[24] The real significance of this treaty is found in the amended, or modified, version in 1954. The modified version will be discussed in more detail later in the chapter.

ISRAEL: THE HINGE POINT OF HISTORY (MAY 14, 1948)

The historical hinge point on our timeline is the establishment of Israel as a nation on May 14, 1948. Beginning in 1948, the momentum of significant changes accelerated in a relatively short period of time. Satan knows his time is short. He has one generation left in which to lie and deceive. He will attempt to destroy anything or anyone to prevent people from having an encounter with Jesus Christ (the Way, the Truth, and the Life), and he will try to destroy the testimony of those who have already accepted Jesus and His free gift of salvation.

Israel is the only nation in history to have experienced total annihilation and dispersal to the far corners of the earth, and then to have experienced the rebirth of the nation.

When other nations were conquered and destroyed, the people of those countries lost their national identities as a result of being dispersed and intermarrying with people from other nations. **For Israel to have retained its identity for two thousand years and then to have been reestablished as a nation in the same geographical location it originally inhabited is nothing short of a miracle. This is a landmark event.** God initiated this for His Name's sake and His glory. He did not bring the Israelites out of the other nations for *their* sake, but for the sake of "His holy name." "… Then the nations will know that I am the Lord …" (Ezekiel 36:23).

God had promised to gather Israel from the nations and bring her back to her own homeland. "For I will take you from the nations, gather you from all the lands and bring you into your own land" (Ezekiel 36:24). The promises of Israel's restoration were dormant for several thousand years until this generation.[25]

The Old Testament foretold the scattering of the Israelites among the nations in Ezekiel 36:19 and their regathering in Ezekiel 36:24, but it did not give a time period. In the New Testament, Jesus made reference to the signs that would precede His Second Coming in Matthew 24. He narrowed the time frame to one generation and then connected that generation to the rebirth of Israel.

> Now learn the parable from the fig tree: when its branch has already become tender and puts forth its leaves, you know that summer is near; so you too, when you see all these things, recognize that He is near, right at the door. Truly I say to you, this generation will not pass away until all these things take place. (Matthew 24:32-34)

The fig tree is a symbol for Israel, as an eagle symbolizes America and a bear symbolizes Russia. "In context, the fig tree is always a symbol for Israel, such as Hosea's statement, 'I found Israel like grapes in the wilderness; I saw your fathers as the earliest fruit on the fig tree in its first season' " (Hosea 9:10).[26]

As mentioned earlier, the Bible refers to a fig tree thirty-three times. In reference to the parable of the fig tree, Matthew 24:32 says, "… when its branch has already become tender and puts forth its leaves, you know that summer is near." Just as this is a reference to the general time frame (summer is near), "so the argument goes, is the restoration of Israel to her land a sure sign the general time of Christ's restoration has arrived." [27]

Jesus narrowed the time frame: first, to Israel becoming a nation; and second, to one generation, from the rebirth of Israel to the Second Coming of Christ. When referring to the nearness of His return, skeptics will often quote Matthew 24:36: "But of that day and hour no one knows …" It is also true that Jesus was giving the "season" of His return. Jesus gave a sign of the time of His return in Matthew 24:32-34, which is only two verses prior to "of that day and hour no one knows." He was not contradicting Himself, only narrowing the time frame to a season or "generation," not the day, the hour, or even the year.

THE LAST GENERATION (1948 TO THE SECOND COMING)

In this last generation, which began in 1948, we can see two of the many prophecies of Daniel unfolding. Both are found in Daniel 12:4, 8-10.

"But as for you, Daniel, conceal these words and seal up the book until the end of time; many will go back and forth, and knowledge will increase." ... As for me, [Daniel] I heard but could not understand; so I said, "My Lord, what will be the outcome of these events?" He said, "Go your way, Daniel, for these words are concealed and sealed up until the end time. ... those who have insight will understand." (Daniel 12:4, 8-10 [brackets by author])

The first prophecy says, "... many will go back and forth ..." If we back up fifty to seventy-five years, this prophecy would not mean much. People have always traveled, but slowly and, for the most part, over relatively short distances. The technology to travel fast and to transport large numbers of people around the globe in a short amount of time has only existed for about the last fifty years. This prophecy makes sense today.

The second prophecy says, "... knowledge will increase." Again, knowledge has increased throughout history, but today the increase is exponential, at a mind-boggling rate. (Refer to **Chart** 8, "Growth of Knowledge" on the next page.)

KNOWLEDGE EXPLOSION

"But as for you, Daniel, conceal these words and seal up the book until the end of time; many will go back and forth, and knowledge will increase." (Daniel 12:4)

Most scholars agree that this reference concerning knowledge is related directly to understanding Daniel's prophecy in the end times prior to the Second Coming of Christ. Daniel did not understand the great prophecies that were revealed to him. Although this prophecy concerning knowledge relates to understanding Daniel's prophecy, there is an interesting parallel to the growth of human knowledge in general.

Human knowledge has been on the increase since the beginning of mankind, so this prophecy could be plugged into any point in history. How does Daniel's prophecy about the increase of knowledge apply to our day and time? The answer lies in the *rate* of increase. According to most experts, the sum total of all human knowledge doubles every two years.[28] (See **Chart** 8 on the next page.)

When we consider the history of mankind and the vast knowledge that has accumulated, this rate is nothing short of phenomenal. Ray

CHART 8

Growth of Knowledge

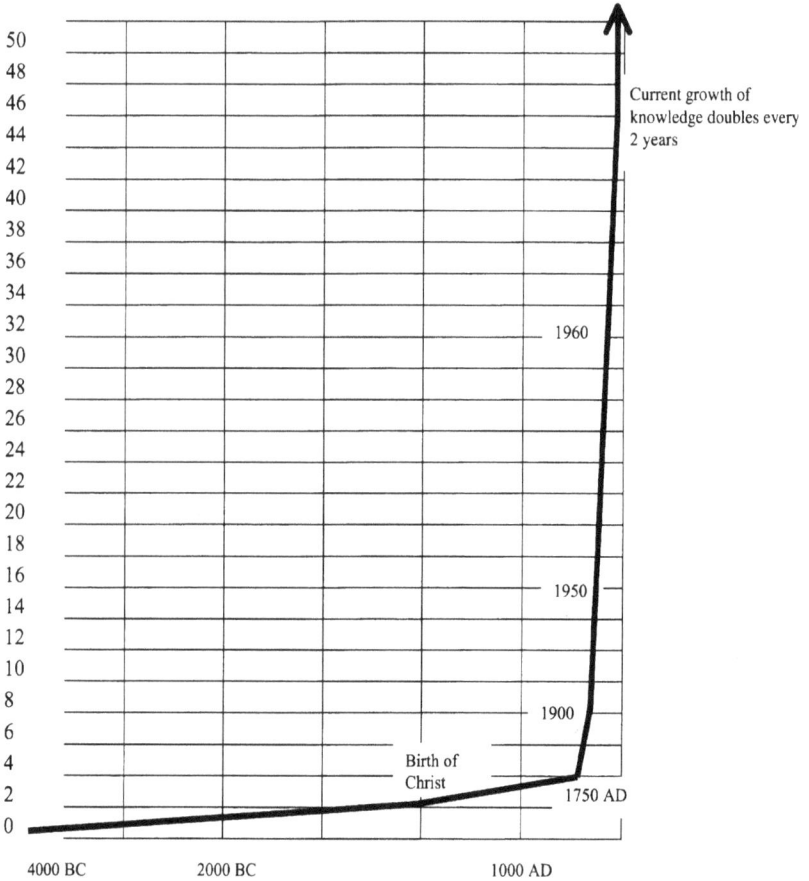

Current growth of
knowledge doubles every
2 years

1960

1950

1900

Birth of
Christ

1750 AD

50
48
46
44
42
40
38
36
34
32
30
28
26
24
22
20
18
16
14
12
10
8
6
4
2
0

4000 BC   2000 BC   1000 AD

STATISTICS:

➤ Doubled once between 4000 BC and birth of Christ (4000 yrs)
➤ Doubled between birth of Christ and 1750 (1750 yrs)
➤ Doubled again between 1750 and 1900 (150 yrs)
➤ Doubled again between 1900-1950 (50 yrs)
➤ Doubled between 1950 and 1960 (10 yrs)
➤ 1960 – doubles every 2 years or less

Chart based on information from Peter and Paul Lalonde,
2000 A.D. (Nashville: Thomas Nelson Pub., 1997) P.23

Kurzweil, inventor, scientist, and futurist, wrote in his article, *The Law of Accelerating Returns*, "... we won't experience 100 years of progress in the 21st century—it will be more like 20,000 years of progress (at today's rate). ... There's even exponential growth in the rate of exponential growth."[29]

This exponential growth in knowledge takes on prophetic significance in light of Daniel 12:9. "He said, 'Go your way, Daniel, for these words are concealed and sealed up until the end time.'" Daniel could not understand the prophetic visions that were given to him (Daniel 12:8). The key to understanding Daniel's prophecy is the tremendous increase in knowledge that is present in the "end times." Prophecy can be understood in light of current events and the exponential increase in knowledge. Prophecy, like a puzzle, begins to portray the real picture.

There is an excellent example that is often used to describe exponential growth. If you paid an income for one month starting with one penny on day one and doubled it each day, by mid-month, or day fifteen, your total is $327.67. By day twenty-five, your total is $335,544.31. Now the amount of money you have accumulated is a big deal. By day thirty-one, the total is $21,474,836.47. **Exponential growth has taken on a new meaning.**[30]

It is those last days of the month that are significant, especially the last three days. The increase of knowledge has demonstrated a similar growth. The "Growth of Knowledge" chart shows that, at the present time, we are in the time that is almost vertical. To use the monetary example, we are in the last three days of the month.

A REAL GENERATION GAP

Historically, a generation gap would explain the reason parents and children did not understand each other. The music was different, along with the hairstyles and clothing styles. The two generations did not speak the same language.

With the exponential growth in both knowledge and technology, this gap has widened considerably. "The technology explosion has created the first true generation gap in human history. In the past, kids wore their hair differently from their parents or listened to different music. But today, they truly live in a different world. They're plugged in, they're online, and they view the world through a lens that the older generation doesn't even know exists."[31]

The first true generation gap makes sense, considering the rebirth of Israel as a nation on May 14, 1948, and considering the words of Jesus, "Truly, I say to you, this generation will not pass away until all these things take place" (Matthew 24:34). If we are the last generation, as the evidence indicates, the exponential increase in knowledge and technology would take place during this generation. Remember that knowledge was doubling every two years as early as 1960. Since then, this rate has again increased.

INTERNET: KNOWLEDGE COMMUNICATION EXPLOSION

Larry Roberts designed the Internet in the early 1960s. It was originally called Arpanet and came into existence as a result of the Cold War. The military commissioned the government to create a communication system that would continue to function in the event of a nuclear attack. Messages were delivered in packets of information that could take alternate paths to reach a destination. As a result, the Internet was born.[32]

Since the Internet "piggybacks" our telephone systems, it was easy to cover most of the world in a short period of time. This technological leap caused a quantum leap in communication in the information age. Remember Daniel 12:4, "... many will go back and forth and knowledge will increase."

We truly have a global communication network in place. Since the Internet was initially dependent on the phone lines, it was not possible to connect the whole world with the Internet. Today it is becoming possible to connect the entire world electronically, due to advances in satellite and cellular phone technologies.[33]

We are now in the process of a wireless revolution. In 1999, a Time magazine advertisement for Agilent Technologies, illustrates the explosion of a global communication network. The ad states, "It took one hundred years to connect the first billion people. The second will only take five. The wireless revolution is at hand."[34] It is here.

Finally, in Daniel 12:9-10, it says, "... these words are concealed and sealed up until the end time" and "... those who have insight will understand ..." In other words, these prophecies will make sense in the end time to the righteous, that is Christians (Daniel 12:3, 9). Today, in this generation, they make sense.

WHAT ABOUT ISRAEL?

God secures Israel's future as a nation. Romans 11:1-2 says, "God has not rejected His people [Israel] whom He foreknew ..." Israel has experienced tough times as a nation, but not as tough as it will experience during the Tribulation Period. In Daniel 12:1, Daniel is told: "Michael, the great prince [archangel] who stands guard over the sons of your people [Israelites], will arise. And there will be a time of distress such as never occurred since there was a nation until that time ..." [brackets by author].

This is a reference to the Great Tribulation, the last three-and-one-half years, when Satan will attempt to exterminate every descendant of Abraham (Revelation 12:15-17). This will be a time of great distress for Israel.[35] God keeps His promises; He will fight for Israel, as seen in the future prophecy concerning Michael, a powerful angel in God's army.

NORTH ATLANTIC TREATY ORGANIZATION (NATO) (1949)

On April 4, 1949, the North Atlantic Treaty Organization (NATO) was signed. The core provision of this treaty (Article 5) was intended to protect the Western European Allies and the United States against an attack by the USSR. It was a collective self-defense recognized under Article 51 of the Charter of the United Nations.[36] The purpose of this treaty was a collective security with a philosophy of Mutually Assured Destruction (MAD). This philosophy perpetuates the arms race. It is only through the Second Coming of Christ at the end of the Tribulation Period that mankind will be rescued from total destruction (Matthew 24:22).

Following two world wars and the advent of the atomic bomb, the world has become an unsafe place to live. Many of the countries that are members of NATO are the same countries (called member states) that are members of the European Union (EU) and the Western European Union (WEU). The headquarters for NATO is in Brussels, Belgium. The EU and the WEU also have their headquarters in Brussels. This is another move toward world unity.

THE WESTERN EUROPEAN UNION (WEU) (1954)

In order to clearly summarize the development of the Western European Union that began in 1954, it is necessary to briefly cover the time span from 1954 to 2005.

In 1954, the Western European Union (WEU) was established as a result of a 1954 amendment to the 1948 Brussels Treaty (Article 5). This became a major modification and had a tremendous impact on the direction and the empowering of the EU. Under Article 5 of the modified Brussels treaty, the WEU became responsible for the collective defense of the EU. This article contained an unconditional defense clause. This put them in a very powerful position.

The WEU became Europe's only Security and Defense Assembly. Its first session was in 1955, but it wasn't until 1984 that the WEU was reactivated to provide a limited military capability. Its first military operation was with the Allied maritime forces during the Gulf War of 1991. The WEU is a growing military power. It is clearly becoming a major player in the EU's influence on the world stage.

Under Article 4, the security of the WEU member states (countries) became linked to NATO. Through the establishment of the WEU Assembly, thirty-seven countries became entitled to send their parliamentary representatives. This includes all of the EU member states, the European NATO countries, Russia, the Ukraine, and all the Balkan states. The Assembly scrutinizes European intergovernmental activities in the areas of security and defense, including armaments cooperation. The WEU is the enforcement arm of the European Union.

Javier Solana has served as the Secretary General of the Western European Union since the year 2000. **This man is extremely powerful. The WEU, under Solana's leadership, is likely to become the ruling arm of the EU.** Geographically, the EU is in accordance with the Bible as the origin or home base of the Final Empire, which will expand to a World Empire. This puts Solana or his successor in a position to become a world ruler.

Solana has an impressive resume. From December 5, 1995 to October 6, 1999, Solana held the position of Secretary General of NATO. In 1995, the same year that Solana started his term as Secretary General of NATO, the WEU became a ten-nation-member state. These same ten countries have full status membership in the EU, NATO, and the WEU. These are the ten Brussels Treaty powers, and it is very likely that they refer to the ten kingdoms or regions that have their origin in the same geographical region as the Roman Empire, referred to by the ten toes in Daniel Chapter 2, and the ten horns and ten kings in Daniel Chapter 7. Solana was also former president of the European Union.

In addition, Solana is the first to hold the newly created position of Office of the High Representative (1999) of the Common Foreign and Security Policy (CFSP). This office is for the European Union. It was created in 1999 to direct common foreign policy towards Russia, Ukraine, and the Mediterranean. Solana, recognizing the importance of this office, left his office as Secretary General of NATO two months early in order to take this new position. In 1999, Solana was also made Secretary General of the Council of Europe, the main decision-making body of the EU.[37]

On November 20, 1999, Javier Solana was selected by the ten member (nation) states, the core of the WEU, to be its Secretary General, pending unification with the European Union.

WHAT ABOUT 666?

The number 666 is mentioned in the book of Revelation. This number represents the name, or the number of the name, of the Antichrist. During the tribulation period, in order to buy or sell, a person must have this number or the name of the Antichrist on his right hand or forehead (Revelation 13:16-18). There seems to be a "providential" connection to Solana and the WEU.

The new office of "High Representative" came as a result of the Vienna Summit in December 1998. Out of 1,150 documents created at the Summit, the document that created this office happened to be number 666.[38] In my research for this book, I came across the number 666 three times involving the political structure or government policy as it relates to Solana, the EU, or the WEU. Coincidence or Providence?

By the year 2000, Solana was serving in the capacity of High Representative, a position created by document 666 of the Vienna Summit, and as Secretary General of the WEU. "On June 5, 2000, the ten-nation WEU, in its Assembly Recommendation 666, noted that under its governing treaties, complete merger could not occur."[39] This recommendation had to do with a continuing relationship with the ten Brussels Treaty Powers (same ten countries), but it did not allow for a merger of the EU and WEU. The WEU Assembly supported a proposal under Recommendation 666. According to Article 12 of Recommendation 666, Solana was allowed to become Secretary General of the ten-nation WEU Alliance. In his role as High Representative, Solana could preside over the Political Security Committee (PSC) and convene the Council of the European Union in the event of an emergency.

Solana is now the Secretary General of the WEU, the CFSP High Representative, and the Secretary General of the Council of Europe. He wears three hats and is allowed to preside over the Political Security Committee (PSC) and convene the Council of the European Union "in the event of an emergency ... All foreign ambassadors of the European Union entity as well as all EU military personnel are ultimately accountable to the Council of the European Union through Javier Solana."[40]

Solana plays two roles and fills two offices meant for two people, with the power to convene the Council of the European Union. He also plays a third role as Secretary General of the Council of Europe. He holds office in three positions and is currently seeking permanent seats on the UN Security Council. If he gains a permanent seat on the UN Security Council (including veto power), it will make him the most powerful man on earth.[41]

Only Recommendation 666 had to do with WEU's continuing relationship with the ten Brussels Treaty Powers (ten full member states of the EU and WEU) and increasing the power of the Office of High Representative.[42] Solana is the Secretary General of the WEU and the High Representative of the CFSP, under the authority of Recommendation 666. Under Article 12 of the Recommendation, Solana, as Secretary General of the WEU and High Representative of the CFSP, has the authority (in the event of an "emergency") to take control of the EU's military machinery.

What constitutes an emergency? The European Union is perceived to be the major power in Europe. The WEU is considered a part of the greater EU. In reality, the situation is reversed. The WEU has more influence and power than the EU. An "emergency" could involve a collapse of the recently signed treaty of Lisbon, the replacement of the European Constitution, which could result in the collapse of the EU. Since nature abhors a vacuum, there is only one logical candidate to step in and pick up the pieces, and Recommendation 666 has already established the framework for the Secretary General of the WEU to step in.[43] This is the second time the number 666 has cropped up. In both cases the number was related to a document number (666) that created a new office (High Representative) and a recommendation number (666) that gave more authority to the Secretary General of the WEU. If Solana doesn't fill the role of Antichrist, the future world ruler, his office is the ideal power base for a successor to fill the role as Antichrist.

The real power is in the hands of the ten full members of the WEU, which are the same ones that are included as full members of NATO. The WEU, with its ten members, are under the authority of Solana, the Secretary General, who also holds the office of High Representative. In reality, the real power is not in the hands of the European Union, but in the hands of the Western European Union that is currently under Javier Solana.[44]

THE TREATY OF ROME (1957/1958)

The Treaty of Rome was signed in 1957 and enforced in 1958. This was the political treaty that created modern-day Europe. It created the European Economic Community (EEC) that was also known as the European Common Market. It also established the European Atomic Energy Commission (EAEC). This was not the treaty that established the European Union.

Europe is rapidly becoming one entity and not just a group of countries that are "member states." It is becoming federalized, as we will see in the next chapter.

CLUB OF ROME (1957)

The Club of Rome is a German-based think tank established in 1957. It is an association of scientists, economists, businessmen, international high civil servants, and former heads of state. The members are from all five continents and include fifty-two countries. It has a limit of 100 active members. The only major country not included is Israel. A vast majority of the world hates Israel, along with any country that supports them, including the United States. The Club's purpose is to figure out ways to solve humanity's problems.

Many years ago, the Club of Rome divided the world into ten regions. Today, regionalization is the new buzz word, with "regions" of countries gaining power and influence. World Federalists, who also advocate world regions, have detailed plans for a world government similar to the Club of Rome.[45]

In 1958, GATT (General Agreement on Trades and Tariffs, 1947), as well as other organizations at the Club of Rome advocating a "One World

Order," divided the world into ten economic centers and called them "Mega Territories" and "Kingdoms." The One World Government would rule the "Ten Kingdoms" of the Club of Rome. The U.S. has recently agreed to the GATT treaty by joining the World Trade Organization (WTO).[46]

In 1974, the Club of Rome submitted a plan to the United Nations for a global government. The plan called for all nations to be divided into 10 political/economic regions.[47] These "regions" are designated on a world map.

Since 1974, we now have almost five completed political/economic regions, called "Unions," and they fit 5 of the 10 designations on the world map proposed by the Club of Rome. They are: the **European Union** (1993), the **African Union** (2002),[48] and the **Mediterranean Union** (July 2008), proposed by President Nicholas Sarkozy of France. The Mediterranean Union includes the countries bordering the Mediterranean Sea, as well as the E.U. member states.[49] This is an obvious expansion of the Revived Roman Empire.

The Union of South American Nations (UNASUR) [or possibly the South American Union] signed a Constitutive Treaty on May 23, 2008. It still needs to be ratified[50] [brackets by author]. These will be followed soon enough by the North American Union.

The division of the world into ten regions by the Club of Rome involves inter-connections with the World Federalists and the World Economy (one of the necessary three pillars of a one world government) through GATT. In 1995, GATT became known as the World Trade Organization (WTO). It is clear that the end time, one world government was in the planning stages as far back as 1958, and it is in the development stage in this last generation.

WHAT ABOUT AMERICA?

This is a common question that perplexes biblical scholars. Nowhere in the Bible is America mentioned. It is a world superpower both militarily and economically, yet it is not mentioned in Scripture. There are some theologians who try to plug it into the Bible, but the majority admit that it is not mentioned. What does this mean?

The conclusion many have drawn is that America, in the last days, will lose its prominence as a world superpower. The question then becomes, "How will the USA lose prominence on the world scene?" The answer may be found in developments that are happening behind the scenes. "Is there an insidious plan to merge the sovereign nations of the United States, Canada, and Mexico into one North American superpower like its counterpart in Europe?"[51] John Corsi gives us insight in his 2007 book, *The Late Great USA: The Coming Merger with Mexico and Canada*, as shown in the following information.

In Waco, Texas, in March 2005, there was a meeting of three of the world's elite leaders. The meeting included President George W. Bush, Mexican President Vincente Fox, and Canadian Prime Minister Paul Martin. The leaders of these three North American countries introduced the Security and Prosperity Partnership of North America (SPP). According to John Corsi, these three men plan to combine the United States, Canada, and Mexico into one giant economic powerhouse, similar to the European Union.[52]

"There are extensive construction projects preparing a 'NAFTA Superhighway' to expedite goods from Lázaro Cárdenas, on the Pacific Coast of Mexico, through Laredo, Texas, to the Kansas City 'Smart Port' (an electronic port of entry to be regarded as Mexico territory), on through Duluth, Minnesota, to Canada."[53] Interstate Highway 35 is under construction from Texas to Minnesota. The simplest explanation for all of this "is that the U.S. is constructing a superhighway along the I-35 corridor to link Canada to Mexico for the SPP."[54]

According to John Corsi, the American dollar will be replaced with new money—the *amero*, "One man has become the face behind the Prosperity Partnership. Corsi exposes the hidden agenda of Robert Pastor, who speaks frankly about what it would take to bring a new North American currency to America—nothing more than an old-fashioned crisis. Pastor recently suggested that another 9-11 might be what it takes to get George Bush refocused on securing the borders of North America."[55]

Let's analyze it through the Bible prophecy lens. Jack Kinsella, a writer with Hal Lindsey's *Last Days Chronicles*, states that:

> Bible prophecy foretells the existence of four spheres of global influence in the last days: the Kings of the East, (China); the Gog-Magog Alliance (Russia, Middle East and North Africa); the Kings of the South (sub-Saharan Africa); and the revived Roman Empire of the antichrist.
>
> There is no mention of a fifth superpower resembling the United States. However, the antichrist's empire is so powerful, compared to the others,

that it qualified as a global government. The antichrist controls the global economy ... and that system will be imposed on a global basis.

The EU fits the description given in prophecy, except it is not yet the superpower the Bible describes it to be. According to both Daniel and John, each of the other global spheres of power come against him [the antichrist] at some point during the Tribulation, but are easily broken by his military power.

The EU doesn't have that power alone, but an alliance with an integrated North America would make it the undisputed and indisputable global superpower extraordinaire.[56]

Perhaps the North American Union will fit into the Club of Rome's plan to divide the world into ten economic regions. **If this SPP takes form, the USA would diminish in power. It would therefore make sense that it is not mentioned in biblical prophecy.**

The next chapter will complete the historical development of the Last Empire, and will also look at the current state of that empire and how it fits into the final days of the Last Generation.

Chapter Five

The Final Empire:
A One World Government

The previous chapter established the biblical foundation for the historical and future development of the "Times of the Gentiles." Daniel Chapter 2 illustrated this through the interpretation of Nebuchadnezzar's dream. Some of the political and historical developments toward the emerging Final World Empire were also covered.

This chapter will cover the current status of the "Revived Roman Empire" and One World Government. It also looks at the current status of the European Union and how the EU fits into the prophetic puzzle.

This chapter will be divided into two parts. The first section will be devoted to completing the political-historical development of the Final Empire and the last section will be devoted to the current status of the One World political system.

COPENHAGEN CRITERIA (JUNE 1993)

Since the Treaty of Rome was signed in 1957, a number of countries in Europe have found the need to unite economically. These countries later became known as "member states" of the EU. By 1981, ten countries had joined. By 1993, there were thirteen member states. In 1995, the number increased to fifteen nations, proposed or accepted. In 2004, the number reached twenty-five countries with ten candidate nations. In 2007, the number of member states has grown to twenty-seven.

By June of 1993, the European Council of the EU decided to set criteria for acceptability of candidates. The criteria included:

1. Stability of institutions guaranteeing democracy, the rule of law, and the respect and protection of minorities.
2. A functioning market economy and the capacity to cope with competitive pressure within the EU.
3. Adherence to arms of political, economic, and monetary union.

These criteria were intended to provide some barriers to entry.[1] The EU paradoxically worked to help countries get past barriers. For example, the Central Bank, established in June 1998, had "Enlargement Committees." By 1999, 67.5 percent of all direct investments from their bank were poured into candidate countries of EU origin.[2]

MAASTRICHT TREATY (NOVEMBER 1, 1993)

The Maastricht Treaty, also referred to as the Treaty of the European Union, was signed on February 7, 1992 and was enforced on November 1, 1993. This treaty replaced the Treaty of Rome and officially gave the name European Union to what was formerly known as the European Economic Community. This was the second major step in the uniting of Europe, the first being the Treaty of Rome.

The EU countries became known as "member states." This began a movement to erase national boundaries. States are usually members of a country. The larger body of government is now called the "European Union" and the countries previously referred to as "European countries" are now referred to as "member states." One wonders if the "states" (countries) in the EU, along with other states/countries outside of the EU, will turn into "regions" of the coming One World Government.

The answer is probably yes. By changing the name, the culture begins to accept the inevitable. Nations lose their sovereignty, and the few people at the top (eventually one man) will be in control.

The rapid expansion of the EU in a relatively short period of time shows the accelerated expansion of the Final Empire. The movement toward the erasing of national boundaries is indicative of a cultural shift in mindset toward a One World Government. This is all happening in this generation.

THE BARCELONA TREATY (NOVEMBER 27, 1995)

Javier Solana, who was then the president of the EU, convened the Barcelona Conference, which established the Barcelona Treaty (also known as the Barcelona Declaration or Process). As mentioned in the previous chapter, Solana is an extremely powerful man who has skyrocketed up the political ladder of success. He may become a name everyone will eventually know. Only time will tell us if he will play a significant role in prophecy.

This treaty established a set of goals designed to lead to a free trade zone in the Middle East by 2010. The treaty became known as Euro-Med or Euromed. One of the first points on the initial agenda included battling religious fundamentalism. This will, in time, include the true Christians and the Orthodox Jews. Anti-Semitism is rampant and is growing, especially in the EU. The Jews are blamed for everything beyond all rational thinking. This can only be due to a demonic influence. Satan hates God's chosen people, which is clearly seen through history. Hitler is just one example of irrational hatred that is demonically motivated.

A second point on the agenda is to achieve mutually satisfying trading terms for the region's partners. The "regions" consist of countries that participated in the trading agreements. The third point is to eliminate or greatly reduce the U.S. presence in the Mediterranean. Biblical prophecy does not appear to include the United States. This is a movement in that direction.

The fourth point is the "Treaties of Association." This is a continuation of the Barcelona Treaty or Euro-Med Policy. These various treaties include but are not limited to the "Treaty of Association" between the EU and Israel, which was signed by Solana and Shimon Peres on November 20, 1995 and ratified June 1, 2000. Those treaties were reconfirmed, including the EU-Israel treaty, at the ninth conference in June 2004.[3] This sounds like a prototype of the covenant that will be made between the Antichrist and Israel. As we shall see in the next section, a single monetary system is a practical necessity in the formation of a One World system.

THE EUROPEAN MONETARY UNION (1999)

Monetary unions have been attempted a number of times throughout history. In the eighth century, Charlemagne established a uniform silver coinage. Napoleon also considered it (1769-1821). Other attempts include the Latin Monetary Union (1865-1926), and the Scandinavian

Monetary Union (1873-1924); both failed.[4]

The euro was proposed in 1999. Concerning the future of the euro, one writer made the following statement: "Within 10 years, the euro should be merged with the dollar to create the eurodollar, a single currency for both the U.S. and Europe, and eventually the rest of the world."[5]

In 2001, the euro was introduced as legal currency. By 2002 the euro had replaced the national currencies in twelve European states.[6] As of January 28, 2008, the Single Euro Payments Area (SEPA) includes 31 member states, created to allow for the European financial infrastructure, creating a zone for the euro where all electronic payments are considered domestic. As of January 1, 2008, twenty-two European countries are using the euro (see www.geography.about.com/od/lists/a/euro.htm). The European states using the euro are referred to as the euro zone. The movement toward a single monetary currency will bring us one step closer to a One World economy that is under the authority of the Antichrist.

According to Revelation 13:16-18, the "beast" or Antichrist will give all people a mark on their right hand or forehead. Without this mark, no one will be able to buy or sell. The mark will be the name or the number of the name of the Antichrist. Our technology has advanced to the point that this could easily become a reality.

With the introduction of nanotechnology, microscopic chips can be implanted under the skin in animals or people that contain a volume of information about the entity, including such things as the owner's name and address in the case of an animal, or the medical history, legal background, and financial status of a person. It is the perfect solution to identity theft and terrorist activities. Stolen social security numbers, credit card numbers, driver's license numbers, etc. is a growing menace.

There is a growing need in our society to link one's identity to the person. By using an implant of some type, it would become impossible to separate a person's proof of identity from the person himself. It is the perfect solution and will become a reality. The problem comes when the solution produces a greater problem. This "mark" discussed in Revelation 13:16-18 will identify the person with the most ruthless person to walk the face of this planet, the Antichrist.

The EU economy is growing rapidly. The euro is growing in value against the U.S. dollar. Over just six years, the EU's total trade increased by 300%. The EU has a trade surplus of 25.8 billion euros per year as compared to a U.S. trade deficit of 435.2 billion dollars. As mentioned

earlier, in 1999 the Central Bank (established in 1998) did direct investments of 67.5 percent into candidate countries of EU origin. In 2005 and
2006, there was a trade surplus of 3.1 billion euros.[7]

The European Central Bank has been stockpiling gold and is pursuing making the euro an asset-based currency. This is in contrast to the
U.S. dollar, which is debt based.[8] "A lot of central banks, Asia in particular, where the most important volumes are located are shifting reserves
from dollar reserves into euros," according to Wemer Becker of
Deutsche Bank). From July 2003 to July 2008, the U.S. dollar reported-
ly went from 1.15 dollars for one euro to 1.57 dollars for one euro.

The United States used to be the world's Superpower. That status is
rapidly shifting to the European Union, the primary power base of the
Final Empire, which originated from the same geographical area as the
Roman Empire.

THE EU–UN CONNECTION

All of the European Union members and candidates are members of
the United Nations. As of January 2007, the number of EU member states
increased from twenty-five to twenty-seven. The number of UN members
increased from 191 to 192 with the inclusion of Montenegro on June 28,
2006. These numbers increased the EU percentages from 13 to 14 percent
of total UN membership.[9]

The UN began with 52 countries. Between 1947 and 1991, this number increased to 191. This large increase was a result of ethnic divisions.
One of the signs of the Second Coming is seen in Matthew 24:7, "…
nation will rise against nation …"

"The Greek word translated 'nation' is *ethnos*, from which we get the
word *ethnic*. The word means 'a race or tribe'—not an inconsistent definition for our modern understanding of ethnicity."[10] By looking at the
verse in context, one of the signs of the end times is that "ethnic group
shall rise against ethnic group." This is describing ethnic unrest.[11] The
multiplication of countries can be attributed to ethnic divisions within
the countries. This sign is being fulfilled in this generation.

As a side note concerning UN membership, prior to January 2007, 190
out of the 191 member countries rotate on the Security Council. Israel is
excluded from this rotation. Yet, Islamic nations, known for terrorist activities, are allowed to be on the Council. Anti-Semitism is a real and growing

issue, especially in the EU. Israel is also excluded from the Human Rights Commission and the International Red Cross. As mentioned earlier, this hatred of the Jewish people is not rational from a human perspective. Satan, who has tried to exterminate the Jews for thousands of years, drives this hatred, and it will escalate during the Tribulation Period.

The EU share of the UN regular budget between the years 2001 and 2003 was 37 percent. The EU only provides 13 percent of the UN membership but comprises 37 percent of the Regular Budget. [As of 2007, those numbers are 14 percent and 38 percent.] The power and influence of the EU over the UN is significant considering its proportion or percentage of the membership. This will increase as the EU, the power base of the Final Empire, continues to gain momentum. [In 2003, the Commission reported that the EU had a common position in almost 95 percent of resolutions in the UN General Assembly.][12] [brackets by author]

PARALLELS BETWEEN THE REBIRTH OF ISRAEL AND THE REBIRTHING OF A REVIVED ROMAN EMPIRE: STARTING IN 1948

Israel was reborn as a nation in 1948, the same year that the Congress of Europe met in Hague, Holland, and adopted seven resolutions on political union. Resolution #7 called for the creation of a United Europe. 1948 was also the year of the Benelux Treaty that became the nucleus for the modern super state of Europe, and it was the year of the Brussels Treaty that added Britain and France to the Benelux countries. The Brussels Treaty was modified in 1954 to become the springboard for the Western European Union. In 1948 the political Roman Empire—Europe—was reborn.[13]

THE MUSLIM CONNECTION

The Muslim population in the EU has increased considerably. Let's take a brief detour that ties together the EU statistics and the anti-Semitism of this chapter with the False World Religion discussed in the next chapter.

Chuck Missler heads up Koinonia House, a biblically-based ministry with a heavy emphasis in the area of biblical prophecy. He gave the following statistics on the Muslim population in the EU: France 7.5%; Netherlands 4.4%; Germany 3.9%; Britain 3.3%; Spain 1.8%; Italy 1.8%; [Denmark, Norway, Sweden 1.4%]. This equates to 13 million Muslims living in Europe. Turkey is a candidate for membership in the EU. Turkey's Muslim population is growing. If Turkey is admitted to the EU, the Muslim population will reach 63 million.

What difference does this make? The Muslim religion is based on the Koran, which does not teach tolerance. They have a hatred for Israel and believe that the Muslims will someday rule the earth. They will not compromise in regard to Israel.

This brings us to the question of how they will fit into an all encompassing false world religious system that has no room for fundamentalism, whether it is true Christianity, Orthodox Judaism, or Islam. The next chapter covers the link between Islam and the False World Religion. This "probable" link is becoming evident today as we add one more piece to the prophecy puzzle.

THE INFAMOUS SOLANA DECISION (2000)

As mentioned earlier, Javier Solana is a very powerful man. By the year 2000, he was Secretary General of the WEU and also held the office of High Representative. As High Representative, he presides over the Political Security Committee (PSC). All of the members seated at that committee hold ambassador rank in the EU.

In the summer of 2000, while many Members of the European Parliament (MEPs) were away on holiday, the European political establishment and the EU Ambassadors slipped in a whole series of secrecy laws. This new code of access to documents became law by the end of August 2000. It was rushed through under something called a "written procedure."[14]

At Solana's request, the EU now withholds information on public security, defense of the Union, military and non-military crisis management, internal relations, monetary stability, court proceedings, inspections, and investigations. This act is in direct violation of the Amsterdam Treaty, which enshrines "the public right of access to EU documents."[15]

This is another move toward a dictatorship. This act also gave further reason to plan an EU parliamentary police force to quell internal problems.[16] This decision empowered Solana and his member states. Information and agendas could now be hidden from public scrutiny. This very act of hiding information from the public, combined with hidden agendas, will be the dominant theme later in the chapter.

It will be interesting to see if Solana eventually takes on the role of the Antichrist. If he doesn't fill this role, it is likely that he has created a powerful political position that could be filled by the Antichrist.

As a side note, true Christians will not know who will fill the role of the Antichrist. We can speculate and make educated guesses, but that is as far as we can go. He will not be revealed until after the Rapture (2 Thessalonians 2:6-8). Unbelievers will know the identity of the Antichrist after the Rapture but, in many cases, will mistake him for the Christ, the Messiah, or the Super Human who will solve the world's problems.

The next section covers one of Solana's recent policies in establishing a broad agreement that includes numerous countries.

EUROPEAN NEIGHBORHOOD POLICY (ENP) (2003)

In June 2003, Solana delivered a ten-page security doctrine at the Greece Summit, titled "A Secure Europe in a Better World." It had three basic parts: 1) Establishing economic and political stability through the EU's neighborhood; 2) Establishing a new international order; and 3) "Increasing the EU's civil and military capacity to combat rogue states and weapons of mass destruction."[17]

The ENP consists of a very large package of different types of deals called "Action Plans" for each participating nation. These action plans include a tailor-made plan to meet the needs of each country and a monitoring program. If a country fails to live up to the agreement, the agreement could be terminated. The ENP actually becomes a way for Solana to activate or reinforce his Euro-Med plan (also referred to as the Barcelona Treaty) and bring the participating nations into compliance.[18] [See The Barcelona Treaty (1995).]

In light of the EU's growing anti-Semitic sentiment, it is interesting to note that Israel was the first to sign the ENP "Action Plan." On the surface this does not seem congruent with an anti-Semitic sentiment. What we do know is that the Antichrist will be a Gentile and will come out of the geographical area once known as the Roman Empire, which is currently part of the EU. We also know that he will make a covenant, or peace treaty, with Israel that will mark the beginning of the seven-year Tribulation Period. He will break that covenant in the middle of that seven-year period. (See Daniel 9:27.) There may be another agenda involved behind Israel being the first to sign the ENP "Action Plan." Only time will tell. The funding of these "Action Plans" began on January 1, 2007, the new seven-year budget plan.

The EU operates on a seven-year budget term. The current term began on January 1, 2007.[19] Solana's people have drawn up a new funding instrument for the ENP. This new instrument will fund all the action plans and deals for these member states. The nations will be monitored with a total review by December 31, 2011, to complete each nation's compliance. "The purpose of the EU's ENP is to revive and confirm an existing covenant with many that was dying."[20]

There are many Bible scholars who believe that Daniel 9:27 actually says that he (the Antichrist) will "confirm" or "revive" an existing agreement for one week (seven years) as opposed to making a new covenant. This is an interesting consideration in light of the ENP plan. It is also interesting to note that Solana plans a total review by December 31, 2011.

Although January 1, 2007, may have marked the start of a new seven-year EU budgeting term, it does not represent the start of a seven-year Tribulation Period. It only marks the date that allows Solana to fund his ENP plan. The Rapture has not occurred, and the Tribulation Period has not begun. If there is a correlation between the two, it is still a future event.

If Solana's review date is December 31, 2011, this is really close to the middle of the seven-year (or "one week") term mentioned in Daniel 9:27. In the middle of the seven-year Tribulation Period referred to in Daniel 9:27, the Antichrist turns against the nation Israel by breaking his covenant with them. If there is a connection between the ENP seven-year plan and the seven-year Tribulation Period, one wonders what Solana will do if the review of the nations in 2011 is not in compliance, according to his definition. If the review date is December 31, 2011, does this correspond to the middle of the Tribulation Period when the Antichrist breaks his covenant with Israel? If so, this would be three and one-half years into the Tribulation Period, which would move the start date later than January 1, 2007. It is food for thought with profound implications.

EUROPEAN PARLIAMENT
THE NUMBER 666 / THE THIRD TIME

Under the heading "What About 666?" in Chapter Four of this book, I mentioned that I had come across the number 666 three times while researching this book. In that section, we saw two of the times. The first was in regard to the Vienna Summit in 1998. Out of 1,150 documents created at the Summit, the document that created the new office of "High Representative" was document 666. Is it coincidence that out of 1,150 documents, document number 666 was the one that created this powerful office that Solana was the first to fill?

The second mention of number 666 was in the year 2000 when the Western European Union (WEU) proposed Assembly Recommendation 666. Under Article 12 of this Recommendation, Solana, as High Representative, was allowed to become Secretary General of the ten-nation WEU Alliance. In his role as High Representative, he could preside over the Political Security Committee (PSC) and convene the Council of the European Union in the event of an emergency. Once again, more power was given to Javier Solana, or possibly his successor.

The third mention of the number 666 is in reference to the seating plan of the MEP (members of European Parliament) in the European Union Parliament. The EU Parliament meets in two locations. It meets in Brussels, Belgium, three out of four weeks and in Strasbourg, France, one out of four weeks. The Strasbourg auditorium is equipped with 750 seats, even though the EU has set a ceiling of 700 seats for its MEP.[21]

A report by Dr. Paisley, a member of the Fifth Parliament Europe in Strasbourg, included a huge painting of the "woman on the beast" on the dome where the Parliament meets in Brussels. It is also by the sculpture outside the EU Council of Ministers office in Brussels.[22] This image is also found in Revelation 17. It is Europe's choice for a national symbol. Coincidence or providence? (This symbol, along with other significant European symbols, will be discussed in more detail later in this chapter.)

According to Paisley, out of the 700 seats (the ceiling set by Parliament), 679 were occupied as of 1999. The seats are allocated to members by name and number. "One seat remains unallocated and unoccupied. The number of that seat is 666."[23] Paisley actually lists each name and seat number from 655 through 679, with seat number 666 left blank. This is the third mention of 666. For more information about 666 and its role in biblical prophecy, see "What About 666?" in Chapter Four of this book.

EUROPEAN CONSTITUTION (OCTOBER 29, 2004)

The EU Constitution was approved and signed on October 29, 2004, but it was never successfully ratified by all twenty-seven member states.

The Convention for the Future of Europe has deleted any mention of God and Christianity.[24] Secularists have contended, "A clearly pluralist modern Europe had moved beyond any reference to any particular religion." (See *Europa Rising*, DVD, presented by Chuck Missler.) Former Irish Prime Minister John Bunton formally proposed including the mention of Christianity, but the proposal failed to muster support.[25]

An agreement was reached on a new treaty titled The Reform Treaty, which became known as The Treaty of Lisbon. An informal agreement was reached on the final text in Lisbon on October 19, 2007, but the treaty still needed to be signed ("Treaty of Lisbon" from Wikipedia, the free encyclopedia).

On December 13, 2007, the leaders of the EU signed the landmark Treaty of Lisbon that redefines foreign policy for the EU and creates an EU president. This treaty enters into force on January 1, 2009, provided ratification occurs ("European Leaders Sign Lisbon Treaty" from Wikinews, the free news source you can write). This treaty will federalize the EU, unifying it and increasing its influence and power. This act adds another piece to the prophetic puzzle, i.e., giving the beast, the EU, or Revived Roman Empire, a more defined sense of recognition.

If the European Constitution or the recently signed Treaty of Lisbon are unable to get full support to be ratified by all member states, what will happen? Could this failure produce a crisis? Is anyone powerful enough in the EU to fill that vacuum?

Under Recommendation 666, Article 12 (see Chapter Four in this book), Javier Solana would be given the power to preside over the Political Security Committee (PSC) and convene the Council of the European Union "in the event of an emergency." As mentioned in Chapter Four, an "emergency" could involve a collapse of the recently signed Treaty of Lisbon, which could result in the collapse of the EU. There is only one logical candidate to step in and pick up the pieces, and Recommendation 666 has already established the framework for the Secretary General of the WEU to step in.[26]

This has been a brief chronological sketch of the political events leading up to the present day. The next section provides an overview of the (often hidden) real power behind the world events that are moving us at breakneck speed toward the Tribulation Period. The believer in Jesus Christ is moved that much closer to the Rapture, which will precede the Tribulation Period. The movement toward the worst period of time the world has ever experienced should produce terror in the unbeliever, but joyful anticipation for the born-again believer.

THE COVERT WORLD EMPIRE:
A SHADOW GOVERNMENT BEHIND THE SCENES

Who is really governing world events? Who is running the show? According to former British Prime Minister Disraeli in 1844, "The world is governed by very different personages from what is imagined by those who are not behind the scenes."[27] Nelson Rockefeller is likely the main financier of the New World Order. In 1962, in *The Future of Federalism*, he wrote: "The nation state is becoming less and less competent ... Sooner perhaps than we realize there will evolve the basis for a federal structure of the free world."[28] The implication is that there are people and money behind the scenes, pulling the strings with an agenda toward a European super power and a One World Government.

HIDDEN HANDS: PULLING THE WORLD INTO A
GLOBAL SUPER STATE

There are covert, rich, and elite Americans who have pushed for a United Europe, according to declassified American documents. In the 1950s and 1960s, the U.S. intelligence community ran a covert operation to push for a United Europe. "It directed and funded the European federalist movement, and behind the scenes were the usual suspects from the Rockefeller and Ford Foundations, long controlled by 'One World' enthusiasts keen to abolish the nation state."[29] As we shall see, the visible rulers are the front men and are not necessarily the ones pulling the strings.

There are a number of Christians who believe that the "end times" arena is in the hands of secret societies and organizations that are behind some world leaders and political movements.[30] There is evidence to back up this belief. For example, one former British army officer believes that Europe's future was decided in 1940.[31] According to a letter to the *Daily Telegraph* (London) that appeared on November 26, 1997, under the heading "Euro Visions," Graham Langmead, of Bogner Regis, West Sussex, England, wrote the following:

The first I heard of a common European currency was from [German] General Von Vietinghoff, to whom as a very junior officer I was an escort at Bologna in April 1945, just after he surrendered the German forces in the central Mediterranean. He was outraged that he was put in the charge of a twenty-year-old Lieutenant, but proceeded to tell Langmead that a Franco-German agreement had taken place in 1940. The agreement was "that Europe would become one state controlled by Germany and France ..." [32]

He went on to tell Langmead that "there would be one currency, which would create a European state under German dominance." [33] According to the German General, that agreement happened in 1940. What he said has already happened in part. There is a European State, the EU, and now one currency, the euro.

In 1970, leading financier Edmund de Rothschild stated: "Western Europe is going to form a political union. The structure that has to disappear, the lock that has to burst, is the nation." [34] This has already happened. We now have the Western European Union (WEU) as well as the European Union (EU). European countries are now called "member states."

One has to wonder if Rothschild was forecasting a future need, or if he was behind the scenes, engineering world events. As we will later see, Rothschild, along with other super-rich financier families have been instrumental, behind the scenes, in directing world governments.

German Chancellor, Gerhard Schroeder, "... called for the creation of a European government and a reformed and more powerful two-tier European Parliament. His ideas were published in April 2001 in a draft party document proposing radical changes in the EU institutions." [35] The plans, which were leaked to the German *Der Spiegel* magazine, were drawn up under his supervision.

The idea is to replicate Germany's system of government at the European level. This would reduce the nation states to local regions. Schroeder has a proposed head or president of the European government for a future election, probably by the MEPs in the European Parliament. This could possibly be a leading candidate for the future Antichrist. [36]

We now have the EU and the Western European Union (WEU). The EU has already reduced nations to member states. There is currently a movement toward "regionalization." This was first seen by the Club of Rome, with plans to divide the world into ten regions, which will characterize the Final Empire.

What are the implications of these events? It is clear that certain rich, elite Americans, the U.S. Intelligence, and Germany have an agenda to move Europe away from being a group of nations and into local regions, with Germany's system of government applied to the government at the European level, and with a proposed head or president.

Part of this agenda is already taking place. The EU now has member states, not countries or nations. The next move may be toward local regions. It is hard to comment on the relevance or the reality of Schroeder's idea of replicating Germany's system of government at the European level. Time will tell.

HISTORICAL DEVELOPMENT OF A COVERT FINANCIAL EMPIRE

In 1797, a man named John T. Robinson wrote the book, *Proofs of a Conspiracy*. He was Secretary General to Scotland's prestigious Royal Society and professor of natural philosophy at the University of Edinburgh. He was an intellectual and a scientist. Science was called natural philosophy at that time.[37] Robinson was a high degree Mason. Whenever he traveled from Scotland to Europe, he always attended the Grand Orient Masonic Lodges.[38]

On one trip he met up with Adam Weishaupt, the founder of a new elite group known as "Illuminism." This new element had penetrated the Lodges. Weishaupt approached Robinson to join this inner circle. Robinson refused due to his loyalty to the royal family of England. He warned them that hidden powers were pulling the strings behind the French Revolution and that it was not an historical accident happening by a whim, but it "was manipulated by brilliant and powerful men who had their own agenda."[39]

The Illuminists planned to stage a revolt of the masses to unseat the "present powers of the hereditary aristocracy" and replace them with an intellectual aristocracy. "This, indeed, was exactly what the French Revolution appeared to be—key people catalyzing great numbers of people."[40]

Adam Weishaupt, a professor of canon law at the University of Ingolstadt, started the Order of Illuminati on May 1, 1776.[41] The *Portman Papers*, a quarterly newsletter that keeps watch on the superstate [EU], said in October 2000: "Eight years before the French Revolution began in 1789 ... Adam Weishaupt, founder of the Illuminati, drew up the blueprint."[42] It goes on to say, "The Reign of Terror claimed over a million victims," and "the terror was justified in the name of democracy."[43]

According to Professor Robinson, the true purpose of the Illuminati was World Domination. It was to have a world order ruled by an elite pretending to represent the common man.[44] Weishaupt's plan was to build a hierarchy of inner circles with one real inner circle who knew the true purpose of the Order.[45]

There is evidence that the Illuminati was not confined to Europe, but had spread to the U.S. In 1797, George Washington made a statement that saying, in essence, that he believed the Illuminati had spread to the United States.[46] By the 1800s, the Illuminists were mentioned in the correspondence of Washington, Jefferson, Madison, and John Quincy Adams. They did not want this plan infiltrating the United States. The pieces of a global world empire ruled by the elite insiders would fall into place rapidly in the twentieth century, 200 years later.

FAST FORWARD TO THE TWENTIETH CENTURY

In 1966, Carroll Quigley authored a book titled *Tragedy and Hope: A History of Our Time*. According to Tal Brooke, author of *One World*, it literally "rocked those who saw it when it first came out." Quigley was a Harvard and Princeton professor emeritus. Today, according to Quigley, the power of a certain group of bankers is colossal.[47]

Quigley confesses to being an insider and confidant of this elite group. **This 1,300 page book named major insider power groups attempting to manipulate a world socialist order.** Quigley supported the plan but no longer wanted to do it undercover.[48]

Tragedy and Hope was Quigley's *magnum opus*. Even though he supported the plan, he revealed too much information.[49] The Macmillan first edition in 1966 literally disappeared almost overnight, even from the public libraries.[50] Quigley's final post was professor of history at the Foreign Service School at Georgetown University.

The inside cover of the book shows Quigley's impressive academic background. He told it like it was. According to the introduction, it took him twenty years to write his book.

As professor at the Foreign Service School, one of his students in the 1960s was William Jefferson Clinton. Clinton was obviously deeply impacted by Quigley, as evidenced by his acceptance speech at the Democratic

National Convention. "[Clinton] reverently mentioned Carroll Quigley, his mentor, as being one of the two people to most influence his life."[51]

In reference to world financial control by the elite and the banking system, Quigley summarizes the insider's grand plan:

> The powers of financial capitalism had a far-reaching (plan), nothing less than to create a world system of financial control in private hands able to dominate the political system of each country and the economy of the world as a whole.[52] ... This system was to be controlled in a feudalist fashion by the central banks of the world acting in concert, by secret agreements arrived in frequent private meetings and conferences.[53]

Quigley traces some of the wealthiest, most powerful families, such as the Rothschilds, Rockefellers, and Morgans. These families would exert their influence over governments by lending money with provisions that called for specific policies. This financial power encouraged governments to become dependent on them.[54]

International Banking Aristocracies were owned by family dynasties. For example, the banking dynasties of Rothschild include five pivotal nations in Europe. The family privately owns the Central Bank of England. The respective governments do not own the Bank of England, the Bank of France, and the Bank of Germany, as most people believe, but "they are privately owned monopolies."[55] According to Quigley:

> It must not be felt that these heads of the world's chief central banks were themselves substantive powers in world finance. They were not. Rather, they were the technicians and agents of the dominant investment bankers of their own countries, who had raised them up and were perfectly capable of throwing them down. The substantive financial powers of the world were in the hands of these investment bankers (also called "international" or "merchant" bankers) who remained largely behind the scenes in their own unincorporated private banks.[56]

Quigley and others reveal the fact that banking houses are owned by the great family dynasties, which are also the banks behind the International Monetary Fund and the World Bank. The goal is a global central bank. Europe has projected a central banking system that is a major milestone toward this goal. Part of this agenda includes America's central bank, the Federal Reserve Bank.[57] It was established in late 1913 as the New York Reserve Bank and became powerful much later.[58]

Some of the key family dynasties behind the Federal Reserve Bank are: Kuhn Loeb, Goldman Sachs, and Lehman Brothers. There is a primary member of the Federal Reserve Bank that is not mentioned with the other international bankers. It is the Rockefellers of the Chase Manhattan Bank and Citibank of New York. Rockefeller's Chase Bank merged with Warburg's Manhattan Bank to become the Chase Manhattan Bank. The above dynasties preside over multiple banks, many of them with interlocking directorates. Most of these banks are private partnerships run by family dynasties.[59]

Diagrammatically, the levels of this financial pyramid would be: **Great Family Dynasties [1]** own **Banks [2]**, which support the **IMF and the World Bank [3]**, with a goal of a **Global Central Bank [4]**. At the base of the pyramid are the **most powerful** of the four listed—the Family Dynasties, which have interlocking directorates with other central banks.

The financial and political powers that are apparent are only "the tip of the iceberg." The real financial power lies beneath the surface.

INTERNATIONAL NETWORK OF INSIDERS (1909-1913)

According to Quigley, there is an "international network" of "insiders" who meet for semisecret discussions. This network is referred to as "Round Table Groups." Quigley reveals the following about this "international network" in *Tragedy and Hope*:

> This network, which we may identify as the Round Table Groups, has no aversion to cooperating with the Communists, or any other groups, and frequently does so. I know of the operations of this network because I have studied it for twenty years and was permitted for two years, in the early 1960s, to examine its papers and secret records. I have no aversion to it or to most of its aims and have, for much of my life, been close to it and to many of its instruments.[60]

This international network of insiders, known as the Round Table Groups, had its origin between 1909 and 1913. In *Tragedy and Hope*, Quigley gives the following account of its origins:

As governor-general and high commissioner of South Africa in the period 1897-1905, Milner recruited a group of young men, chiefly from Oxford and Toynbee Hall, to assist him in organizing his administration. Through his influence these men were able to win influential posts in government and international finance and became the dominant influence in British imperial and foreign affairs up to 1939. Under Milner in South Africa they were known as Milner's Kindergarten until 1910. In 1909-1913 they organized semisecret groups, known as the Round Table Groups, in the chief British dependencies and the United States. These still function in eight countries. They kept in touch with each other by personal correspondence and frequent visits, and through the quarterly magazine, *The Round Table*, founded in 1910 and largely supported by Sir Abe Bailey's money. In 1919, they founded the Royal Institute of International Affairs (Chatham House) for which the chief financial supporters were Sir Abe Bailey and the Astor family (owners of *The Times*). Similar institutes of International Affairs were established in the chief British dominions and in the United States (where it is known as the Council on Foreign Relations) in the period 1919-1927.[61]

Tracing some of the roots of the existing powers that underlie the visible world governments provides a better feel of where we have come from, where we are going, and how this fits into prophecy. The international network of insiders known as the Round Table Groups paved the way for similar institutes of International Affairs. In the United States, the Council on Foreign Relations was born.

THE COUNCIL ON FOREIGN RELATIONS (JULY 29, 1921)

According to Professor Quigley, the Council on Foreign Relations (CFR) was the result of the Round Table meetings that formed several semi-secret groups to help promote globalism. The CFR was the semi-secret group for America.[62] The stated purpose of the CFR is to advise the President on foreign matters. The CFR's real purpose, or primary agenda, is not to advise the President but to promote a "New International Order."

The CFR traditionally divulges very little about its aims and purpose. On one occasion, something did leak out. On November 25, 1959, CFR's *Study No. 7* was published. It openly declared the CFR's real purpose: "... building a New International Order [which] must be responsive to world aspirations for peace, [and] for social and economic change ... an international order [code for world government] ... including states labeling themselves as 'Socialist' "[63] [brackets by Tal Brooke].

Finances for the CFR came from John Rockefeller, J.P. Morgan, Bernard Baruch, Otto Kahn, and Jacob Schiff. The founders included many of those who were present at the signing of the Treaty of Versailles after World War I.[64] The roster of CFR members is impressive and "so are the power groups who have representatives in it."[65]

International banking organizations currently have men in the CFR. "The CFR is totally interlocked with the major foundations (Rockefeller, Ford, Carnegie) and the so-called think tanks (Rand, Hudson Institute, Brookings Institute)."[66] "The CFR and the financial powers behind it ... promote the New World Order as they have for seventy years. The CFR is the promotional arm of the Ruling Elite in the United States of America."[67]

The real power behind the world governments rests in the hands of the elite. Felix Frankfurter, Justice of the Supreme Court (1939-1962), said, "The real rulers in Washington are invisible and exercise from behind the scenes."[68] In a letter to an associate dated November 21, 1933, Franklin Roosevelt said: "The real truth of the matter, as you and I know, is that a financial element in the large centers has owned the government since the days of Andrew Jackson."[69]

The Elite, working behind the scenes, not only have the power to direct government policy and decision-making, they have the power to start wars, instigate revolutions, and remove dictators from power. The following incident is only one of many examples that could be cited. In October 1964, David Rockefeller, who was chairman of the CFR and the Chase Manhattan Bank, decided for some odd reason to make a trip to Russia. The story is cited as follows:

> A few days after Rockefeller ended his only vacation to Russia, the head of Russia, Nikita Khrushchev, was recalled from a vacation at a Black Sea resort to learn that he was no longer premier of the Supreme Soviet. He had been fired—Khrushchev, who pounded his shoe on the desk at the United Nations General Assembly, the killer from the Ukraine who said to the capitalists, "We will bury you." He was fired after David Rockefeller's visit—amazing.[70]

As previously mentioned, this incident is only one of many where the elite super rich engineered the course of history from behind the scenes.

The role of the Illuminati (in the French Revolution), quotes from very credible witnesses, and the mysterious job loss of Nikita Khrushchev evidence the invisible powers pulling the strings in governmental policy decisions. Elite family dynasties, the Illuminati, and the international bankers have enormous power over the world governments.

Up to this point, we have discussed the "hidden hands" pulling the strings of governmental affairs, but we haven't spoken of the core "inner circle." This inner circle is where the real power originates. Like an onion, the surface of the onion, the outer layer, is totally visible. The next layer down isn't visible unless exposed by peeling off the top layer. We touched on the layer under the surface, but the power eminates from the core, the "inner ring." Let's take a brief look at that "inner ring."

THE DARK EMPIRE

"... the god of this world has blinded the minds of the unbelieving so that they might not see the light of the gospel of the glory of Christ, who is the image of God" (2 Corinthians 4:4).

C.S. Lewis pointed out in "The Inner Ring," a lecture given at Oxford, that those who make the inner circle will have to pledge their very souls, and at some point, they too will begin summoning the dark god.[71] The deepest "inner circle" moves into the realm of the demonic mafia or underworld. This realm includes professionals, politicians, and Hollywood directors. There are rewards for being in this "inner circle," but the price tag is high.

The supernatural or apocalyptic picture is totally removed from the naturalistic worldview. It makes no sense to those who have rejected anything beyond the five senses. "But others in the younger generations have been more receptive to the possibility of the supernatural."[72] Hollywood often sets the pace. Over the last twenty-five years, there has been a considerable increase in movies involving the supernatural, the occult, and UFOs. Our culture is primed for supernatural occurrences.

A contemporary portrayal of the supernatural through a fictional lens can be seen by two famous directors of our time, Stanley Kubrick and Roman Polanski. Tal Brooke, author of *One World*, said: "Both directors in their own way may have stumbled into this dark international cabal [conspiratorial group of plotters], perhaps taking risks to warn of this reality (or conditioning the public to accept this eventuality). There has been some speculation that Kubrick, at one point, got a glimpse of this secret world."[73] If anyone were in a position to have contact with such an elite group, or at least know about them, it would be Kubrick, as shown below.[74]

EYES WIDE SHUT

"Stanley Kubrick's *Eyes Wide Shut* is like a final telegram to the world. It was completed just two weeks before he died a mysterious and untimely death. The famed director had filmed most of his final opus under absolute secrecy in England."[75]

Eyes Wide Shut deals with a frightening kind of power. It deals with the hidden realities that escape the common man whose eyes are wide shut. Critics were intent on downplaying it as a satire or a flop. According to Tal Brooke, "The message is too threatening for self-satisfied and urban materialistic agnostics secure in believing there really is no devil."

The movie is a sobering experience once you realize it is not fiction. It portrays what is really going on to which the common man is blinded (thus, the title, "Eyes Wide Shut"). Evidence of the movie's reality was Kubrick's mysterious and untimely death two weeks after the movie was completed. The conditions in which the movie was made is further evidence of its reality—it was filmed in absolute secrecy in England. **Someone or certain groups did not want this movie made. They did not want the exposure.**

The setting of the movie was on a palatial estate on Long Island, "perhaps suggesting the even larger Rockefeller estate in nearby Upstate New York." An ambitious Manhattan doctor manages to walk in on a massive midnight gathering. Wearing black robes and hoods were a hundred or more of the "most powerful people in the world." One cannot help wondering who are behind the masks: perhaps a statesman, or a powerful Wall Street broker negotiating a merger between two corporate giants, or public figures like Kissinger, Rockefeller, or Greenspan.[76]

What followed was an event that suggested a satanic mass. Following this religious ritual was an orgy throughout the estate. All moral barriers in the outside world were broken in contempt against the rigid morality of a holy God.

In the end, the doctor, played by Tom Cruise, was rescued from possibly becoming that evening's human sacrifice. "He was in over his head and did not have a clue what kind of world he had just entered. **Kubrick's message was direct and to the point: They Exist."**[77] Once you enter Satan's domain, you have no protection, even if your mind outright rejects what you saw or heard as being impossible. "You are in the most vulnerable position imaginable."[78] When you do not know your enemy or even believe that he exists, your eyes are wide shut.

Does such a meeting place exist as portrayed by the palatial Long Island estate in *Eyes Wide Shut*? There is such a place in the redwood trees of Northern California that the movie seems to implicate. "The French-sounding chant during the ritual scene in *Eyes Wide Shut* suggests the inscription on the gate at the Bohemian Grove."[79] The next section describing this estate is extracted from the book, *One World*, by Tal Brooke.

BOHEMIAN GROVE

There is some speculation that Stanley Kubrick was once a guest at the elite Bohemian Grove's annual gathering.[80] The Bohemian Grove is an estate on 2,700 acres. For two weeks, a virtual who's who of over two thousand of the world's wealthiest and most influential gather, many arriving in their corporate jets. There is plenty of gourmet food, drugs, sex, and expensive wine.[81]

During this two-week event, starting on July 15, security is extremely tight. Almost no one has been able to penetrate the tightly guarded grounds "until Alex Jones, a journalist, somehow got in with a camcorder (infowars.com) long enough to record one of the ceremonies. His footage was played in England on BBC 4's *World of Wonder*."[82]

Tal Brooke, head of Spiritual Counterfeits Project, and a friend attempted to gain access to Bohemian Grove, but were met by armed guards and told to leave immediately. Armed guards patrolled the area, and the high fences made the place practically impossible to penetrate.[83]

From August 31 to September 6, the *Orlando Weekly* reported on the Bohemian Grove when the founder of *USA Today*, Al Neuharth, and Newt Gingrich were among the speakers. The following excerpt is from that report:

> Al Neuharth spoke at Bohemian Grove, the all-male encampment in Northern California where much of America's government and corporate elite gather each summer for two weeks of speeches and activities like

mock-Druid fire rituals. The official program described Neuharth's topic as "a look inside media newsrooms and boardrooms."[84]

According to *The Orlando Sentinel*, "Neuharth was among the 2,200 men who heard an address by House Speaker Newt Gingrich. And what did Gingrich have to say? 'I'm sorry,' Gingrich staff writer Robert George told us. 'We do not have a copy of that speech, and it will not be transcribed. The Bohemian Grove events are basically private functions.' "[85] The *Orlando Sentinel* went on to say:

> A week later, former President George Bush [Senior] spoke at Bohemian Grove. In fact, every Republican president since Coolidge has been a member. In modern times, participants have included Secretaries of State Henry Kissinger, George Shultz, and James Baker; Jimmy Carter; William Randolph Hearst Jr., Walter Cronkite, David Gergen, and David Rockefeller. Notables have also included the presidents of CNN and the Associated Press.[86]

Tal Brooke continues, "Occasionally ... At Bohemian Grove, for example, members can be seen lighting torches [and] wearing black robes with hoods during midnight ceremonies. Druids march in procession chanting to the Great Owl (Moloch) before a funeral pyre with 'corpses.' It is the 'Cremation of Care' ritual, in which the club's mascot is burned in effigy. 'A harmless Canaanite cult?' But why go to such trouble if it is all just a meaningless ritual? 'Male bonding?' That can happen at the golf club or duck hunting."

Brooke states that the entire assembly is obviously not composed of practicing Satanists, but it "does not exclude the possibility of an inner-circle monitoring events, which is usually the case in secret societies where neaphytes [*sic*] are being evaluated and recruited. The *Santa Rosa Sun* reported in July 1993 that several recruits have fled Bohemian Grove, reporting people disappearing in the woods as well as ritual human sacrifices."[87]

The rituals are exciting for ambitious newcomers, especially when seen as a harmless "means of greater inclusion within the global elite with incredible privileges and rewards—a seemingly small price to pay."[88] In reality, the price is great. To restate a quote by C.S. Lewis, "Those who make the inner-circle will have to pledge their very souls. At some point they, too, will begin summoning the dark god."

ROSEMARY'S BABY

Roman Polanski directed the occult classic, *Rosemary's Baby*. "Polanski took a varied approach to the same theme as *Eyes Wide Shut*: that a dark, hidden cabal at the highest reaches of society operates virtually undetected—due to unbelief—controlling huge sectors of the world from a hidden vantage point. The cunning internationalist devil worshippers blend in with the rest of society, outwardly looking harmless."

Rosemary was to be the host for Satan and his messiah. She was impregnated with a satanic fetus. The internationally-known Dr. Saperstein was treating her with various potions needed by the satanic fetus. The coven included the doctor. No one believed Rosemary, not even the doctor she saw for a second opinion. The coven consisted of average middle- or upper-class people. Rosemary was portrayed as paranoid and delusional. No one believed her about this group of Satanists next door. No one, that is, but another Satanist. She realized she had a losing hand.[89] According to Brooke, "The film either exposed the blinding power of unbelief or, on a deeper level, was a paean to Satan's power." Shortly after the film's released, the Manson gang entered Polanski's home and murdered his wife, Sharon Tate.[90]

Satan is a master of deceit. He accommodates the culture or the individual. He either works through a naturalistic worldview (denying the existence of the supernatural), where nothing is real to the individual beyond the five senses, or through the acceptance of the occult and Satan worship (direct, power for allegiance). For those directly involved, he promises money and power, but primarily power. Through deception and the power of unbelief, he controls the family dynasties, international bankers, the super rich, and the elite. Ultimately, he is moving the world toward a supernatural mindset for the end times, preparing the world for a dark messiah, or the Antichrist.

Up to this point we have covered the historical development of the coming One World Government with the primary emphasis on the European Union. We have reviewed the overt development through treaties and governmental policies, and we have also looked at the covert development through the elite, the family dynasties, the international bankers, and the demonic underground connection with high profile people, i.e., professionals and politicians. The next section will show the connection between the EU, the Roman Empire, and the Babylonian Empire.

BABYLON AND THE ROMAN EMPIRE:
A MERGER WITHIN THE EUROPEAN UNION

The Book of Revelation deals primarily with prophecy, or the future of our planet, and eternity. The Book of Genesis is a book of origins, although it also contains prophetic predictions. The Book of Revelation tells us about the fulfillment of those prophetic predictions. The Book of Genesis tells us about the first world government. The Book of Revelation tells us about the last world government. The two have a common link called Babylon.

EUROPEAN UNION AND THE BABYLON LINK

The association between Babylon—the first world government—and the European Union—the seat of the coming world government—can be seen in the EU's symbols and pictures. For example, the EU issued a poster showing the Tower of Babel and carrying the slogan, "Many tongues, one voice."

In order to understand the link between Babylon, the Tower of Babel, and the EU, it is essential to return to the Book of Genesis and review the development of man's first attempt to form a world government. This account is found in Genesis 9 through 11.

THE FIRST ATTEMPT AT A ONE WORLD GOVERNMENT

Following the flood, God commanded the sons of Noah and their descendants to populate the earth.[91] According to their genealogies, they were to become nations on the earth.[92] In disobedience, they chose to stay together and build a city and a tower "lest we become scattered abroad over the face of the earth."[93]

World governments have leaders, and the world's first government was no exception. A man named Nimrod led the people in rebellion against God. The beginning of his kingdom was known as Babylon,[94] which was located in the "land of Shiner," or modern-day Iraq. "Nimrod" is connected with the verb "to rebel." Tradition has identified him with tyrannical power. "He was the founder of the earliest imperial world powers in Babylon and Syria."[95] The Bible does not give us a lot of information about Nimrod. Through traditional accounts, accounts other

FIGURE 1

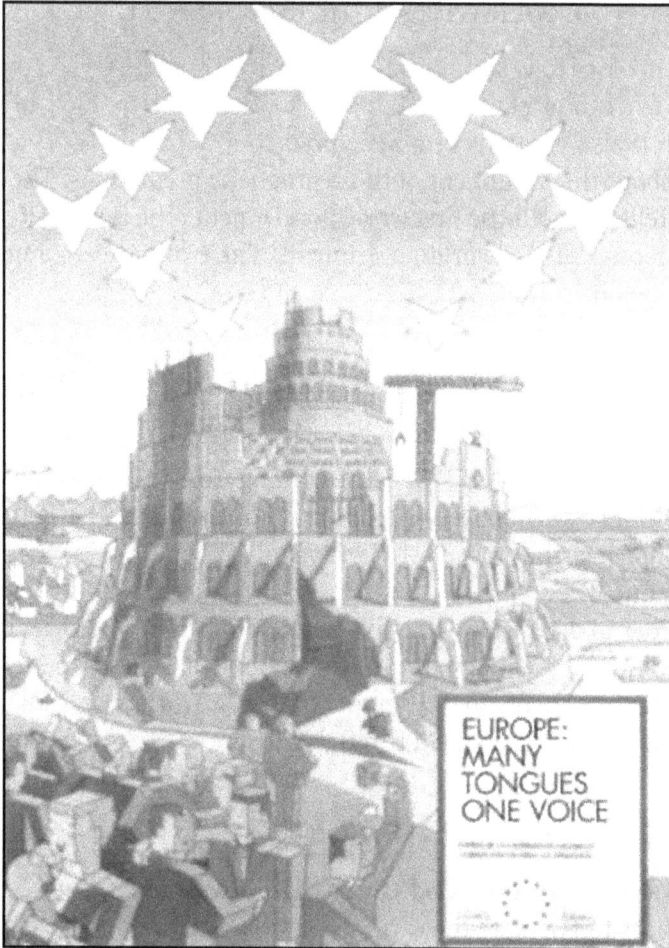

Note that the stars are inverted, pointing down, which is typically satanic.

than biblical, and the biblical account, we have a good profile of Nimrod. He was a prototype of the Antichrist who will rule the Final World Empire or government.

The Babylonians, under Nimrod's leadership, decided to build a city and a tower for the purpose of establishing an empire and staying united in opposition to God. Their decision not only involved disobedience to God, but the sin of pride was also involved. This can be seen in the following passage from Genesis 11:4: "They said, 'Come, let us build for ourselves a city, and a tower whose top will reach into heaven, and let us make for ourselves a name; otherwise we will be scattered abroad over the face of the whole earth.' " [96]

Note the phrase, "let us make for ourselves a name." Pride is the sin that caused Lucifer's (now called Satan) rebellion against God, resulting in Lucifer's downfall and name change. It is one of the sins that caused the fall of Adam and Eve. It will also play a prominent role in the last world government.

The building of the Tower of Babel was an attempt to keep from being scattered and was rooted in pride. "In those days the whole earth used the same language and the same words." [97] The Lord promptly took care of their disobedience and pride by confusing their language. Genesis 11:7-10 states the following:

> [The Lord speaking] "Come, let Us [Trinity implied] go down and there confuse their language, so that they may not understand one another's speech." So the Lord scattered them abroad from there over the face of the whole earth; and they stopped building the city. Therefore its name was called Babel [or Babylon, from the Hebrew means *confuse*], because there the Lord confused the language of the whole earth; and from there the Lord scattered them abroad over the face of the whole earth. [brackets by author]

The EU shows the same prideful spirit as Babylon in its EU-issued poster showing the Tower of Babel and the slogan, "Many tongues, one voice." This appears to be an attempt to reverse God's judgment on Babel when He "confused the language of the whole earth." A crane is shown in the background as if it is attempting to rebuild the tower. [98]

This was the world's first attempt to have a One World Government. Some of the links between Babylon and the EU are becoming obvious. It is as if the EU is attempting to reverse God's judgment, rebuild the Tower of Babel (i.e., by expanding its boundaries and adding more member states), and to complete the project in the Final World Government. This brings us to the current EU and the Babylon connection.

THE CURRENT EU: THE BABYLON CONNECTION

A Congress of Europe met in 1948 at The Hague, Holland. Seven resolutions on political union were adopted. Resolution seven states:

"The creation of a United Europe must be regarded as an essential step towards the creation of a united world."[99] This occurred sixty years ago as of the writing of this book, in 1948, the year Israel became a nation. It is the same year that marked the beginning of the last generation.

In 1995, under the terms of the Barcelona Treaty, also known as the Euro-Med agreement, the EU was expanded through its connection with twelve Mediterranean states (countries). The European Neighborhood Policy (ENP) in 2003 expanded the Euro-Med agreement of 1995. The EU is like a hungry beast that is growing by leaps and bounds through its addition of member states (formerly called countries) and its "treaties of association" with additional countries. It is not hard to envision a man who will someday have absolute power, first over the EU, and then extending worldwide. This man will be the Antichrist (the modern-day Nimrod).

This quest to empower one man to lead the whole European Union was expressed by Paul-Henri Spaak, former Belgium prime minister and president of the Consultative Assembly of the Council of Europe nearly fifty years ago. He made a chilling statement: "We do not want another committee. We have too many already. What we want is a man of sufficient stature to hold the allegiance of the people, and to lift us out of this economic morass in which we are sinking. **Send us such a man, be he God or the devil, and we will receive him.**" Many Europeans have been thinking along these lines for years.[100]

Spaak made a profound statement, a prophetic statement without realizing it. Upon further examination, he said that he was tired of committees and the political hassles involved in running a national government. He expressed total frustration, as voiced in his willingness to let one man call all the shots. This frustration reached a point of exasperation, as can be seen by the statement, "[B]e he God or the devil, we will receive him."

In other words, it doesn't matter if he is good or evil, ethical or unethical, as long as he can "lift us out of this economic morass." He also expressed where the burden was, "this economic morass." The economy is one of the three pillars of the coming One World system and is the primary source that sets the stage for the other two pillars: World Government and World Religion. This is the perfect mindset for the Antichrist to move into office.

According to Alan Franklin, British author of *EU: Final World Empire*, many Europeans have been thinking along these lines for years. Franklin

FIGURE 2

The European national symbol, as adapted above, is the same symbol used in the Book of Revelation—the harlot riding the beast. The woman rider represents the false world religion and the beast represents the Antichrist and his empire.

is a professional journalist who has researched the EU's role in biblical prophecy, and he is a European. He has a sense of the European mindset.

Babylon was the first attempt at a world government. It was also the origin of the Babylonian mystery religions. Paganism and idolatry have their roots in Babylon. In Revelation 17:3-6, reference is made to the "woman sitting on a scarlet beast" (v. 3). **She is referred to as "Babylon the Great, The Mother of Harlots and of the Abominations of the Earth" (v. 5).** She represents the false religious system in the last days. It is pagan in its origins as seen in her name "BABYLON THE GREAT."

She is characterized as being "drunk with the blood of the saints, and with the blood of the witnesses of Jesus" (v. 6).

Although the spirit of Babylon is characteristic of the Tribulation Period, it can be seen in the current European Union in different forms, such as posters with the unfinished Tower of Babel in the process of being completed, with the slogan: "Many tongues, one voice." The EU Parliament building in Strasbourg, France, has a very large replica of the unfinished Tower of Babel placed in the center of the building. Even the secular press could not miss the connection between the old and new towers of Babel, labeling the new structure, "The Tower of Eurobabel."[101]

It can also be seen in the European national symbol, a woman riding a bull. This represents the mythological image, Europa, riding the bull. The bull was actually the god, Zeus, disguised in the form of a bull.

Babylon and the European Union are linked in images as well as common denominators. Babylon was the world's first attempt to establish a world empire or government. The EU will be the last world empire before the Second Coming of Christ. Nimrod was the first ruler of an attempted world empire, Babylon. He was a rebel who defied God in disobedience. The people under Nimrod pridefully wanted to make a name for themselves.[102] The Antichrist, who has not yet been revealed, will also defy God and will display himself as being God.[103]

There is a link between the Book of Genesis and the Book of Revelation. Genesis gives the account of the first attempted world government and the building of the Tower of Babel. Revelation gives the account of the final world government, symbolized as a woman with a name written on her forehead, "BABYLON THE GREAT, THE MOTHER OF HARLOTS AND OF THE ABOMINATIONS OF THE EARTH" (Revelation 17:5). The woman was riding a beast. She represents the false world religious system. The beast represents the Antichrist and the final world empire.

Just as Babylon is linked to the EU, Genesis is linked to the Book of Revelation. The origins and first world government are linked to the end times and the final world government. This brings us to the Roman Empire link to the European Union.

THE EUROPEAN UNION / ROMAN EMPIRE CONNECTION

The association between the Roman Empire and the EU can, like Babylon, be seen in the EU's symbols and pictures. For example, the

European national symbol of a woman riding a bull originates from mythology. The myth involves the abduction of the woman Europa by the god Zeus who is disguised as a bull. Zeus takes Europa to the island of Cyprus where he rapes her. Although the myth comes from Greek mythology, the imagery ties it to Revelation 17:3, which makes reference to the "woman sitting on the scarlet beast." The European national symbol ties the EU to the Tribulation Period, which occurs during the Final One World Empire.

In order to understand the link between the Roman Empire and the EU, it is necessary to look first at the biblical foundation. The "Times of the Gentiles" is a reference to Daniel Chapter 2. In Daniel 2, King Nebuchadnezzar, the king of Babylon at that time, had a dream of an "image." God disclosed the dream and its interpretation to Daniel, one of the wise men. This interpretation prophesied four successive empires. The fourth empire was the Roman Empire, the final empire culminating with the Second Coming of Christ.

This Roman Empire was never really defeated, but broke into pieces. These pieces or tribes were never able to reestablish a Roman Empire or any empire to replace it. The European Union has been successful at recreating a "Revived Roman Empire." This has been a regrouping of the pieces of the Roman Empire. The next step is to look at common characteristics shared by the original Roman Empire and the European Union, the Revived Roman Empire.

TIMES OF THE GENTILES

Understanding how the EU fits the description of the Final One World Empire requires an understanding of where it fits on the prophetic time line. In Chapter Four of this book, we reviewed the image and its interpretation in Daniel Chapters 2, 7, and 8. A brief overview will show where the EU fits on the historical time line.

Daniel Chapter 2 summarizes a dream by King Nebuchadnezzar, the king of Babylon, about a giant image of a man. He was unable to interpret the dream, and his "wise men"—magicians, conjurers, sorcerers, and the Chaldeans—were also unable to interpret the dream. When Daniel heard about the king's dilemma, he prayed to God for the interpretation, and his prayer was answered. The following is a brief summary of Daniel's interpretation:

1. The Head is made of gold and represents the Babylonian Empire.
2. The Breast and Arms are made of silver and represent the Medo-Persian Empire.
3. The Belly and Thighs are made of bronze and represent Greece.
4. The Legs are made of iron and represent the Roman Empire. The feet and toes are made of iron and clay. This is still part of the Roman Empire, similar yet different from the original Roman Empire. This most likely symbolizes a Revived Roman Empire.

The Roman Empire is the last of the four empires before the Second Coming of Christ (see Daniel 2:34-35, 44-45). It was never defeated, but broke into pieces. The ten toes in Daniel 2:42 parallel the ten horns in Daniel 7:24, which also represent ten kings. There were never ten kings ruling the Roman Empire simultaneously, so this has to refer to a future event. Bible scholars often refer to the EU as the "Revived Roman Empire." [See Chapter Four for a more detailed explanation.]

THE ROMAN EMPIRE, THE EUROPEAN UNION, AND THE COMMON DENOMINATORS

The two legs of iron represent the Eastern and Western divisions of the Roman Empire. In A.D. 284, during the Imperial Age or Empire Period, the empire split into two parts. The capital of the Eastern Roman Empire was Constantinople, named after Emperor Constantine. The capital of the Western Roman Empire was Rome.

The EU now has a Western European Union (WEU). Although both are considered part of the EU, the WEU is taking on a more powerful and significant role. Could this possibly be a continuation of the Eastern and Western Roman Empire, i.e., feet and toes, representing a Revived Roman Empire? Remember the feet and toes are made of iron and clay, not just iron like the legs.

In the beginning, the Roman Empire was multicultural. In the end, it was an empire ruled by Emperors from Rome.[104] In the beginning, the area now known as the EU was multicultural, a mixture of cultures or nations known as Europe. It is now unifying into member states as the European Union (EU).

The Roman Empire created the First Universal Declaration of Human Rights. This was actually an abstraction of civil rights.[105] The more recent

Universal Declaration of Human Rights was drawn up in 1947. While it was not intended to lay a philosophical foundation for the coming EU and the One World Government, we can see that in the last 30 to 40 years it has done so. It recognized the state/government as the Supreme Authority in determining a person's rights, instead of God. This was significant. The foundation has been laid for the Antichrist to take the stage. The Roman Emperors declared themselves to be gods and demanded the worship of the people. The Antichrist "opposes and exalts himself above every so-called god or object of worship, so that he takes his seat in the temple of God, displaying himself as being God."[106]

The Roman Empire "developed different formal and informal relationships with neighboring cities, states, territories, peoples, and empires."[107] The EU established a European Neighborhood Policy (ENP) in 2003 that provides for individual alliances with different countries with tailor made "action plans."

In A.D. 330, Emperor Constantine established Christianity as the official Roman religion, although paganism was still tolerated. Constantine had a loyalty to both. As we shall see later, this divided loyalty resulted in Christianity, as practiced officially in the Roman Empire, incorporating pagan elements and their overtones for years to come. The false world religion, symbolized as the "woman on the scarlet beast" in the Book of Revelation, will become the official religion during the Tribulation Period. (See Chapter Six of this book for more details on the current development of the false world religion.) People who refuse to worship the image of the beast will be killed.[108] This false world religion will originate out of the EU. This will be a time of mass Christian martyrdom as practiced and well documented in the Roman Empire, only to a much greater extent.

The Roman Empire had a universal currency. The EU also has a universal currency with the introduction of the euro in 2001. By 2002, it had become the national currency in twelve member states (countries). As mentioned earlier, in January 2008, the SEPA now includes 31 member states. The pieces of the puzzle are falling into place rapidly. The Roman Empire had a single government that operated according to a consistent set of written laws. The EU also has a central government with a written set of laws and the Treaty of Lisbon that will be completely ratified by all the member states by January 1, 2009.

Geographically, the Roman Empire during the time of Christ included most of Europe, the Mediterranean countries, North Africa, Egypt, Syria, and Israel. This is very similar to the geographical area currently covered by the EU. The Roman Empire grew to include a larger geographical area. The EU is also expanding very rapidly. As a point of interest, a large portion of a map of the Roman Empire during the time of Christ looks very similar to a current map of the EU.

SUMMARY OF COMMON DENOMINATORS, OR "IT'S ALL IN THE FAMILY":

Babylon, the Roman Empire, and the European Union

Although there are differences between the members of a biological family, there still exists a common denominator, the gene pool. There is a connection, and there are similarities among the members. Babylon, the Roman Empire, and the European Union are similarly connected.

1. **Babylon:** The people wanted to stay together, build a one world government, and speak the same language. The EU consists of many countries coming together with a centralized government expanding toward a One World government. They identify themselves through a poster with a picture of the Tower of Babel and carrying the slogan, "Many tongues, one voice."

2. **Babylon:** The building of the Tower of Babel was led by one man, Nimrod. The EU is moving in the same direction, as expressed over 50 years ago by Paul-Henri Spaak, former Belgium prime minister and President of the Consultative Assembly of the Council of Europe. He said, in essence, that all we want is one man "to lift us out of this economic morass ... be he God or the devil, we will receive him."

3. **The Roman Empire:** It had a single currency. The EU has a single currency—the euro.

4. **The Roman Empire:** It had a written set of laws. The EU now has the Treaty of Lisbon, which replaces the EU Constitution. It has been signed but has not yet been ratified by all member states.

5. **The Roman Empire:** geographically it covered most of Europe as well as other countries in North Africa and around the Mediterranean. The EU covers an area that is very close to being geographically identical to that of the Roman Empire.

6. **The Roman Empire:** religion was paganism and then Christianity. The EU is primarily Christianity influenced by paganism.

All of these similarities show the connecting links between the EU, Babylon, and the Roman Empire. These similarities were not evident prior to 1948. They have all occurred during this generation, which is the last generation before the Second Coming of Christ.

EU SYMBOLS: PROPHETIC BIBLICAL SYMBOLS

1. **Official European Symbol: Europa Riding on a Bull**
   A. Chosen by the euro planners to represent Europe without regard to the biblical implications.
   B. Based on a myth: The details of the myth were discussed under the European Union/Roman Empire Connection.
   C. Biblical symbol: The "beast" (counterpart to the bull) is described in Daniel 7:19 as "exceedingly dreadful." In Revelation 13:1, 16-18, it is described as a "scarlet beast" with seven heads, ten horns, and full of blasphemous names. The beast represents or symbolizes the Antichrist and his kingdom (Revelation 17:7, 16). The woman who sits on the scarlet beast represents the apostate religion (she was drunk with the blood of the saints and witnesses of Jesus) (Revelation 17:6). Her name is "BABYLON THE GREAT, THE MOTHER OF HARLOTS AND OF THE ABOMINATIONS OF THE EARTH" (Revelation 17:5).
   D. The woman riding on the beast was one of Hitler's favorite symbols.[109]
   E. The chosen symbol came from pagan mythology, but it ties in with the events of the last generation and the Book of Revelation. Coincidence or Providence?

2. **The European Flag**
   A. Consists of twelve stars in a circle. Although the EU has more than twelve member states, the number remains at twelve. This is consistent with Revelation 12:1, which describes the Woman of the Apocalypse.
   B. According to Leon Marshall, a former Secretary General of the Council of Europe, the stars represent those of "The Woman of the Apocalypse."[110]
   C. Even the European flag has religious significance, not in the Christian sense, but in the pagan sense, as will be shown later.

3. **European Union Poster**
   A. It shows a partially built Tower of Babel with a crane in the background rebuilding the Tower. It has twelve eurostars above it that are "inverted and shaped like pentagrams, as in witchcraft, with the central points downward."[111]
   B. The twelve stars are tied to the "Woman of the Apocalypse" as portrayed in Revelation 12. There is a link to the Babylonian "Mystery Religions" and the name of the "Woman on the Beast" in Revelation 17.
   C. The Tower of Babel slogan is "Many tongues, one voice." "This appears to be an attempt to reverse God's judgment."[112]

4. **The Virgin Mary Under a Halo of Twelve Stars**
   A. This is found in the stained glass window of the Council of Europe at the Strasbourg Cathedral in France. "The Vatican is playing a major role in the creation of a new Holy Roman Empire."[113]
   B. This symbol and its significance will be explained as it fits into the dominant theme of the next chapter.

This chapter illustrates how close we are to the return of Christ. We have traced the historical development of the Coming One World Government with an eye toward the future. We have also traced the economic development toward the Coming One World Government. This covers two of the three pillars that have to be in place during the Tribulation Period. The next chapter will focus on the third or final pillar, the Coming One World False Religion.

Chapter Six

The Coming One World Religion

*"... and on her forehead a name was written, a mystery,
'BABYLON THE GREAT, THE MOTHER OF HARLOTS AND
OF THE ABOMINATIONS OF THE EARTH.'"*
— Revelation 17:5

The previous chapter covered the development and current status of the coming world *government*. This coming world government and its leader, the Antichrist, are symbolized in the Book of Revelation as a "beast."

This chapter will focus on the development and current status of the coming world *religion* as symbolized by the woman who is riding on the beast (Revelation 17).

Some of the information contained in this chapter will be upsetting to some people. Because of the controversial subject matter, I gave serious consideration to the omission of part of the chapter. After prayerfully seeking God's will, I have decided to include all of it.

My prayer is that the reader does not personalize any comments about any religious denomination. This is not about a group of people or any particular individuals; it is about the doctrinal positions to which those religious denominations ascribe. My research and the findings are based on very credible sources. This chapter begins by examining common characteristics of a false religion.

HALLMARKS OF A FALSE RELIGION

One must have a reference point or standard for what is true in order to understand what is false. In Christianity, the Bible is our standard for truth. Anything that contradicts the Bible is false. Second Timothy 3:16 says, "All Scripture is inspired by God and profitable for teaching, for reproof, for correction, for training in righteousness."

Anything that is added to the Bible is false. If anything is subtracted from the Bible, it also results in something false. The Book of Revelation states: "I testify to everyone who hears the words of the prophecy of this book: if anyone adds to them, God will add to him the plagues which are written in this book; and if anyone takes away from the words of the book of this prophecy, God shall take away his part from the tree of life and from the holy city, which are written in this book" (Revelation 22:18-19). Although this is a direct reference to the last book of the Bible, the Book of Revelation, the implication is for a broader application to the whole Bible (God's Word).

Having established the biblical standard for truth, we can now look at what constitutes false religion. In order to have the unity required for a *false* one world religion, it would have to involve at least four characteristics: 1) it must contain a compromise of doctrine; 2) it must be experience based in order to be believable; 3) it must provide a broad road to salvation; and 4) it must include counterfeit miracles.[1] It would also be based on sources outside of the Bible that are not compatible with Christian doctrine. False religions manifest themselves in the ways listed below.

COMPROMISE OF DOCTRINE

One of the key phrases used in the European Union, as well as in the United States, is "Unity in Diversity." This sounds good on the surface. It means we are a unified but diverse group of people—all of the hallmarks of tolerance. To have this kind of unity in a world religion necessitates a compromise of doctrine, whereby different religious groups have to compromise their beliefs.

Tolerance is promoted in almost every area. The major exceptions are fundamental Christianity and Judaism. The developing world religion will be tolerant of everything but the truth. This will be seen in its ultimate form during the Tribulation Period. The false world religion, symbolized by the harlot sitting on the scarlet beast in Revelation 17:1-6, is "… drunk with the blood of the saints, and with the blood of the witnesses of Jesus." This is in reference to the martyred believers in Jesus. It is an example of the ultimate expression of intolerance. Unity in diversity is "the key for globalization to unlock the door to the New World Order, in this case, a New World Religion."[2]

BASED ON EXPERIENCE

"Show us a sign and we will believe" (John 6:30 paraphrased).

There is an escalating trend worldwide toward an experienced-based religion and an experienced-based Christianity. "More people are traveling to many different places where they say God is manifesting Himself through signs and wonders."[3] These manifestations are many times apparitions of Mary or of angels, but rarely Jesus. It is important to keep in mind that biblically-based Christianity is always founded on a personal relationship with Jesus Christ.[4] True faith is evidenced by hearing and doing God's Word.[5]

Paul exhorts the Galatians not to be fooled by people who want to distort the gospel of Jesus Christ. He states: "But even if we, or an angel from heaven, should preach to you a gospel contrary to what we have preached to you, he is to be accursed!" (Galatians 1:8). Paul also warns in Colossians 2:18 against taking a stand based on visions someone claims to have seen. The Bible warns us repeatedly to be on guard against false prophets and teachers. **It is important to remember that "Satan disguises himself as an angel of light" (2 Corinthians 11:14). He has the ability to work miracles and make it appear to be a manifestation of God (disguised as an angel of light).**

One example of a supernatural demonstration of Satan's power can be seen in the Book of Exodus. The Israelites were captives in Egypt and were being oppressed as slaves. God called Moses to return to Egypt and bring the Israelites out. He instructed Moses in all that he was to do when he arrived in Egypt. Moses, along with his brother Aaron, confronted Pharaoh to "let the sons of Israel go out of his land" (Exodus 7:2). When they made this request, Pharaoh responded as the Lord had predicted by asking them to do a miracle.

Now the LORD spoke to Moses and Aaron, saying, "When Pharaoh speaks to you, saying, 'Work a miracle,' then you shall say to Aaron, 'Take your staff and throw it down before Pharaoh, that it may become a serpent.' " ... and Aaron threw his staff down before Pharaoh and his servants, and it became a serpent. Then Pharaoh also called for the wise men and the sorcerers, and they also, the magicians of Egypt, did the same with their secret arts. For each one threw down his staff and they turned into serpents. But Aaron's staff swallowed up their staffs.[6]

The Lord "won the contest," as He did with other miracles, some of which were counterfeited by Satan. Remember, God is always victorious!

BROAD ROAD TO SALVATION

A rapidly growing belief system is that of Universalism, which is another lie. It promotes the belief that there are many paths to God. While this may be a "politically correct" theology in our day, it is the neo-paganism of the New Age. People who buy into universalism are risking where they will spend eternity on a gamble that the Bible is wrong.[7] Jesus said, "... I am the way, and the truth, and the life; no one comes to the Father but through Me" (John 14:6). Any other way to God violates Holy Scripture, the Standard, which says the road to salvation is narrow.[8]

COUNTERFEIT MIRACLES

The events that occurred in Egypt when Moses and Aaron confront-ed Pharaoh is a clear case of Satan's power to perform miracles and to counterfeit miracles from God. Obviously, God's power is superior to Satan's power. God was victorious over Satan then and will continue to defeat him, even during the Great Tribulation Period when Satan's power is poured out full strength. The miracles performed in Egypt illustrated an obvious demonstration of good over evil.

These events not only illustrate Satan's power to perform miracles, but his tendency to counterfeit or copy God's miracles. Scripture tells us that Satan disguises himself as an "angel of light." He can perform miracles, he can counterfeit God's miracles to some degree, but he is a liar, the father of lies and of all that is false. There is no truth in him (see John 8:44 AMP).

The present generation is oriented toward the experiential and the miraculous. Over the last ten to fifteen years, there has been a greater orientation toward the supernatural. This gives Satan an open door to perform visions and apparitions that appear to come from God. As a result, hundreds of thousands of people are flocking to see them. **The impact of these apparitions has been so powerful that they have cut across religious denominations worldwide, including Islam.**

A false one-world religion is rapidly taking shape, and, as we will see, its home base will be in the European Union. This can be seen in many ways but is most obviously seen through the European symbols.

MADONNA OF THE APOCALYPSE?

In a cathedral in Strasbourg, France, you will find the "Woman of the Apocalypse" portrayed in a stained-glass window. The woman has a halo of twelve stars. The EU poster also shows twelve stars, known as "eurostars," along with a picture of a partially built Tower of Babel. The twelve stars are also found on the European flag.

This symbol originated from the Woman of the Apocalypse in the Book of Revelation, which is often called the Apocalypse: "… a woman clothed with the sun, and the moon under her feet, and on her head a crown of twelve stars, and she was with child …" (Revelation 12:1-2). The woman described here is not a reference to the Virgin Mary but to the nation of Israel. The twelve stars symbolize the twelve tribes of Israel. Israel is symbolized as the woman who gave birth to Jesus Christ.[9] Jesus was of Jewish heritage.

The same imagery is found in Genesis 37:9-10. Joseph had a dream that involved his future and his family's future: "… the sun and the moon and eleven stars were bowing down to me" (Genesis 37:9). It was clearly understood as a reference to Joseph's parents (sun and moon) and his eleven brothers (stars).[10]

It is not coincidental that the twelve-star halo above the woman in the stained-glass window in Strasbourg just happens to be on the EU poster that also illustrates a partially built Tower of Babel. Nor is it coincidental that the twelve stars are also on the European flag.

These twelve stars do not represent the EU member states. There has never been a connection between the twelve stars and the number of member states. There are currently twenty-seven member states.

The Roman Catholic Church interprets the woman of the Apocalypse as the Virgin Mary. This interpretation fits neither the context nor the symbolism. It is obvious that the Vatican is playing a major role in the creation of a new Holy Roman Empire.[11] The religious symbolism of the Apocalyptic woman is linked to the EU through the twelve stars found on the poster and on the European flag. There is a clear connection between the church, Roman Catholic, and the state, the EU.

As shown in Chapter Five of this book, the national symbol of the EU is a woman representing Europa riding a bull. This image originated in Greek mythology. Although the euro planners did not choose this symbol from the Bible, the Book of Revelation presents a similar image of a woman described as a "harlot" riding a "beast." The EU image of Europa riding on a bull is the national symbol. The woman riding on a beast is a biblical symbol. The similarity between the two images is striking. They are linked. Just as there is a connection between the EU national symbol and the biblical symbol, there is also a definite connection between paganism and mythology. This will become clear later in this chapter.

The next section focuses on the relationship between the biblical image of the woman on the beast that is found in Revelation 17 and the coming world religion. It will also identify the woman rider and what she symbolizes.

THE RIDER FROM HELL

In the same way the Apocalyptic woman described in Revelation 12 was symbolic of the country of Israel, the woman rider in Revelation 17 symbolizes the coming false world religion. This can be determined by looking at her identity, her character, her influence, and her behavior.

Her title and description allude to her character.

> The woman was clothed in purple and scarlet, and adorned with gold and precious stones and pearls, having in her hand a gold cup full of abominations and of the unclean things of her immorality, and upon her forehead a name was written, a mystery, "BABYLON THE GREAT, THE MOTHER OF HARLOTS AND OF (T)THE ABOMINATIONS OF THE EARTH." (Revelation 17:4-5)

Her adornment describes the religious trappings of ritualistic churches today.[12] Her name makes reference to "Babylon" and the "Mother of Harlots." This links her to the Babylonian religion. The Bible is full of information about Babylon as the source of false religion, beginning with the Tower of Babel.[13]

In regard to her behavior, she is described in verse 2 as committing "acts of immorality" and in verse 6 as being "drunk with the blood of the saints, and with the blood of the witnesses of Jesus." So far, she has been characterized as religious, antichristian (martyrs the followers of Jesus), immoral and powerful (commits acts of immorality with the kings of the earth). If you are a true Christian, this is not the kind of woman you would want to associate with. This tells us a lot about her character, but this alone still does not tell us what she symbolizes.

The woman rider is further described in Revelation 17:1 as "... the great harlot who sits on many waters." John, the author of the Book of Revelation, explains how to interpret the "waters." Verse 15 says, "... The waters which you saw, where the harlot sits, are peoples and multitudes and nations and tongues." This further indicates her identity as a religious system that is worldwide.

In verse 18 she is referred to as "... the great city, which reigns over the kings of the earth." She also sits on "seven mountains" (v. 9).

Based on the description of the woman rider portrayed in Revelation 17, we can see at least three implications:

1. "The woman as a great city" is another link with ancient Babylon, this time regarded as a religious center for false religion.[14]
2. Her influence and power cover many nations, but her center or home base is a city on seven hills. Rome is a city on seven hills. It is also the home base of the Roman Catholic Church.
3. There is a connection between ancient Babylon (the origin of false religion) that began with the Tower of Babel and consummates with the coming One World (false) Religion.

In essence, we are dealing with two Babylons. The first one is ancient Babylon where the Tower of Babel was built and is considered the origin of false religions and paganism. The second and last Babylon has characteristics of the first Babylon but will be worldwide. It will be an expanded, much grander version of the first one. This will occur during the Great Tribulation Period, a segment of time that will literally be the worst time imaginable since the flood.

The next section traces the origin of the coming World Religion. The focus is on ancient Babylon, its characteristics, how it branched out into the different pagan religions, and how it has influenced the Christian Church today.

ANCIENT BABYLON TO MODERN BABYLON

The ancient Babylonian "mystery religions" never really died. They had their beginnings in the Book of Genesis, which gives the account of the building of the Tower of Babel under the leadership of Nimrod. It reaches both its zenith and its destruction in the Book of Revelation.

The False Prophet, referred to as "another beast," "exercises all the authority of the first beast [Antichrist] in his presence. And he makes the earth and those who dwell in it to worship the first beast."[15] The False Prophet heads the coming World Religion under the authority of the Antichrist. The Babylon "mystery religions," in a disguised form, comprise this false religious system. These mystery religions are the alpha and omega of paganism and idolatry.

Babylon of the Old Testament and Babylon of the New Testament are related and can be linked and traced. The mystery pagan religions originated in Babylon, spread to different countries, and took on different names. Nevertheless, it is still the same Babylonian religious system.

The following historical information includes elements of mythology in some accounts. It is important to remember that mythology is usually a distortion of actual facts. The historical facts occur, but the memory of these facts results in truth being transmitted or myth being transmitted. Sometimes it is a combination of myth and truth.[16]

ORIGIN OF THE MYSTERY RELIGIONS OF BABYLON

The following information is drawn from the Bible and accounts outside of biblical sources. As a brief overview, the key characters will be listed and further explained by showing their connections to certain pagan deities and some common denominators that run through the different cultures. The chart on the next page shows the specific names of pagan deities associated with the original pagan characters. This will simplify the following section.

The three original key characters are Nimrod, Semiramis, and Tammuz. The following chart indicates the spread of the Mother-Child

Babylonian cult throughout other localities with the names of the gods and goddesses that originate from these three key characters. It will be easier to follow the names and their connections in the following sections by referring to this chart.

These were the original names of the Mother-Child cult. Semiramis was Nimrod's wife, and Tammuz was her son.

We know that Nimrod was the founder of Babylon.[17] It was Nimrod's

CHART 9

ORIGIN OF THE MYSTERY RELIGIONS OF BABYLON		
SEMIRAMIS . . . . NIMROD		
Queen of	**TAMMUZ**	*Husband*
Heaven	*Son*	
Mother		**Son**
Isis . . . . Egypt. . . . . Osiris		
Ishtar . . . . Assyria . . . . Bacchus		
Isi . . . . India. . . . . Iswara		
Cybele . . . . Asia . . . . Deoius		
Aphrodite . . . . Greece . . . . Eros		
Venus . . . . Rome. . . . . Cupid		
Rhea . . . . Babylon . . . . Zero-ashta *(the seed)*		
Ashtoreth . . . . Phoenicians . . . . Tammuz		
		Ninus *(Son or Husband)*
		Lamented One *(Son)*

Adapted from chart on p. 292, *One World: Economy, Government, & Religion in the Last Days,* by Ron J. Bigalde Jr., and *The Two Babylons* by Alexander Hislop, p. 5.

Different countries and cultures changed the names. Some of the other names given to the Mother/Child cult includes: 1) The Egyptian Madonna, Isis, and the little sun god, Horus.[18] Sometimes it is Isis and Osiris when Osiris plays the role of husband and son. 2) The Phoenicians changed the name Semiramis to Ashtoreth, but Tammuz remained the same. The names then became Ashtoreth and Tammuz instead of Semiramis and Tammuz. The Phoenicians were carried to the ends of the earth with Ashtoreth and Tammuz as the mother and child of these adventures.[19] 3) In Greece, it was Aphrodite and Eros. 4) In Italy, Venus and Cupid. 5) There are many other names in many different places.[20] However, the focus of this section is on the names listed.

wife, Semiramis, who founded the secret religious rites of the Babylonian mystery religions. Semiramis claimed that she conceived, through an alleged miraculous conception, a virgin-born son who would be the salvation of mankind. She named him Tammuz. In effect, this was a false fulfillment of the promise of the Seed, given to Eve in Genesis 3:15.[21]

Hislop's book, *The Two Babylons*, chronicles the spread of the ancient Babylonian cult of the mother and child throughout other nations and civilizations.[22] Hislop also researched the Babylonian worship of the queen of heaven. Jeremiah warned the Israelites against offering sacrifices to the *queen of heaven* (Jeremiah 7:18; 44:17-19, 25).

According to Hislop's research, the Babylonian worship of the queen of heaven found its origin following the death of Nimrod, which put Semiramis in shock. Although she had shared the throne of Babylon with her husband, his death had given a rude shock to her power. Her resolution and unbounded ambition, however, were in no wise checked.[23] It was through this supposedly miraculous conception and the son she bore that she gained her power.

"In life, her husband had been honored as a hero; she will have him worshipped as a god; yea, as the woman's promised seed, 'Zero-ashta,' who was destined to bruise the serpent's head, and who, in doing so, was to have his own heel bruised."[24] It was well known by the patriarchs that the ancient world was well acquainted with the grand primeval promise of Eden. They "knew right well that the bruising of the heel of the promised seed implied his death, and that the curse could be removed from the world only by the death of the grand Deliverer."[25] Semiramis declared Nimrod "the promised seed," and, through his death ("bruised heel"), he became the grand Deliverer. Satan attempted to counterfeit the prophecy concerning Jesus.

Semiramis, the wife, was worshipped as Rhea, the "Mother Goddess," by the Babylonians. Her connection with her husband, under the name of Ninus, or "The Son," originated the peculiar worship of the "Mother and Son." This "Mother and Son" worship was found throughout the nations of antiquity. This explains the fact, which has so puzzled inquirers into ancient history, that Ninus is sometimes called the husband and sometimes called the son of Semiramis. The same confusion can be seen between Isis and Osiris, the mother and child of the Egyptians. One of Osiris' titles of honor and dignity was the name "Husband of the Mother."[26]

Mythology and paganism come further into play when the story goes on to say, according to tradition, that Tammuz was killed by a wild animal and was then restored to life.[27] This was a satanic anticipation and counterfeit of Christ's resurrection. It becomes more distorted, according to classical literature, when Tammuz becomes known as "Bacchus," or the "Lamented One." The Lamented One is exhibited as the child in his mother's arms, yet is also considered to be the husband of Semiramis, named Ninus or "The Son." As we have already seen, Ninus is identified with Nimrod. The biblical and historical facts have now become distorted into myth that is incorporated into paganism.

"MOTHER AND CHILD" AS GOD CULT:
DISTORTION OF THE TRINITY

This cult was one of the major Babylonian religious practices. It was built upon worshipping a "Mother" god who had a "divine baby," a son supposedly born of a miraculous conception.[28] This practice showed up in different pagan religions, each using its own unique names. The mother and child cult, which had its origin in Babylon, spread to other religions with name changes, as shown earlier. It became very popular.

The Mother/Goddess cult eventually supplanted the worship of the Father God. This was the result of a distortion of the Trinity. The Trinity was represented in some form in very ancient paganism. This unity of the Father, Seed (or Son), and Holy Ghost "was the original way in which pagan idolatry had represented the Triune God."[29] This notion of a Triune God survived until the time of Sennacherib, King of Assyria (704-681 B.C.). There is evidence that, at a very early period, an important change had taken place in the Babylonian notions in regard to the divinity, and that "the three persons had come to be the Eternal Father, the Spirit of God incarnate in a human mother, and a Divine Son, the fruit of that incarnation."[30]

The first person of the Trinity, or Godhead, was practically over-looked. "As the Great Invisible, taking no immediate concern in human affairs, he was 'to be worshipped through silence alone,' that is, in point of fact, he was not worshipped by the multitude at all."[31]

Worship of the "King Eternal and Invisible" is almost extinct throughout Europe where the Papal system is completely developed, while the Mother and the Child are the grand objects of worship. This was also true in ancient Babylon. The popular view of the Babylonians was the worship of a Goddess Mother and a Son as represented in pictures and images.[32]

"In China and Japan, the Jesuit missionaries were astonished to find the counterpart of Madonna and her child as devoutly worshipped as in Papal Rome itself; Shing Moo, the Holy Mother in China, being represented with a child in her arms, and a glory around her, exactly as if a Roman Catholic artist had been employed to set her up."[33] In the following section, we will trace the roots of the resemblance and association between the Chinese images of paganism and the Catholic religion, which so astonished the Jesuit missionaries.

THE PAGANIZATION OF CHRISTIANITY

After the Persians took over Babylonia in 539 B.C., they discouraged the continuation of the mystery religions of Babylon. As a result, the Babylonian cultists moved to Pergamum (or Pergamus) where one of the seven churches of Asia Minor was later located.[34]

The chief priests of the Babylonian cult honored the fish god by wearing crowns in the shape of a fish head.[35] The crowns bore the words, "Keeper of the Bridge." According to Wolvoord and Zuck, authors of *The Bible Knowledge Commentary*, this was symbolic of the "bridge" between man and Satan (see endnotes 35 and 36). The Roman Emperors adopted the Latin title Pontifex Maximus, which means "Major Keeper of the Bridge."[36] The bishop of Rome later used the same title. The pope today is called pontiff, which means pontifex. Even today the term Pontifex Maximus can be found throughout the Vatican and numerous cathedrals in Rome. When the teachers of the Babylonian mystery religions later moved to Rome, they were influential in paganizing Christianity.[37] The Roman Empire included the geographic area known today as the European Union.

To grasp this discussion, it is important to remember that the early Christian Church was the persecuted church. There was a clear distinction between good and evil. During that era, the Roman Empire was characterized by paganism, which involved the worship of many false gods. The Emperors burned Christians at the stake for entertainment. If you were a follower of Christ, you were the enemy of the Empire. There was no confusion between Christians and pagans. This leads us to ask the question, "What went wrong?"

The first mistake was the joining of church and state. It was under Emperor Theodosius (A.D. 379-395) in the year A.D. 381 that Christianity was recognized as the state religion. In effect, Constantine legalized the practice of Christianity and Emperor Theodosius made it the state religion. This resulted in a threefold problem:

1. Constantine claimed to be a Christian, yet he still held on to pagan practices. This raises the following question. Is it possible for a person to be a true "born again" Christian while continuing to embrace paganism? The clear dividing line between Christianity and paganism became blurred.
2. The glorification of Mary as "Queen of Heaven" and the worship of the Mother/Child religion had entered the Christian Church from the mystery religions of Babylon.
3. The evangelistic zeal to spread Roman Catholicism to the heathen lands resulted in a compromise with paganism. The native myths and beliefs were incorporated into Roman Catholicism.

When Constantine converted to Christianity and granted the "Freedom of Worship" for the citizens of the Roman Empire, this freedom of worship opened the door for Christians to practice their faith without persecution. Unfortunately, Constantine's conversion to Christianity also included a loyalty to paganism.

Christianity became interwoven with the Babylonian mystery religions. This new form of paganized Christianity was now endorsed as the official state religion. It was not the pure, unadulterated gospel of Jesus Christ as taught by the Apostles. Martyrdom characterized the conviction of the disciples of Jesus Christ. Prior to this time, it was easy to determine who the Christians were and who the pagans were. This was no longer the case.

The mystery religions were now part of the Christian Church, which included the pagan Mother/Child cult. This cult was going strong for many centuries prior to the life of Mary and the birth of Jesus.

As paganism was infiltrating Christianity (beginning in Constantine's era), the Roman Catholic Church declared Mary the "queen of heaven" as a result of the miraculous birth of Christ. In the Old Testament, God condemned the worship of the queen of heaven. Jeremiah 7:18 says, "The children gather wood, and the fathers kindle the fire, and the women knead dough to make cakes for the queen of heaven; and they pour out drink offerings to other gods in order to spite Me."

Catholics began to evangelize the pagan world.[38] As they traveled to heathen lands on mission trips, they would find temples built to false gods. They would also find Madonna statues of Isis or Semiramis holding a child. In spite of the fact that the statues were pagan deities and Madonna figures, "the Catholic evangelists simply renamed them as Mary holding the child Jesus. They let them keep their gods and merely changed the names. Instead of 'pagans,' they were renamed 'Catholics.' "[39]

The pagans kept their Madonna statues of Semiramis, Isis, and a host of other goddesses portrayed with a child. In essence, the Catholic missionaries did a trade off. They allowed the "heathens" to keep their pagan mother/child statues as long as they renamed them "Mary and Jesus." This intertwining of paganism and Catholicism has resulted in a subtle yet progressive contamination within the Catholic Church.

What we are seeing today in the Roman Catholic Church is a movement toward an ecumenical world religion. It falls under such titles as "tolerance" and "unity in diversity." This One World Religion will be built on compromise. Many people will be attracted to this One World Religion as a result of their experiences. Many people are having experiences, especially through apparitions. This will be seen in the following sections.

POPES IN THE FINAL COUNTDOWN

There are two key figures that will come to power in the end times. The Bible refers to these key figures as two beasts (Revelation 13:11-15). The first one is the Antichrist. He will be a political and economic messiah. The second one is the False Prophet who will be a religious leader and miracle worker. Prophecy scholars have taught for many years that the False Prophet will be a final apostate pope. Only the pope would have the power and influence necessary to bring all religions together.[40]

The pope, also considered the "bishop of Rome," is the head of the Catholic Church. His authority is placed above biblical revelation. He can make doctrinal changes in the Catholic Church even if it is contrary to the Bible. The various popes have made different contributions, but our primary focus will be on Pope John Paul II and Pope Benedict XVI.

POPE JOHN PAUL II

Pope John Paul II was the most instrumental pope in history. Two central themes characterize his time in office: his role in elevating Mary to a much higher position than previously recognized and his attempt to bring together all religions and faiths. He was known as the "great unifier."[41] This would also be indicative of the end times' One World Religion.

His devotion to Mary was made evident by his motto, *Totus Tuus*. In Latin this means "totally yours." This is not a reference to Christ but to Mary.[42] His total consecration to Mary was an established fact. He had the letter "M" embroidered on all his garments, showing his devotion to Mary.[43] He did everything within his power to elevate Mary to a divine status as co-redeemer with Jesus. He promoted this doctrine in an attempt to elevate it "to the level of dogma through an infallible papal proclamation."[44] He was dissuaded by his advisors due to their fear that it would undermine their ecumenical attempts to draw Protestants into a working cooperation with the Catholic Church.[45]

Pope John Paul II was, without a doubt, the most Marianistic pope of all time. He credited Mary with saving his life during the 1981 assassination attempt, which deepened his devotion to her.[46] He actually credited the picture of "Our Lady of Fatima" with saving of his life.[47]

On May 13, 1981, the pope appeared before an audience at St. Peter's Square. The pope noticed a little girl wearing a picture of the Mary of Fatima on her lapel. At the moment he leaned over to look at the picture, a Turkish assassin named Mahomet Ali Agca fired two bullets at his head. The bullets missed by several inches because the pope had bent down to look at the picture of Our Lady of Fatima on the little girl. The next two bullets hit John Paul's body, disabling him for many months.[48] John Paul later gave serious consideration to the Fatima vision and the fact that the assassination attempt occurred on the exact anniversary of the day that Mary supposedly appeared to the three children at Fatima in Portugal.[49]

This event had a great impact on the pope, especially regarding Mary's elevated position. He states in his book, *Crossing the Threshold of Hope*, "After my election as pope, as I became more involved in the problems of the universal church, I came to have a similar conviction on this universal level. If victory comes, it will be brought by Mary. Christ will conquer through her."[50] He goes on to say, "Christ will conquer through Mary because He wants the church's victories now and in the future to be linked to her."

While Pope John Paul II was recovering from the assassination attempt, he began to seriously consider the Fatima vision and its meaning to his life and mission. He "believed that his personal destiny was to rule the Catholic Church during the crisis described in the 'Third Secret of Fatima,' which was based on the Marian apparitions of Fatima."[51]

A Catholic theologian named Malachi Martin wrote a book titled, *The Keys of This Blood,* subtitled, *Pope John Paul II Versus Russia and the West for Control of the New World Order*. Martin, who was respected by Pope John Paul II, "wrote and believed that the pope's belief was based on the Fatima visions, a miraculous appearance of Mary in the future, to be in connection with a spectacular astronomical event."[52] In Martin's book, he makes the following statement concerning Pope John Paul II.

> He's waiting for an event that would fission human history, splitting the immediate past from the oncoming future. It would be an event on public view in the skies ... it will involve our human sun ... but on the day of this event, it [the sun] will not appear merely as the master so-called star of our solar system. Rather, it will be seen as the circumambient glory of the woman whom the apostle describes as, "clothed with the sun."[53] [brackets by author]

We have previously discussed the Woman of the Apocalypse (Revelation Chapter 12). Pope John Paul was referring to this woman. He believed that a supernatural sign involving the sun and the Virgin Mary would bring in a kingdom of peace. He believed it would be a global apparition that would astonish the world's population. According to Martin, the pope believed that this phenomenon would give him the authority to create and reign over a new religious church-state world government.[54]

In the year 2000, Pope John Paul II gathered 1,500 bishops from around the world, the largest group to assemble since Vatican II. He proclaimed the third millennium as the "Great Jubilee."[55] They were there to entrust the world and the millennium to "Our Lady of Fatima," not to Jesus, not even to God, but to Mary.[56] In commemoration of this event, in October of 2000, he ordered the actual statue of "Our Lady of Fatima" to be moved from Fatima, Portugal, to St. Peter's Square to signify "his great devotion to Mary."[57]

It is obvious that Pope John Paul II is the most Marianistic pope of all time. This does not sound like biblical Christianity. Jesus is not glorified, but Mary is honored and exalted. The Catholic Catechism states: "The Immaculate Virgin, preserved free from all stain of original sin—when her earthly life was finished, was taken up, body and soul, into heavenly glory, and exalted by the Lord as Queen over all things."[58] Mary has been exalted to the position of "queen of heaven," which is condemned in Scripture. This title does not describe Mary, the mother of Jesus. The "queen of heaven" referred to in Scripture is a pagan goddess.

The second central theme that characterizes Pope John Paul II is his role as the "great unifier." He had a great talent for public relations. He used this gift very effectively and has thoroughly deceived millions of people.[59] He was the great unifier, which required him likewise to play the role as the great compromiser. This is a necessary role in the formation of a One World religion. This can be seen in a number of his speeches and visits to other countries.

In 1986 in Assisi, Italy, the pope met with a group of false religious leaders, including the Dalai Lama (who basically says he is God). "In Tibetan Buddhism, he is God."[60] The pope joined in a circle to pray and meditate with snake handlers from Togo, Shamans and witch doctors from Africa, Hindu gurus from India, Buddhist monks from Thailand, and liberal Protestant clergymen from Great Britain. They were all included.[61]

The *Associated Press* gave an account of Pope John Paul's visit to the African country of Benin. The article was titled:

POPE MEETS WITH VOODOO BELIEVERS

"Pope John Paul II, on Thursday, sought common ground with the believers in voodoo suggesting that they would not betray their traditional faith by converting to Christianity. 'Christians also revere their ancestors in the faith, from the apostles to the missionaries.' "[62]

The pope's statement goes beyond compromise. To say that they can retain their voodoo beliefs while joining the Catholic Church borders on heresy. Voodoo worshippers believe in many deities. The article goes on to say, "Voodoo priests warmly welcomed the pope." Sossa Guedehoungue, head of Benin's Voodun community, said, "I have never seen God, but today, when I have seen the pope, I recognized that I have seen the good god who prays for all the vooduns."[63] The head voodoo doctor met the pope and said, "I've seen the eyes of God."[64]

Pope John Paul II's "compromising" approach to other religions, which include Shamans, witch doctors, Hindu gurus, Buddhist monks, and now voodoo, sounds very similar to the approach of the Catholic evangelists in the early days of Christianity. The pagans were allowed to keep their statues of Isis and Horus, or other Mother/Child statues, and rename them Mary and Jesus. Pope John Paul II was using the same approach previously used, which allowed paganism to enter the Catholic Church and has now set the stage for the establishment of a One World Religion.

POPE BENEDICT XVI

Prior to becoming Pope Benedict XVI, Cardinal Joseph Ratzinger was head of the Roman Catholic Church's Congregation for the Doctrine of the Faith (CDF) back in 1984.[65] During that time, he made the following statement: "One of the signs of our times is that the announcements of 'Marian apparitions' are multiplying all over the world."[66] The pope clearly saw this as a significant sign of our times. The Marian apparitions play a significant role toward completing the prophetic puzzle, which will be covered in more detail later in this section.

Pope Benedict XVI's age was clearly a factor among the cardinals who selected him as a transitional pope. They chose someone who "could skillfully lead the church as it absorbs John Paul II's legacy, rather than a young cardinal who would wind up with another long pontificate."[67]

Pope Benedict XVI made it clear that his pontificate would follow the trajectory of his predecessor Pope John Paul II. He wanted to continue in a sincere dialogue with other religions and do everything in his power to improve the ecumenical cause. His pledge was to work to unify all Christians and all religions.[68] He continued in Pope John Paul's footsteps toward a One World (False) Religion.

Jewish leaders were encouraged by the prospect of Benedict continuing to build relations between Christians and the Jewish nation.[69] In light of the fact that anti-Semitism is at an all-time high, especially in Europe, this would be very appealing to Jews. They would, understandably, be very open to such a pope. This would also fit the prophetic picture.

The Antichrist and the False Prophet who gives allegiance to him will be supportive of Israel but will turn on them halfway through the Tribulation

Period. This can be found in Daniel 9:27, which supports the timing of this betrayal of Israel. Jesus speaks of this event in Matthew 24:15 when He said, "Therefore when you see the ABOMINATION OF DESOLATION which was spoken of through Daniel the prophet, standing in the holy place (let the reader understand), then those who are in Judea must flee to the mountains." Jesus confirms Daniel's prophecy.

This event has not yet occurred. It is an event that involves a total desecration of the Jewish Temple, similar to the desecration that happened under Antiochus Epiphanies during the Inter-Testament period. This also implies that a Jewish Temple is in existence. *That Temple does not currently exist.* The Romans under Titus destroyed it in A.D. 70 as Jesus had predicted. We can therefore conclude that this reference to the Abomination of Desolation refers to a future Temple. It will have to be erected at the sight of the Dome of the Rock, an Islamic shrine. As impossible as it may seem, according to Scripture it will happen, and it is impossible for Scripture to be broken.

When he became pope, Cardinal Ratzinger modeled his name after Benedict XV (1914-1922). He chose this name to honor him. Benedict XV was very active in an attempt to negotiate and mediate peace during World War One. He also embraced the Muslims, which was an unprecedented choice for his time. He was in many respects the first modern pope. Ratzinger chose this name for a very important purpose.[70] As Pope Benedict XVI, he has likewise embraced the Muslims, but as we will see, there will be a very different outcome that will eventually lure them into the coming One World Religion.

THE MUSLIM CONNECTION: THE MISSING LINK

There is a direct connection between Pope John Paul II, Pope Benedict XV, and Pope Benedict XVI. All three popes reached out to the Muslim community, and they have responded with open arms. An *ABC News* report stated the following:

MUSLIMS WELCOME BENEDICT: HOPING HE WILL PROMOTE HARMONY BETWEEN THE TWO RELIGIONS

In part, the article said, "… there were widespread hopes that Benedict will follow in the path of John Paul in reaching out to the

Islamic world."[71] "A day after reaching out to other Christians and to Jews in his installation mass, Pope Benedict XVI met Monday with the members of the Muslim community ... assuring them that the Church wanted to continue to build bridges of friendship that would foster peace in the world."[72]

The pope is seeking world peace and "is destined to bring the Roman Catholic Church and Muslims together!"[73] When considering the intolerant and uncompromising nature of the fundamental Islamic religion, this may seem like an impossible task. Prophecy scholars have struggled with this issue for years. The perplexing question is: *How can the Islamic religion blend into a One-World Religion?* A closer look at current events, along with historical events, provides the answer.

MARIAN APPARITIONS

According to Cardinal Ratzinger, "... Marian apparitions are multiplying all over the world."[74] This is the new pope who considers the Marian apparitions as "one of the signs of our times." Stories abound regarding visions of Mary. One of the stories involves a remote cornfield in Georgia where a so-called prophetess claims to receive a message from Mary once a year. Over 100,000 people patiently wait for the "prophetess" to get this apparition from Mary. She then comes out and supposedly tells them what Mary said.[75]

Numerous messages have been given by the apparitions of Mary. In one of the so-called messages, Mary said: "Tell this priest, tell everyone, that it is you who are divided on earth. The Muslims and the Orthodox, for the same reason as Catholics, are equal before my son and I. You are all my children."[76]

The underlying message, according to Mary, is: "All religions are the same. We are the ones causing divisions. There are no real differences." In order to give credibility to these apparitions and messages, it is necessary to answer two questions: 1) How do we determine the validity of the message? 2) How do we determine the validity of the messenger?

In order to determine the validity of any message that is religious or spiritual in nature, there has to be a standard to measure it by. The Bible is our standard. In the gospel of John, Jesus made the following statement: "... I am the way, and the truth, and the life; no one comes to the Father but through Me" (John 14:6). It is clear that the Word of God invalidated the message supposedly given by Mary. Colossians 2:18 says, "Let no one keep defrauding you of your prize ... taking his stand on visions he has seen ..."

The message from "Mary" leaves room for salvation to occur through paths other than Jesus. If she is speaking for her "son" as well as herself, then Jesus is contradicting Himself. When a person bases his beliefs on a vision that contradicts what the Bible says, he is ignoring Colossians 2:18. If Mary, the mother of Jesus, were really the messenger, she would not contradict her Son's words. Both the message and the messenger failed to live up to the standard, God's Word.

In an apparition of Mary in the village of Medjugorje, Bosnia-Herzegovina, Mary supposedly stated in part:

> I invite you to become carriers and witnesses of my peace to this unpeaceful world. Let peace rule in the whole world. (understandingthetimes.org, "Queen of Rome," p. 3)

Both Pope John Paul II and Pope Benedict XVI made reference to Mary's role in the last days. The assassination attempt on Pope John Paul II resulted in the Fatima connection and the dedication of the third millennium to Mary. Pope Benedict XVI made a statement in his previous position as Cardinal Ratzinger concerning the Marian apparitions as being "one of the signs of our times."

The apparitions of Mary are appearing worldwide and the message is peace, unity, and tolerance.[77] These statements by "Mary" put the emphasis on her, not Jesus. She said (in part), "I want you to become carriers and witnesses of my peace." Whatever happened to Jesus?

MARIAN APPARITIONS IN EGYPT AND AFRICA

An apparition of Mary was viewed by millions of Muslims. It was at a Coptic Orthodox Church in Zeitoun, Egypt, a suburb of Cairo. There was an apparition of a woman that onlookers believed was Mary. She supposedly performed signs, miracles, and healings. The apparition appeared for several nights each week for years. Since most of the spectators were Muslim, this apparition of "Mary" appeared to millions of Muslims.[78]

The following is a word-for-word description of the events concerning the Zeitoun apparitions.

The Zeitoun apparitions were seen by everyone present. The persons present at apparitional events there varied from several thousand to over two hundred thousand per night. Total witnesses perhaps numbered into the millions. Several nights each week, thousands of Muslims, who constituted most of the crowds, fell to their knees on prayer rugs ... all witnesses agreed that the Lady seemed to be composed of light that usually was intense ... The apparitions of Mary, the Mother of Jesus, were serenely animate.[79]

According to a British-Catholic magazine, "A Marian revival is spreading throughout Africa with alleged apparitions of Mary, finding a following among the Muslims."[80] Although African Muslims are supposedly seeing apparitions of the Virgin Mary, they "are not required to become Christians to follow her."[81]

MARY, THE MISSING LINK

Bishop Fulton Sheen, who back in the 1950s was the first Catholic on television, wrote a book predicting that Islam would be converted to Christianity.[82] In the same era, the 1950s, Bishop Sheen also wrote a book titled, *The World's First Love*. In his book, he stated: "But after the death of Fatima (Muhammad's daughter), Muhammad wrote, 'Thou shall be the most blessed of all women in paradise after Mary.' " This connection with the Muslims, through Mary, was predicted about fifty years ago.

Bishop Sheen also made the following statement:

Through a summoning of the Muslims to a veneration of the Mother of God ... the Koran has many passages concerning the Blessed Virgin. First of all, the Koran believes in her immaculate conception and also her virgin birth. Mary then is for the Muslims the true saeta or lady. The only possible serious rival to her in their creed would be Fatima, the daughter of Muhammad himself. But after the death of Fatima, Muhammad wrote, "Thou shall be the most blessed of all women in paradise after Mary."[83]

Bishop Sheen was ahead of his time, at least as it relates to the future of Islam. The Muslims will be included in the coming One World Religion, but it will not be Christianity. It will be a global religion that is characterized by a "harlot" who martyrs the followers of Christ.

THE MARY/FATIMA CONNECTION

The key players in this scenario are: Mary, the mother of Jesus, and Fatima, the daughter of Muhammad. The Portuguese village of Fatima is named after Muhammad's daughter. Bishop Sheen made mention of "how remarkable it was that our lady had the foresight to appear in the Portuguese village of Fatima, named after Muhammad's daughter, and thus became known as Our Lady of Fatima, the same lady that the pope took the image of in the year 2000 and dedicated humanity to her—the very same."[84]

The apparitions of Mary are seen as Christian miracles. It is important to remember that Satan also has the power to work miracles. This will be demonstrated through the False Prophet and the Antichrist prophesied in Revelation 13:12-15. It is also important to remember that "Satan disguises himself as an angel of light" (2 Corinthians 11:14).

The Koran exalts Mary and minimizes Jesus. Surah 3:42 in the Koran says, "Behold! the angels said: 'Oh Mary! God has chosen thee and purified thee; chosen thee above all women of all nations.'" Mary is exalted. Surah 5:75 says, *"Christ the son of Mary was no more than an Apostle; many were the Apostles that passed away before him. His mother was a woman of truth."*

The implications here are tremendous. If Muslims and Roman Catholics both exalt Mary, then she becomes a common denominator. "Unity in Diversity" can exist through a false world religion, which includes Muslims, as well as other religions, and allows them to remain Muslim and yet become a member of this One World Church or Religion.

There is a clear connection between the Roman Catholic Church and the Muslim faith. The common denominator between them is Mary, the mother of Jesus. One of the problems with the Mary connection is the credibility of the apparition. Using the Bible as our standard, the apparitions of Mary lack credibility. In the next section, we will look at the pope's role and how he fits into the end times.

TWO POPES FROM JUDGMENT DAY

The following prophetic account is not a biblically based account. The content of the account, however, and the predictions, are not contrary to the Bible. The fulfillment of the predictions has an amazingly high success rate; they are too accurate to be ignored and are therefore worth our consideration.

In 1139, a Catholic bishop named St. Malachy set out for Ireland on a pilgrimage to Rome. "On sighting the eternal city, he fell to the ground and began murmuring Latin verses, each signifying the future destiny of the popes. His words were suppressed for over three hundred years by the Vatican, yet, to this day, ninety percent of the saint's prophecies have come true, unfolding in chronological sequence ... for Malachy foresaw an end to the Roman Catholic Church and predicted the fates of the popes until judgment day." [85]

St. Malachy worked all night by candlelight until he concluded the 111 Latin phrases. He explained that God had given him a vision of every pope to reign after the current pontiff, which was Innocent II, until the end of time when God would judge the world. There is controversy concerning whether the phrases were composed in 1140 or by someone in the 1590s, and there is controversy that it was fabricated later under a pseudonym of a medieval saint. [86]

"If his assertion is true, the papal succession is finite ... we are but two popes away from Judgment Day." [87] This was written while Pope John Paul II was still alive. If this prediction is true, we are now one pope away from Judgment Day. Assuming that John Hogue, author of *The Last Pope: The Decline and Fall of the Church of Rome*, is right about his predictions being ninety percent accurate, the reign of the present pope, Benedict XVI, will be short, since he is seventy-eight years old and frail. The final pope may very well fit the role as the False Prophet. This may be further evidence that we are indeed living in the last generation, and we are close to the end of that generation.

In Hogue's book, St. Malachy's 111 Latin phrases are cryptic phrases written in a blend of Medieval Latin and Latinized Italian. "These cryptic phrases were rarely more than three words in length and are believed to contain a number of clues to the reign of each pope until doomsday." All 111 prophecies make one small identifying statement. Each one can be validated through the years in regard to the successive popes. They were written over 800 years ago on a piece of parchment paper. [88]

It is of interest to note that John Hogue is not a Christian and is "certainly not a Catholic either ... He is a New Age advocate. Yet his conclusion is that these prophecies are legitimate." [89]

Hogue makes the following prediction: "And the whole world will come into a New Age. It's the end of their world. What the Church sees as its final persecution could actually be the next quantum awakening of human intelligence." He calls it, "a new spiritual revolution."[90]

He went on to say, "Thus we may hope that a better religious life is waiting for us when the labels Protestant, Orthodox, or Catholic, or the labels of three hundred other religions are discarded and religion as we have known it comes to an end."[91] This quote by Hogue sounds very similar to a statement by Mary during one of her apparitions. She said, "… The Muslims and the Orthodox, for the same reason as Catholics, are equal before my son and I." The content of the two quotes are not identical but are very similar. One was by a New Age author and the other was supposedly by "Mary." The reader can draw his own conclusions.

THE APOSTATE POPE

To review, according to St. Malachy, there are three final popes. Pope John Paul II was the 110th pope. He is referred to as "the Marian Pontiff." His devotion to Mary is legendary. "Even the seal of his pontificate and his coat of arms depicts the arching letter 'M' for her."[92]

Pope Benedict XVI is the 111th pope. He is referred to as "The Glory of the Olive." As Cardinal Ratzinger, he wrote a book called, *God in the World*. The following quotes are from both Ratzinger's book and Hogue's book, *The Last Pope*. Ratzinger's book illustrates that he has a special interest in Israel, which is symbolized by the olive branch:

> "That the Jews are connected with God in a special way, and that God does not allow that bond to fail is entirely obvious. We wait for the instant in which Israel will say yes to Christ" (Ratzinger, Cardinal Joseph, *God in the World*). In *The Last Pope: The Decline and Fall of the Church of Rome*, Hogue writes that St. Malachy indicates, "We see the 'glory of the olive' in the first decade of the new century, trying his best to apply the lessons of the past to a new age that rejects the past."[93] "His motto implied that he will be drawn into the political and religious quagmire of the Middle East as the 'Glory of the Olive Branch,' or 'Peacemaker.' The olive branch is a symbol of Israel … the motto might imply that this pope will champion the cause of the Jews."[94]

The Apostate Pope is the 112th pope. St. Malachy lists 111 phrases plus a final prophetic declaration naming an apostate pope and calling him "Peter of Rome." Some believe that means there are 112. There is some controversy over whether the 111th pope will be the final pope.[95] "The Roman Catholic Church's official position is that there could be many popes between 111 and the final one."[96]

This does not seem like a reasonable position on the part of the Roman Catholic Church. If St. Malachy has been right on 111 popes in a chronological sequence, why would there be "many popes" between the 111th and the 112th pope? This sounds like desperation on the part of the church. "They certainly would not place their official stamp of approval upon any declaration that states their church is soon to end."[97]

St. Malachy's final prophetic declaration states:

> "During the last persecution of the Holy Roman Church, there shall sit *Petros Romanos* (Peter of Rome), who shall feed the sheep amidst many tribulations" (he will be the tribulation pope), "and when these things have passed, the city of the seven hills shall be destroyed."[98]

Pope number 111 will probably not live long, considering his age. This means pope number 112, if we give credibility to St. Malachy's predictions, may very well be the final one before judgment day.

THE CATHOLIC—MUSLIM CONNECTION: PUTTING IT ALL TOGETHER

Millions of Muslims have claimed that they have viewed the Marian apparitions. The Koran exalts Mary, as does the Roman Catholic Church. It would be reasonable to conclude that the "apparitions of Mary" will link two religions that take in a sizeable portion of the human race. This will be instrumental in the coming False One World Religion. As mentioned earlier, the New Age Movement will also be instrumental in this False One World Religion. The following section will show the connecting links among the end times, the New Age Apostasy, and the coming False One-World Religion.

NEW AGE APOSTASY

The New Age Movement, which started mushrooming in popularity in the 1960s, is very broad and hard to define because it is a mixture of

Eastern philosophies, religions, and mysticism combined with Western beliefs. It includes the occult and areas such as extrasensory perception (ESP), parapsychology, psychic phenomena, Transcendental Meditation, mind control, and the UFO movement, to name a few. It also includes more subtle areas such as many self-help books, and movies like *Harry Potter* and *The DaVinci Code*. New Agers have also coined many "buzz" words and phrases such as Higher Consciousness, Christ Consciousness, the Cosmic Christ, Global Village, the Force (used in the movie "Star Wars"), Co-Creators with the Universe, New World Order, and the Age of Aquarius.

One of the hallmarks and attractions of the New Age Movement involves deification of Self combined with an emphasis on experience for determining reality. **It usually involves a mixture of truth and lies.**

The New Age Movement has permeated most disciplines, including psychology and counseling. It has infiltrated colleges and seminaries, attacking the Bible and evangelical Christianity.

It is very subtle and deceptive and has desensitized Western civilization and countries established on Christian principles. Christians can be deceived by it. This author, a counselor by profession, can personally testify to its deception after spending ten to fifteen years dabbling in it and attempting to blend it with Christianity. The two would not blend and were never meant to be compatible. If it can happen to me, having a Christian background with a master's degree from seminary, it can happen to others. (See Appendix A: New Age Apostasy: Departure from the Faith.)

THE COMING ONE WORLD SYSTEM:
RECAP OF THE THREE-PILLAR FOUNDATION

The formation of a One World System requires the development of three pillars: 1) A World Government, 2) A World Economy, and 3) A World Religion. These three pillars had their beginnings in 1948, the same year that Israel became a nation.

1. **FIRST PILLAR: A World Government**
   The first pillar of the coming One World System is the world government.
   A. The first root of this was the establishment of the United Nations in 1945, but its Constitution was not established until 1948 under the Universal Declaration of Human Rights (UDHR). The

UDHR was designed to set up the lofty principles of the U.S. Bill of Rights. Its purpose was to empower the UN with the authority to govern all nations.[99]

B. The second root in the establishment of a world government was the Benelux Treaty in 1948. This treaty laid the foundation for the Western European Union through the Brussels Treaty of 1954. By 1957, under the Treaty of Rome, three more European nations joined—Italy, Britain, and West Germany—to form the European Economic Community (EEC).

   By 1980, the WEU had grown to ten nations. In 1993, the Maastricht Treaty created the current European Union (EU). There are currently two European Super states, the WEU and the EU. Modern Europe is an empire in every sense of the word. It is rapidly growing to a single entity.[100]

   The ten original member-states of the WEU also comprise the original member-states of the EU. These ten original member-states have full status. The rest of the twenty-seven members are on the associate level.

2. **SECOND PILLAR: A World Economy**
The second pillar of the coming One World System is the world economy. This first began to form in 1948, the year the computer age was born.

A. Bell Labs and AT&T developed the transistor in 1948. This opened the door to the creation of the modern computer.[101] Once computers became commonplace in the banking system and the financial institutions were linked to one another, geographical borders began to disappear. The global economy was born.[102]

B. Along with the global economy, there arose a need for a global authority. This gave rise to another root of the global economy, the General Agreement on Trades and Tariffs (GATT) in 1948.

   As GATT matured, it was eventually replaced by the World Trade Organization (WTO) founded in the 1990s. The WTO serves as an oversight committee of the second pillar, the world economy. The United States is under its authority through the "Vienna Law of Treaties" passed in 1948. Under WTO rules, the U.S. has equal weight to a third world country.[103]

C. Two more contributors to the expansion of the global economy were the creations of the World Bank and the International Monetary Fund (IMF) in 1948.[104] This pattern of events that had its origin in 1948 eventually led to the creation of the euro. This has become the common currency of the European Union.

3. **THIRD PILLAR: A Global Religion**
The third pillar of the coming One World System is the world religion. This is the continuing theme of this chapter.

A. The World Council of Churches (WCC) was founded in 1948 in Amsterdam. One of the purposes of the WCC was to develop a milder, gentler, all-inclusive religion.[105] *Tolerance* and *inclusion* are the key words.

Historic Christianity as described in the New Testament has been diluted by organizations such as the WCC. The WCC takes an "all roads lead to Rome" approach. According to Jesus, there is only one way (road) to the Father (God), and it is through Jesus (John 14:6). The WCC and the Gospel of Jesus Christ clash.

B. The United Religious Initiative (URI) is an organization that seeks to become the dominant voice of the United Nations. Bishop William Swing, an Episcopalian from San Francisco, heads it.[106]

According to Bishop Swing, all religions are guilty of fostering terrorism. He said, "… We have to hold the religions' feet to the fire for the violence and terror within them" (Swing, URI). His goal: "… to address the problem of fundamentalism in our own groups …"[107]

The URI was founded in the mid 1990s and is active in fifty-eight countries. It is composed of Protestants and Catholics, as well as witches, druids, and members of the New Age Movement.

Swing is hostile toward traditional and conservative faiths. At one point, he said, "… proselytizing will be illegal in the United Religious zone."[108]

When this becomes illegal, sharing the Gospel of Jesus Christ will be illegal. This religious system is well underway and is taking shape. Bishop Swing's statement will become a prophetic reality. During the Tribulation Period, Christians will be martyred for their faith. The Gospel, preached or shared, will become illegal in the "United Religious Zone." During the

Tribulation Period, Christian martyrdom will be at its peak. What occurred during the first two centuries of the Roman Empire will pale in comparison. This time, the persecution and martyrdom will be on a global scale.

There is one prophetic event that occurs just prior to the seven-year Tribulation Period. This event, known as the Rapture, could occur at any moment. Chapter Seven describes what the Rapture is, when it occurs, who is involved in it, and the possible explanations that will be given by the people who will be "left behind."

Chapter Seven

Vanished!
Milestones in the Race to Armageddon

"But when these things begin to take place,
straighten up and lift up your heads, because
your redemption is drawing near."
— Luke 21:28

The preceding three chapters have established the foundation for the remaining two chapters, which will cover prophetic future events and current world events, climaxing with the glorious Second Coming of Jesus Christ. This chapter will cover a major event called the Rapture and the possible preceding "trigger events," which will either precede or occur simultaneously with the Rapture. Three such trigger events, as well as the Rapture, from both biblical and New Age perspectives, are the focus of the first two-thirds of the chapter. The final third of the chapter will focus on a "post Rapture" deception designed to explain away the Rapture. This New Age deception will possibly become one of the greatest worldwide deceptions mankind has ever experienced.

THE STAGE IS SET

The stage is set to activate all three pillars of the one world system—world government, world economy, and world religion. These three pillars will be fully activated during the Tribulation Period. The next step requires a catalyst or a cataclysmic event to occur (see Appendix B: The UFO Grand Deception). The current status, as of the writing of this book, could be compared to completing the electrical wiring of a large building. Nothing is left undone. In order to activate the power within the building, a switch must be thrown. In this case, "throwing the switch" could be a number of possible events. It is these possible current events and belief systems that threaten the very existence of our civilization. These events and belief systems, along with biblical prophecy, provide the basis for this chapter.

THE ULTIMATE VANISHING ACT

The Rapture does not require any signs or events to precede it. This is called the doctrine of imminence. It is a signless event. Farther in the chapter, trigger events will be discussed. "Trigger events" are major current events that are moving the world at an accelerated pace toward the Tribulation Period and Second Coming of Christ. By implication, the time of the Rapture is much closer on our prophetic time line since it occurs prior to the start of the Tribulation Period. Paul, in his letter to the church of Corinth, refers to the Rapture event as a "mystery." "Behold, I tell you a mystery; we will not all sleep [die], but we will all be changed, in a moment, in the twinkling of an eye, at the last trumpet; for the trumpet will sound, and the dead [in Christ] will be raised imperishable, and we will be changed" (1 Corinthians 15:51-52 [brackets by author]).

The Rapture will occur prior to the seven-year Tribulation Period. The Second Coming of Christ will occur at the end of the seven-year Tribulation Period. Jesus gave His disciples specific signs in Matthew 24 and Luke 20 that precede His Second Coming. **The Rapture and Second Coming of Christ are two separate events.** It can be assumed that any reference to the Rapture comes from a pre-tribulation Rapture position. This interpretation of a "pre-trib" Rapture is based on a literal interpretation of the Bible.

There are many prophecies concerning Israel in the Old Testament. For example, the scattering of the Israelites among the nations was predicted in Ezekiel 36:19; the regathering of Israel was predicted in Ezekiel 36:24. Both of these prophecies have been fulfilled. Just as these and numerous other prophecies concerning Israel were fulfilled (see Chapter Three of this book for a more detailed explanation), so will the remaining prophecies be fulfilled.

Although it is impossible to know the time of the Rapture since it is a signless event, we can predict the general season of the Second Coming of Christ through the signs that precede His return. If that time is close, and it appears to be, the Rapture is at least seven years closer.

According to Hal Lindsey, "[T]he Rapture has become one of the most controversial doctrines in Christianity and is therefore ignored by most Christian churches." [The Rapture, no matter when it happens, is very controversial. Most churches believe only in a Second Coming.] There are a number of reasons for this. Space will not allow for a full and detailed explanation of the controversy; however, a brief explanation summarizing the objections is offered below.

Those holding a pre-trib Rapture position interpret the Bible literally, as did the Christians in the early church. Many of them believed that the promised restoration of Israel and the return of Jesus Christ would happen in their lifetime. A few hundred years passed and Israel was not restored as a nation, nor had Jesus returned. As a result, many Christians began to reinterpret these prophecies. They spiritualized the promises made to Israel by applying them to the Church (born again believers). The Church became the New Israel.

Once this interpretation became widespread, by implication the promises and prophecies concerning Israel became void. Christians today who either believe in a post-tribulation Rapture or deny the existence of the Rapture take this position. This position is not compatible with a pre-trib Rapture interpretation, which consummates the Church Age and begins the seventieth week of Daniel, completing God's timetable for dealing with the Jewish people (see Chapter Three for a more thorough explanation).

What the early Church, as well as many Christians today, did not understand concerns the mystery of the Church and the Rapture. God made known to us the "mystery of His will" (Ephesians 1:9). **A "mystery" is a previously hidden truth unveiled by God's revelation.**

The Church Age was a mystery. It is never referred to in the Old Testament. The Rapture was also a mystery. It is never referred to in the Old Testament. Paul tells us in 1 Corinthians 15:51, "Behold, I tell you a mystery; we will not all sleep ..." By contrast, the Second Coming of Christ is referred to numerous times because it is not a mystery.

The Church Age will reach an end at the time of the Rapture. The Church will not go through the Tribulation Period. People will be saved during the Tribulation Period, but the Christians who are part of the True Church will be raptured prior to that time. This is why the word "Church" is not mentioned after the third chapter of the Book of Revelation (Chapters 4 through 18 describe the judgments of the Tribulation Period). It is only mentioned one other time in Revelation 22:16 as the close of a letter to the "churches." The Church is composed of all born-again Christians who died "in Christ" or who are alive at the time of the Rapture. They will be "translated" or "changed" (bypass death) and will be raptured.

The Rapture itself will be the ultimate cataclysmic event in the acceleration of the prophetic clock toward the final seven-year Tribulation Period. This will leave the door wide open for the switch to be thrown that activates the three world pillars.

Preventing that activation process is the Holy Spirit. He restrains the Antichrist from being revealed before his time (2 Thessalonians 2:6-8), as well as restraining the activation of the three pillars. The Bible is referring to the Holy Spirit by implication as the "Restrainer."

The Bible teaches that the Holy Spirit indwells every true Christian (Romans 8:9-10, 14; 2 Corinthians 1:22). The removal of the Holy Spirit, the Restrainer, happens at the time of the Rapture when all believers who are alive at that time are instantly taken to be with the Lord and are given a glorified "imperishable body" (1 Corinthians 15:51-52). In other words, they will bypass death.

This last generation of believers who are alive prior to the start of the Tribulation Period will be Raptured. They will not have to go through the Tribulation Period (Revelation 3:10). Noah and his family were protected from the flood, which was the first worldwide judgment. In the same way, all true believers who accept Christ as their personal Savior prior to the Rapture will be protected from the seven-year Tribulation Period, which will be the second and final worldwide judgment (Matthew 24:21). The Rapture will be a cataclysmic event; millions of people will appear to vanish instantly to those who are left behind.

The next section discusses some trigger events, such as terrorism, that will accelerate the process toward activation of the three pillars of world government, world economy, and world religion. Later, the chapter will review the deception of the UFO movement and how it may be used to explain away the Rapture to those who "did not receive the love of the truth so as to be saved" (2 Thessalonians 2:10-11).

CHART 10

Primary Distinctions Between the "Rapture" and the "Second Coming"

THE RAPTURE	THE SECOND COMING or "THE REVELATION"
1. A "mystery" truth revealed only in the New Testament (1 Corinthians 15:51).	1. A central truth revealed in both testaments (Jude 14).
2. Pre-Tribulation (Revelation 3:10).	2. Post Tribulation (Revelation 19:11-21).
3. Christ comes in the air (1 Thessalonians 4:15-17).	3. Christ comes to the earth (Zechariah 14:4, 9; Matthew 25:31).
4. Christ comes for the saints (John 14:1-2; 1 Thessalonians 4:15-17).	4. Christ comes with the saints (believers) (1 Thessalonians 3:13; Revelation 19:14).
5. Earth and nations not judged.	5. Earth and nations judged (Revelation 19:15-21).
6. Imminent, signless (1 Corinthians 15:52; 1 Thessalonians 4:16).	6. Not imminent; follows definite predicted signs (Matthew 24:29-31; Mark 13:14-26,29; Acts 2:19-21; Rev.1:7; 6-19).
7. Before the day of wrath (Revelation 3:10).	7. Climaxes the time of wrath (Revelation 6:10; 19:11).[1]

TRIGGER EVENT #1:
TERRORISM AND ISLAM
ACCELERATE THE PROPHETIC CLOCK

The Last Hour, my first book on biblical end times prophecy, was released in 2001 just prior to 9/11. Since then, many significant events have taken place, and it is apparent that we are much closer to the end times.

I can remember 9/11 as if it was yesterday. Following the news event, I recall making the following statement to my wife: "This will be the trigger event that will accelerate the setting of the stage for the Antichrist to rule." In many ways, 9/11 marked the beginning of the end. That has been demonstrated in the months and years that followed.

It appears there are three reasons why we cannot win the battle against organized terrorism, primarily Al-Qaeda. The first problem is "Security." We have focused most of our resources in this area.

The United States, as powerful as it is, is virtually helpless to defend itself against organized terrorism. From the U.S. perspective, the terrorist enemies have crossed our national borders and natural barriers. In many ways, the oceans have served to insulate us from a military attack. The European countries do not have that advantage. This played a significant role in the ultimate formation of the European Union. They became keenly aware of their vulnerability after two world wars.

Terrorists were usually Mideastern in origin, but now include other nationalities. The reference here is primarily to terrorists who have a tight worldwide network, such as Al-Qaeda. It is essential to remember that 9/11 was not the random act of a few terrorists.

Our enemy is within the borders of the U.S. as well as in other countries, especially the European Union. The enemy could be a neighbor next door or a customer in a bank line waiting for the next teller. We are used to the enemy wearing a uniform from an identifiable country.

Our attempt to increase border security through airline security, airport security, cargo security, screening border crossings, trucks, trains, etc., has been helpful but will never solve the problem. It would be impossible to totally secure our borders. Our borders are considered porous, to put it mildly. Even if it were possible to totally secure our national borders, this does not address the fact that many of the terrorists are already inside our borders.

In regards to the enemy inside our borders, there is evidence that forty-eight "nuclear suitcases" were smuggled into the U.S. by Al-Qaeda over a period of several years prior to 9/11. The depressing reality is that they most likely could have accomplished the same thing after 9/11. Paul L. Williams, former consultant to the FBI on terrorism and author of the book, *Osama's Revenge: The Next 9/11*, tells of a man named David Z, the boss of the Chechen clan in Coney Island. Williams states:

> In 1996, David Z and his Mafia associates in Chechnya allegedly purchased a shipment of Special Atomic Demolition Munitions (SADMs), or "nuclear suitcases," from former KGB officials who preferred *perestreika* (the Russian word for "shootout") to *perestroika* (Mikhail Gorbachev's word for "reform").

The compact nukes represented the most desirable weapons for customers from such countries as Iran, North Korea, Libya, and representatives of the World Islamic Front who wanted a big bang for their buck. The Chechen Mafia purportedly sold twenty nuclear suitcases in Grozny to representatives of Osama bin Laden and the mujahadeen. For the weapons, bin Laden paid $30 million in cash and two tons of heroin ...[2]

Williams writes, "In 2002, *Al-Majallah* (a Saudi weekly published in London) published an update, claiming that bin Laden had succeeded in obtaining a total of forty-eight nuclear suitcases from the Russian Mafia over the course of several years."[3] Williams also tells about a closed-door session in 1998 between Alexander Lebed, the former Russian security secretary under Boris Yeltsin, and the members of the U.S. House of Representatives. Lebed "admitted that forty nuclear suitcases had disappeared from the Russian arsenal and could be in the hands of Muslim extremists."[4]

According to an August 1, 2005, *WorldNet Daily* report, Michael Chertoff, the Homeland Security Secretary, stated: "The foremost concern for the nation's security now is the threat of a larger chemical, biological or nuclear attack."[5] Chertoff's statements seem to support the credibility of the widespread reports about "suitcase nukes." These portable nuclear devices have been smuggled into America and are hidden in key locations until the time arrives to detonate them simultaneously in our population centers.[6]

The second problem we face in winning the battle against organized terrorism has to do with Al-Qaeda's money supply. If the money supply can be cut off, the terrorist's activities would be seriously hampered if not halted. Money is the pipeline that fuels organized terrorism.

The authorities have a difficult time catching and prosecuting terrorists. This is due in part to the financial complexity of the operation and the loopholes used to get around the law. "With no paper trail, investigators are at a loss."[7] Patrick Jost, a former Treasury official, said, "It's like a hydra with 200 heads. You cut one off, and it grows two more."[8]

Al-Qaeda also has the financial backing of the drug trade. Osama bin Laden's home territory lies in the heart of the Golden Crescent that covers Iran, Pakistan, and Afghanistan. This area has vast poppy fields producing opium gum; in primitive conditions, it can produce "number three" heroin. "Osama took over the fields and built sophisticated laboratories near Kabul. 'Number three' heroin was processed into the highly marketable 'number four,' a fluffy white powder that can be dissolved and injected."[9]

Williams states: "The laboratories soon became capable of producing five thousand metric tons of heroin a year, making bin Laden the world's largest supplier of the new international drug of choice. By 1997, the poppy harvest in Afghanistan soared ... and revenues began to pour into the coffers of Al-Qaeda at a rate estimated between $5 billion and $16 billion a year."[10] The bottom line is that Al-Qaeda has an unlimited budget.

One has to wonder about bin Laden's religious views. Muslims do not believe in the consumption of alcohol or intoxicants, yet he is increasing the production and consumption of opium to fight his holy war. While he is fighting this "holy war," he is using illegal gain. This gain comes from a product that destroys lives and is more dangerous than alcohol, all in order to support his "holy war." How is this holy? There is something terribly wrong with this picture.

The third problem we encounter in fighting terrorism is the most difficult. It is the religious belief system of the terrorists—the Islamic religion. They are motivated by the fundamental Islamic faith. **It is extremely hard to fight against an enemy who believes that Islamic domination of the world is their manifest destiny.** Along with this mindset is the belief that "chaos" must precede the Islamic domination.[11] Muslims also believe they can speed up the process by instigating chaos. They have been very successful in creating chaos.

Randall Price, author, speaker, and Bible scholar in the area of prophecy and Middle-Eastern studies, gave a talk at the 2006 International Prophecy Conference on March 1, 2006, titled "Islam and Prophecy." He said that the president of Iran, Mahmoud Ahmadinejad, spoke to the UN and said Islam would dominate the world, and Iran will do what is necessary to pave the way.[12] Ahmadinejad said, "Israel should be wiped off the earth."[13]

This religious belief system makes negotiations with the Islamic terrorists or the Palestinian Authority an exercise in futility. History has confirmed this repeatedly. The whole Palestinian question is not a political issue. It is an Islamic religious issue. In the prophet Mohammed's words, "War is deception. Negotiate peace with your enemy until you are strong enough to annihilate him."[14]

Islamic fundamentalists believe that the Koran is divinely inspired by Allah. They interpret it literally and follow it closely. Many Muslims believe that judgment day is at hand, for "they believe that their nuclear fire will purge 'the earth of all but the righteous of Islam.' "[15]

Osama bin Laden is considered a messiah figure. "His attendants bow before him and greet him as the 'awaited enlightened one …' He is more than a mighty warrior or a religious leader. To his followers, he is the rightly guided caliph—the Mahdi—who will appear during the last days of human history."[16]

According to the Shia, a sect of Islam, there were eleven Imams. An Imam is one of a succession of religious leaders whom the Shi'ites believe are divinely inspired. The Shi'ites believe the Imams were all direct descendents of Mohammed. The Sunnis allegedly murdered the first eleven Imams. The son of the eleventh one (the Twelfth Imam) "disappeared" as a youth in A.D. 878 in the cave of the great mosque at Samarra, Iraq. This mosque was bombed in February 2006, either by the Sunni Muslims or by members of Al-Qaeda in an attempt to provoke a civil war between Sunnis and Shi'ites in Iraq.

The Twelfth Imam is supposed to be the final Imam, the last in line of legitimate successors to the prophet Mohammed. According to Islam, the Twelfth Imam will reappear at the end time when the world is in chaos. He will then lead the Islamic warriors to conquer the world for Islam. Sunni Islam also shares in the belief of an end time warrior, but refer to him as Al-Mahdi, "The Guided One." The Twelfth Imam and the Mahdi refer to the same great warrior. Shi'ites call him the Twelfth Imam, and Sunnis call him the Mahdi.

Randall Price gives a brief review of Islam, the Twelfth Imam, and the entimes. The final period of the Twelfth Imam's hiding is known as the "Great Occulation," which began in A.D. 941 when all contact with the world was broken off. Iran is now ready for the Twelfth Imam to reappear. Iran's President Ahmadinejad claimed in 2005 that he has been in touch with the Twelfth Imam who "will definitely return in two years." This would bring us to the year 2007. According to Islam, he will remain for seven years, then die, and Muslims will pray over him (Sunab Abu Dawud, Book 36, Number 4273, Narrated by Ummul Mu'minin). In the beginning of his reign he will make a peace treaty with the Jews for seven years and then he will die.[17]

There is an interesting parallel between the prophetic beliefs of Islam and Christian biblical prophecy. The Antichrist ("prince to come," "man of lawlessness") will also make a seven-year covenant with Israel (Daniel

9:27). Price says, "Islam has its own version of the Antichrist, the Dajjal, who it sees as a Jewish opponent of Islam." Satanic deception will be rampant as the world is being set up to accept a false messiah. The end times are at hand from both a Christian and a Muslim perspective. The two interpretations of what that means and what will happen in the final days and years are very different, but the timing is very similar.

The Muslim terrorists are highly motivated by their religious beliefs and are willing to die for their faith, as demonstrated by their suicide bombings. There is a motivation for these suicide bombers. They are taught that it guarantees them a ticket to heaven. It really does matter what they believe, even if it is false. Their belief system has a worldwide impact. The Islamic fundamentalists' two primary enemies are Israel and the United States. Iran is in the process of building a nuclear arsenal and has even laid out an order of destruction—first the U.S. and then Israel.[18] Iran denies it is building a nuclear arsenal.

To fight terrorism, the world governments have to find a way to provide security for the masses, cut off the money supply of the terrorists, and somehow deal with the belief system of the terrorists. The answer lies in a world system that is under the absolute control of a dictator. This system will come about, but it will be at the expense of human freedom.

During the Tribulation Period, the Antichrist will gain absolute control worldwide (Revelation 13:17). He will provide "peace and safety," but it will be followed by a horrible Tribulation Period described as coming upon them suddenly like "… labor pains upon a woman with child, and they will not escape" (1 Thessalonians 5:3).

TRIGGER EVENT #2:
IRAN, RUSSIA, AND NUCLEAR WEAPONS:
PROPHETIC ACCELERATION INCREASES EXPONENTIALLY

At the time of the writing of this book, Iran was still in the process of enriching uranium, which is necessary in order to make a nuclear bomb. This is a six-step process. Once this six-step process is complete, the enriched uranium becomes the core of a nuclear bomb.[19]

Two well-known authors, Joel C. Rosenberg and John Hagee, have independent sources in Israel that confirm the fact that Iran, as of April 2005, was in stage five of this enrichment process. These sources include, among others, high-level political, military, and intelligence officials.

Iran's claim is that they only want to develop nuclear energy, not nuclear weapons. This is hardly believable in light of a report by the *Associated Press* on March 4, 2007. It stated: " 'Iran is still refusing UN requests to put up cameras with a full view of the site where the Islamic Republic is assembling what it says will be 54,000 uranium-enriching centrifuges,' diplomats said ahead of a key meeting on Iran's nuclear program."[20]

Why not? What are they hiding? If they really wanted to have nuclear power for civilian use alone, there would be nothing to hide. The time is close. Iran does not appear to have nuclear weapons at the time of this writing, but that does not really mean they do not have such weapons.

On April 13, 2005 the Associated Press released the following:

Israel Shares Intel with US on Iran Nukes

Israeli Prime Minister Ariel Sharon pressed the US to threaten Iran with international sanctions, warning Iran was quickly approaching a point of no return in its nuclear program. The White House said it agreed that Iran is pursuing nuclear weapons "under the guise of a civilian program" but wants to continue the current diplomacy strategy to solve problems.[21]

A senior Israeli official traveling with Sharon said while they were guests at President Bush's ranch: "There has to be immediate action taken against Iran. There is a time limit because Iran will soon reach a technological point of no return. Beyond this point of technological no return ... it will be too late."[22] As of the time of this writing, it does not appear that Iran has the nuclear bomb. Estimates range from several months up to two years. "Iran will be 'at the point of no return' in which they will acquire specific scientific expertise and perhaps fissile material to manufacture nuclear weapons" (*Andre de Nesnera's Focus Report*, Voice of America [voanews.com], Washington, DC, February 23, 2006, "Is Iran Building a Nuclear Bomb?"). If Iran has reached this point of no return, the general population is not aware of it.

"In a secret policy review, the Bush administration ordered the Pentagon to draft contingency plans for the use of nuclear weapons against at least seven countries, naming not only Russia and the 'axis of evil' (Iran, Iraq, and North Korea), but also China, Libya, and Syria."[23] Adding to this, the U.S. Department of Defense was also told to make preparations for the possible use of nuclear weapons, which may be required in a future Arab-Israeli crisis. The department was to develop plans for using nuclear weapons in retaliation against chemical and biological attacks, as well as "surprising military developments" of an unspecified type.[24]

On April 17, 2005, Netanya Academic College in Israel conducted a conference at the Strategic Dialogue Center with the topic, "Multinuclear Middle East—Iran, the Bomb, and Israel." One of the highlights of the conference was a telephone interview between Ronen Bergman, a journalist with *Yediot Achronot* newspaper, and Dr. Manouchehr Ganji, a former Iranian Scientist Minister under the Shah of Iran before the Shah's overthrow by the Islamic Republic of Iran.[25]

In that telephone interview, Dr. Ganji made the following statement regarding the Iranian government: "The clerics are in charge and they wish to have nuclear weapons. They will use the exercise, the so-called principle of *tabi' yeh*, their concoction of an Islamic principle that permits them to lie whenever it's in their interest. They have been constantly lying, and they will lie until they get what they want."[26]

ISRAEL'S POSITION

Israel claims that it will defend itself against Iran (or any other country for that matter) with a pre-emptive strike. When Israel has reason to believe that Iran is close to, or has the potential, to make a successful attack against Israel with nuclear weapons, they will attack first.

It is important to understand the Iranian mindset in order to understand Israel's position. Iran's president, Mahmoud Ahmadinejad, believes Allah has appointed him to set the stage by bringing on the apocalypse and paving the way for the twelfth Imam (the Mahdi) or Muslim Messiah to be revealed.[27] He would be playing a "John the Baptist" role.

Israel has demonstrated their willingness to carry out a pre-emptive strike, as shown in 1981 when they successfully bombed a reactor in Iraq. "Time has proven that Israel did the right thing for the world by destroying Saddam Hussein's ability to manufacture nuclear weapons. When America went to war in Iraq in 1992 (during Desert Storm), our troops would have faced nuclear weapons that would have birthed the Battle of Armageddon."[28]

This pre-emptive strike on Iran is inevitable. From a human standpoint, this can only be prevented by the successful diplomatic efforts of other countries. It is unlikely that UN sanctions would stop Iran from aggressively pursuing nuclear capabilities. One of the problems in passing a UN resolution against Iran is the Russian influence. "… Russia is a permanent member of the UN Security Council with veto power. A UN resolution against Iran would get nowhere."[29] Russia, as we will see, has a strong link with Iran. If the UN is unsuccessful in its attempts to get Iran to halt its nuclear program, Israel will take action, i.e., a pre-emptive strike. Israel has also said that if any country decides to use Weapons of Mass Destruction (WMDs) against them, they will retaliate with a nuclear strike.

THE SAMSON OPTION

Israel is known to have a large nuclear arsenal, and the other Islamic countries, such as Iran, are keenly aware of it. As far back as the late 1960s to 1970s, Israel made a decision concerning the use of its defense arsenal. They decided to use it as a deterrent. **They called their decision** *The Samson Option.*

This is based on the Old Testament story about Samson and the Philistines. God blessed Samson with supernatural strength. Samson, an Israelite, became involved with a Philistine prostitute. One day he woke up with the prostitute to find himself surrounded by the Philistine army; he was then taken captive, and his eyes were gouged out.

The Philistines put him on display for all the rulers and some 3,000 people to see as they prepared to sacrifice him to Dagon, their god. Samson was not going out peacefully if he could help it. "O Lord GOD, please remember me and please strengthen me just this time, O God, that I may at once be avenged of the Philistines for my two eyes."

Then Samson pushed against the two pillars on which the temple rested. He pushed against the pillars and said, "Let me die with the Philistines!" He died and killed many Philistines along with him (Judges 16:26-30).

Israel is considered a "One Bomb" nation. A single nuclear strike against them would have a devastating effect on the country. Israel's cry of "Never Again!" is a resolve that takes on new meaning when one bomb promises to bring a nation to its knees ("Atomic Iran Excerpt: *The Samson Option, Israel's Preemptive Strike*" by Dr. Jerome Corsi, www.freerepublic.com/focus/f-news/1367264/posts, March 21, 2005).

Israel's enemies are aware of the Samson Option. If Israel is backed into a corner or encounters a nuclear strike, they will retaliate with full force. They will be destroyed, but their enemies will go with them. God has other plans for Israel. He will deliver them from their enemies, and He will get the glory (Ezekiel 38:18 - 39:7).

THE RUSSIAN CONNECTION

In order to understand the link between Russia and Iran, it is important to look at a very brief history of Russia. When the Soviet Union broke up, it was economically devastated. All Russia had was a vast supply of WMDs and a nuclear arsenal.

Russia did not want to deal with the Muslim countries. Under the Soviet Union, these Muslim states were forced to live in an atheistic society. The Muslim countries could be very disruptive to them as shown by Muslims in the little state of Chechnya.[30] An Islamic-motivated revolt, like in Chechnya, was the last thing Russia needed. Russia foresaw the threat of this happening in countries such as the Muslim-dominated Republic, Kazakhstan, which had a large number of the former Soviet Union's nuclear tipped ICBMs buried in silos on its soil.[31]

Iran, a Muslim country, had a fanatical dedication to Islam; this was very attractive to Muslims who had been forced into an atheistic society for over seventy years. Russia knew that in order for the Russian leaders to get what they wanted, Iran would have to get what it wanted. In February 1991, Moscow offered Tehran a deal that resulted in a pact between Russia and Iran.[32]

Russia needed money and wanted power. They also wanted to be free of disruptive Muslim revivals and revolutions. Iran wanted help building nuclear warheads. They wanted power in order to ultimately bring the world under Muslim domination. Some of the points of this 1991 Russian/Iran Pact follow:

THE RUSSIAN/IRAN PACT

1. Russia supplied Iran with materials and world-class nuclear and missile experts. They would also help Iran build its nuclear warheads and delivery systems.
2. Iran would agree not to encourage in any way an Islamic revival in the former Soviet Republics and also would not interfere with Russia's efforts to put down any such revivals.

3. Russia agreed to fight alongside Iran against the West in the event they invaded Iran, invaded other Muslim nations of the region, or sought to interfere with the internal affairs of the Muslim nations of the region.[33]

The results or implications of this pact are far reaching. This Russian/Iran pact sets the stage for the Russian Invasion of Israel prophesied in Ezekiel 38-39. Several countries will be allied with Russia when they invade Israel. These are primarily Muslim countries (or a Muslim Confederacy). The Russians will help the Muslims in order to establish leadership over them. This prepares the way for Russia to lead the prophesied invasion against Israel.

Vladimir Putin was not only empowering Iran as a nuclear country, he was also empowering other Islamic countries to go nuclear. He cut a deal with Moroccan King Mohammed VI to build a nuclear site in that North African Islamic state, according to an article on Joel Rosenberg's website, dated September 18, 2006 (joelrosenberg.blogspot.com).

Russia is also eager to help Turkey go nuclear despite the fact it is drifting away from the West and is growing increasingly closer to the new Iranian regime (*Ibid*). Turkey is one of the Islamic countries that will be allied with Russia in the coming Russian/Islamic invasion. Turkey is the modern day name for "Gomer" listed in Ezekiel 38:6.

Russia is now Turkey's second largest trading partner (*Personal Update Newsletter*, by Chuck Missler, August 2006, Vol. 16, No. 8, p. 14). Once Turkey allies itself with Russia, everything is in place from a prophecy standpoint for the Russian-led invasion of Israel. The Kremlin has already made the decision to invade Israel. The only thing lacking, according to prophecy, in regards to the Russian-led invasion of Israel was the inclusion of the country of Turkey (International Prophecy Conference 2006, presentation by Missler, March 3, 2006). **When Turkey is in place as an ally of Russia, the time of this invasion will be rapidly approaching.**

The most likely time of this invasion is midpoint during the Tribulation Period, that is after three-and-a-half years. The Bible does not specify the time of this invasion. It could possibly happen prior to the Tribulation Period or between the Rapture and the start of the Tribulation Period. (This is discussed in more detail in the next chapter.) It does happen at a time when Israel feels secure. In Ezekiel 38, God is addressing Russia and its leader (referred to as Magog and Gog). It states:

"... in the latter years you will come into the land that is restored from the sword, whose inhabitants have been gathered from many nations to the mountains of Israel which had been a continual waste; but its people were brought out from the nations, and they are living securely, all of them." (Ezekiel 38:8)

This security that Israel will experience will be based on a false sense of security. It will most likely result from the signing of a covenant between the Antichrist and Israel. It will also mark the beginning and the mid-point of the Tribulation Period (Daniel 9:27; 1 Thessalonians 5:2-3).

This pact insures that Russia would be drawn into a war against the West on behalf of its Muslim allies. The two most powerful countries in the world are the U.S. and Russia. This pact insures their collision at some point unless the U.S. loses its position of power. This may very well happen, as the European Union is united, is growing in size and strength, and will ultimately serve as the power base of the Antichrist and the one world government. In addition to this, the U.S. is not mentioned in the Bible. The reason it is not mentioned may be related to its decline as a world super power.

Going back to 2002, under the headline, "Russia to Expand Nuclear Aid to Iran," dated July 27, 2002, the *Washington Post* stated that Russia announced "... a dramatic expansion of its cooperation with Iran on building nuclear power plants, ignoring administration concerns that the program could help Iran build a nuclear bomb." Russia has a high financial stake in Iran. Russia accumulates hard currency in exchange for weapons, especially Weapons of Mass Destruction (WMDs) and nuclear weapons. It is also gaining in prestige, power, and influence as it invests in the nuclear empowerment of other Muslim countries. The stage is set and the stakes are high.

IRAN'S CURRENT POSITION

Iran's population is primarily composed of Shi'ite Muslims. A Shi'ite is a member of the Shi'a sect of Islam, which is the principle minority sect of Islam. They regard the heirs of Ali, the cousin and son-in-law of Mohammed, as the legitimate successors of the Prophet. A Sunnite is a member of the Sunni branch of Islam, which is the majority branch of Islam. They follow orthodox tradition and accept the first four caliphs (the secular and religious heads of the Muslim state) as the rightful successors of Mohammed.

This may seem like a moot point to the Westerner, but Muslims kill each other over these doctrinal differences. Most of the Islamic countries hate Iran, but they have a common enemy they hate more than each other. That enemy includes Israel and America, a supporter of Israel. This common enemy unites the two branches.

As previously mentioned, the government of Iran is run by the Muslim clerics (religious leaders) and lying is considered permissible if the Muslims determine it is in their best interest. The Iranian president, Ahmadinejad, has tied his religious beliefs with the nuclear issue. According to an Iranian analyst in *Asia Online*, "The danger of such a radical statesman [Ahmadinejad] is that by knotting religious beliefs with the nuclear issue, it makes for an explosive issue that will explode in the face of all Iranians."[34]

Following Ahmadinejad's election in 2006, he vowed to ignite a worldwide Islamic revolution. Just weeks after his election, he addressed a conference in Tehran with a message titled, "A World without Zionism," and made the following statement: "… we shall soon experience a world without America and Zionism …"[35] As mentioned earlier, the president of Iran has an agenda. He wants to destroy two countries, the U.S. and then Israel.

Iran's president, Ahmadinejad, has a "resume" that should cause great concern. He has been identified by three Americans held hostage in the 1979 seizure of the U.S. Embassy in Iran as one of their interrogators. Army Colonel Charles Scott, seventy-three, also recognized Ahmadinejad as one of his former captors.[36] Former political prisoners have also identified him as the executioner at Evin prison.[37] In short, Iran's current president is dangerous.

Iran is currently on the verge of having atomic weapons and has the missiles necessary to deliver them. They have a nuclear plant at Bushehr (Iran) that Russia helped build.[38] They also have twelve underground nuclear facilities.[39]

In addition to this, Ahmadinejad has declared on international television via *Fox News* that his intentions are to share Iran's nuclear power with all Islamic nations.[40] On February 3, 2004, the *Daily Telegraph* of London, England, had the following headline:

Confession of the Father of Pakistan's Atomic Bomb:
"I've Sold Nuclear Secrets to Libya, Iran, and North Korea"

Ahmed Rashid, author of this article, confirmed that "the father of Pakistan's atomic bomb [Abdul Qadeer Khan] has confessed to selling nuclear weapons secrets to some of the world's most notorious 'rogue states,' which included Iran, Libya, and North Korea."[41] This has widespread implications. **Basically, every Islamic terrorist group is going to have the opportunity to use atomic weapons.**[42]

According to an intelligence report in 2005, Iran was at that time in the process of developing the Electromagnetic Pulse (EMP) designed to be used against America in a time of war.[43] The EMP does not kill people —it kills electrons. It stops every form of electricity instantly for months and maybe years.[44] The EMP works in the following way. A missile transports a bomb containing several pounds of enriched uranium to the targeted country. At an altitude of approximately 280 miles, the bomb explodes releasing the enriched plutonium, which blankets the area (in this scenario, the U.S.) with gamma rays. In a billionth of a second, every form of electricity is instantly cut off—computers, lights, radios, refrigerators, cars, trucks, trains, phones, etc.

The U.S. would cease to be a superpower and would be set back to the conditions of the 19th century. In a few days, the U.S. would be paralyzed. Not even our military would be able to communicate with each other.[45] Both North Korea and Iran have the capacity to use the EMP.[46]

According to the *Congressional Report*, "Even primitive SCUD missiles could be used for this purpose [electronic blankets]. Top U.S. intelligence officials reminded members of Congress that there is a glut of those missiles on the world market. They are currently being bought and sold for about $100,000 apiece."[47]

It is important to understand the religious belief system of President Ahmadinejad and the Muslim sect of the Shi'ites. Some of their beliefs were previously summarized under the heading "Trigger Event #1: Terrorism and Islam Accelerates the Prophetic Clock."

President Ahmadinejad believes that the Twelfth Imam is about to reappear and that Allah has specifically appointed him to pave the way. Since world disorder and chaos is a prerequisite for this to happen, he along with many Muslims can hasten this reappearance by instigating war, revolution, and chaos. This is especially dangerous since Iran has

Russian backing and nuclear capabilities.

It does not matter that Ahmadinejad's beliefs are false. What does matter is that he is in a position of power and believes them. As a civilization, we are at risk. This threat is the result of false religious belief systems, such as Islam, combined with WMDs and nuclear capabilities.

Another example of a current false belief system is the joint Russian/Iranian UFO Study. The belief system driving a major country's leadership has a powerful influence on world events.

Where does the belief in UFOs fit into this scheme? Taking into consideration the UFO belief system of these two major countries, our risk/threat level increases. Our world is rapidly getting primed for the Tribulation Period, as shown in the last section of this chapter.

JOINT RUSSIAN/IRANIAN UFO STUDY

According to the *World Net Daily* (April 2005), Russia and Iran have agreed to a joint study of the UFO phenomenon and to work together in the construction of satellites and space research.[48] WND stated in April [2005] that Iran was suddenly struck with "UFO fever" after Reuters reported that the state-run television "broadcast a sparkling white disc flying over the capital of Tehran, and that people from eight towns ran outside to witness 'bright extraterrestrial lights.' "[49]

The *Jerusalem Post* also stated that, "Flying object fever has gripped Iran," and reported that there were shoot-down orders issued for any "unknown or mysterious objects" in Iran's airspace.[50] This response was a result of "so many of the reported hundreds (according to Whitley Streiber's unknowncountry.com) of UFO sightings occurring over Iran's nuclear installations."[51]

Related articles concerning sightings and Iran's aggressive stance have appeared in mosnews.com (i.e., *Moscow News*), *Resalat*, as well as the Islamic Republic News Agency and the Associated Press.[52] Streiber's Unknown Country site mentions parallels between the dramatic increase in UFO activity around Iran's nuclear installations and the "UFO flaps associated with American nuclear installations in the 1940s, 1950s, and 1970s ..."[53] [Consideration as to UFOs, what they mean and how the phenomenon may relate to biblical prophecy, is discussed in more detail in the final section of this chapter and in Appendix B, The UFO Grand Deception.]

WILL ISRAEL EXECUTE A PRE-EMPTIVE STRIKE?

As mentioned earlier, Israel did execute a pre-emptive strike against Iraq in 1981 when it bombed Iraq's nuclear reactor. The bombardment was a localized operation and Israel had the benefit of total surprise. In contrast, to knock out Iran's current nuclear sites involves a much more complex endeavor. According to former IAI chief Major General (ret) Eitan Ben-Eliahu, "… this issue does not concern Israel alone, as 'the political and military response must be carried out with international cooperation and coordination.' "[54] This pre-emptive strike may not be against Iran. Consider the following section.

RUSSIAN-SYRIAN-IRANIAN AXIS

On June 22, 2006, the Hezbollah in Southern Lebanon took two Israeli soldiers hostage. Approximately one month earlier, the Palestinians took one Israeli soldier hostage in an attempt to negotiate a prisoner exchange. The Hamas/Hezbollah proposal was an exchange of three Israelis for 1,000 Palestinian prisoners. By June 23, 2006, Israel retaliated and took action against the Hezbollah in Southern Lebanon. Although there was a cease-fire in August 2006, tension in the area continues.

The background to this conflict, which has threatened the balance of power in the Middle East as well as the world, involves an Iranian-Syrian pact signed on June 15, 2006, by the leaders of Iran and Syria. This pact was a defense agreement between the two countries against Israel and the West.

This pact takes on a much larger significance than appears on the surface. A report by Hal Lindsey lays out the implications of this pact. His report is based on personal, unnamed, intelligence sources that confirm the Debka's intelligence report. Lindsey states that the Debka intelligence sources unveiled a disturbing clause in the agreement [June 15] that was reported to Bush by U.S. intelligence.

The clause speaks of more than one battery of upgraded SHEBA-3 surface-to-air missiles to be deployed on the 13,000 foot Jabal Ash Shanin ridges towering over central Syria … Senior intelligence officials warned the U.S. President that the deployment would not just throw the entire Middle East balance of strength out of kilter, but directly menace American bases as far away as West and East Europe and the Central Asian republics ... This puts all of Europe within range of the soon-coming nuclear tipped Iranian missiles ...[55]

The Russian-Muslim Confederation of countries that will eventually invade Israel is falling into place. As we will see later, Syria is not mentioned in this list of countries. This may indicate its destruction prior to that time, as prophesied in Isaiah 17.

There are reasons to believe that a pre-emptive strike against Iran may very well turn out to be a pre-emptive or retaliatory strike against Syria. There is one unfulfilled prophecy that heretofore has been given very little attention by prophecy scholars until recently. It concerns the destruction of Damascus.

TRIGGER EVENT #3:
THE DEMISE OF DAMASCUS

"... Behold, Damascus is about to be removed from being a city and will become a fallen ruin ... The fortified city will disappear from Ephraim ... " — Isaiah 17:1-3

The city of Damascus is the capital of Syria and is "reputed to be the oldest continuously existing city in the world."[56] It has been conquered by other countries but never destroyed. As a result, we know that this prophecy has not been fulfilled.

Syria is known as a training ground for terrorists. Damascus, the capital of Syria, is believed by many to be the base of operations for a number of terrorist organizations, including Al Qaeda, Hamas, and Hezbollah. Syria is directly linked to Iran, Russia, and Iraq.

Weapons of Mass Destruction (WMDs) were never found in Iraq, but not because they did not exist. They were smuggled out of Iraq and into Syria. Satellite pictures showed them being transported to Syria.[57] Someone had pictures of the serial numbers of the weapons, which were smuggled by fifty-six commercial planes with the seats removed. The claim by Iraq was that they were "planes of relief to Syria for a tragedy," but, in actuality, they were Weapons of Mass Destruction.[58]

These facts are further supported by retired Iraqi General, Georges Sada, "I know how and when they [WMDs] were transported and shipped out of Iraq. And I know how many aircraft were actually used and what types of planes they were …" [brackets by author] (*Saddam's Secrets* by Georges Sada, Integrity Publishers, 2006, p. 252).

Saddam Hussein was warned three days ahead of the inspection. Both Hussein and the head of Syria were members of the Bath Party. This incident was never leaked to the press since four countries were involved in helping Iraq with the WMDs, and they did not want the exposure.[59] It is also interesting to note that Russia and France stalled UN negotiations to allow time for the WMDs to be smuggled to Syria. Otherwise, they would be exposed for their financial support of billions in arms and munitions to Iraq.[60]

A major turning point in Russia's diplomatic relations with Israel followed the 1967 Six-Day War. At that point, Russia severed diplomatic relations with Israel. Russia then aligned itself with Arab Nationalist regimes and provided financial support to the Palestinian militants.[61] During the Soviet era, there was a dramatic resurgence of anti-Jewish sentiment. When Putin took power in 1999, he fueled this anti-Semitism.[62]

After the Russians lost the Middle East foothold provided by Iraq under Saddam Hussein's leadership, the Russians built a new axis of power based on its ties with Turkey, Iran, and Syria. Russia has strengthed its ties with Iran by supplying nuclear-related technologies. Russia and Syria have increased diplomatic and military cooperation. In the arms arena, Russia plans to sell SS-26 and SS-18 missiles to Syria. The SS-26 is highly mobile. "With a range of 180 miles, it can carry a 1,000 pound warhead to most targets in Israel."[63]

Russia signed a $1 billion contract with Iran in December 2005 to sell its advanced Tor-M1 system, which has the capacity to destroy guided missiles and laser guided bombs from aircraft. The guided missiles and laser-guided bombs are among the weapons Israel might use if it launched a pre-emptive strike against Iran's nuclear facilities.[64]

Syria is one of the countries on the U.S. State Department's list of countries that sponsors terrorism. It provides "substantial amounts of financial, training, weapons, explosives, political, diplomatic, and organizational aid" to terrorist groups such as Hezbollah and Hamas, as well as other radical Islamic and Palestinian organizations. Many of these organizations are headquartered in Damascus.[65] "Many experts believe that a large scale confrontation between Syria and Israel could be on the near horizon, which makes Syria's growing relationship with nations such as

Iran and Russia even more concerning."[66]

Syria has recently accumulated more rockets and placed them on Lebanon's southern border. Estimates range from 1,000 to 3,000 rockets financed by Iran. The Syrians and Hezbollah are also strategically placing rockets in Syria and Lebanon (*International Intelligence Report* by Hal Lindsey, March 16, 2007).

It is significant to note that Syria is not listed in the Russian-led Muslim/Confederacy invasion. Perhaps its omission is because it will be destroyed as prophesied in Isaiah 17. Because of the total devastation described in Isaiah 17, the destruction will probably be nuclear. The most likely country to destroy Damascus is Israel. Damascus would likely use WMDs or a Dirty Bomb against Israel. Israel's leaders have already stated that they would react with a nuclear bomb. This could happen any day. The Rapture may be very close.[67]

ON THE EDGE

What does all of this mean? When we consider the reality of the tensions, the conflicts, the threat of nuclear weapons, and the influence exerted by the Islamic belief system in the Middle-East countries that surround Israel, the prospects of peace becomes dismal at best. Consider the following quotes given by some very credible sources:

Eugene Habiger, former Executive Chief of Strategic Weapons at the Pentagon, said that the event of nuclear mega-terrorism on nuclear soil is "… not a matter of if but when."[68]

Warren Buffet, from the private sector, calculates odds against cataclysmic events for major insurance companies; he draws the conclusion that an imminent nuclear nightmare within the U.S. is "virtually a certainty."[69]

Paul Williams, a former consultant to the FBI on terrorism, indicates that empirical evidence does exist to substantiate if Al-Qaeda possesses nukes.[70] He also reports that there isn't just one team of terrorists but at least seven.[71] The seven have been identified as: New York, Miami, Houston, Las Vegas, Los Angeles, Chicago, and Washington, D.C. These attacks would occur simultaneously at all seven sites.[72]

Dr. Graham Allison, Harvard professor and director of Harvard University's Belfer Center for Science and International Affairs, said: "Is nuclear mega-terrorism inevitable? Harvard professors are known for being subtle or ambiguous, but I'll try to be clear. 'Is the worst yet to come? My answer: Bet on it. Yes.' "[73]

Three trigger events have been reviewed thus far that would cause the prophetic clock to speed up in the countdown toward end time events and the final seven years known as the Tribulation Period. The first two triggers are already activated: 1) Terrorism and Islam; 2) Iran, Russia and Nuclear Weapons. The third trigger—The Demise of Damascus—has not yet occurred. This does not exclude the possibility of other major events happening prior to the Rapture, nor does it mean that the destruction of Damascus must happen prior to the Rapture. This last trigger may very well be the fulfillment of Isaiah 17, since this would be a major event and would most likely involve nuclear warfare; it does not, however, have to be. The evidence from both a secular and biblical viewpoint supports the fact that the Rapture is not far off.

The next section deals with the "delusion" that is mentioned in 2 Thessalonians 2:10-11. It says in part: "... because they did not receive the love of the truth so as to be saved. For this reason God will send upon them a deluding influence so that they will believe what is false ..."

A GRAND DECEPTION

It is possible that this deluding influence mentioned in 2 Thessalonians 2:10-11 may involve a widespread belief in UFOs. This section will deal with the reality of UFOs (or lack thereof), explanations of what they really are, and how they may be used to delude the unbelievers following the Rapture.

Belief in UFOs is not confined to the superstitious, the uneducated, or the mentally ill. Many highly intelligent people, including politicians, professionals, scientists, and pilots, believe in UFOs and, in many cases, are currently acting on that belief. The following material will review the evidence, the different interpretations applied, and the implications of those interpretations.

DO UFOs REALLY EXIST?

In the 1940s, it was rare to find anyone who believed in the existence of intelligent extraterrestrial life or UFOs from outer space. According to a 1947 Gallup poll, "Most thought they were illusions, hoaxes, secret weapons, or phenomena that could be explained."[74] Contrast this with a more "recent Gallup poll which revealed that seventy-two percent of Americans believe in extraterrestrial life, forty-eight percent believe in UFOs, and fifteen percent believe they have seen a UFO. According to other polls, up to three percent believe they have been abducted by a UFO."[75]

The UFO-Extraterrestrial phenomena is a current reality accepted by many. The belief in UFOs has increased in popularity over the last fifty years. This growing acceptance of the UFO phenomena and extraterrestrial life is based on mountains of evidence, reported sightings, and accounts of abductions. Excluding newspapers, the number of professional articles exceeds 6,000 in English, 2,200 in foreign journals, and 1,350 periodicals on UFOs.[76]

Despite many unconfirmed testimonies, frauds, and disinformation, there is too much solid, credible evidence to ignore it. The next section reviews a few examples out of the thousands reported.

APOLLO 11 SIGHTINGS

Astronauts Neil Armstrong and Edwin Aldrin reported UFO sightings after reporting their lunar landing. Their reports on July 21, 1969, were dismissed and went unconfirmed for years, as shown by the following excerpt.

According to Otto Binder, a former NASA employee, the agency has a long standing policy of blocking sensitive transmissions through secret, non-public frequencies. According to Binder,[77] an unnamed ham radio operator picked up the following transmission on a public bypass channel when Apollo 11 landed in the Sea of Tranquility:

MISSION CONTROL: "What's there? … Mission Control calling APOLLO 11."

APOLLO 11: "These babies are huge, Sir … enormous … Oh, God, you wouldn't believe it! I'm telling you there are other spacecraft out there … lined up on the far side of the crater edge … they're on the moon watching us …"

In 1979, the former chief of NASA communications, Maurice Chatelain, confirmed Otto Binder's account.[78]

In spite of Chatelain's senior position at NASA, it still denied his claims. In his book, *Our Cosmic Ancestors*, Chatelain makes a number of startling claims about UFO sightings during NASA missions.[79] See Appendix B: **The UFO Grand Deception**, for further documentation, which includes: The Mexico Flap, The Israel Flap, and The Roswell Incident.

OTHER CREDIBLE WITNESSES

There are a number of credible and notable people who have reported UFO sightings. For example, Jimmy Carter, then former governor of Georgia, reported a UFO sighting in 1969. As a presidential candidate in 1976, he pledged: "If I become President, I'll make every piece of information this country has about UFOs available to the public and the scientists." After he became President, he never said another word about it. He didn't deny it or confirm it. He ignored it.[80]

Other notable men who were convinced that UFOs needed consideration include: General Douglas MacArthur, former Senator Barry Goldwater, former President Dwight D. Eisenhower, Lester B. Pearson (former Prime Minister of Canada), and Malcolm Muggeridge of England.[81] It is also noteworthy that former President Ronald Reagan made eighteen references to UFOs in his speeches. Both he and Nancy Reagan claimed they had witnessed a UFO.[82] (DVD titled: "UFO Conspiracy" by I.D.E. Thomas and Dave Hunt.)

We have only looked at the tip of the iceberg concerning UFO evidence and documentation. Of the thousands of cases of UFOs reported over the last 50 years, "more than 700 of the cases have been reported by airline and military pilots."[83] Most of the evidence in these cases is related to the credibility of the witness. Airline and military pilots are very credible witnesses when it comes to UFO sightings.

It is interesting to note that the government and the military have attempted to cover up the UFO reports. One wonders why they want to cover it up. The government attempts to cover it up or explain it away in the "interest of national security." The implication of this cover-up is that the government fears how the general public would react if the truth was disclosed.

The general belief in UFOs and extraterrestrials is so prevalent that people are conditioned to accept the whole UFO and ET phenomena. What does this belief mean, and how does it affect us personally?

According to Missler and Eastman, authors of *Alien Encounters*, if these things are real, it "will lead to the biggest challenge ever faced by mankind. If they aren't real, they bear evidence of a gigantic delusion— one that is being orchestrated with a political end in sight ... what lies behind these strange events will soon affect every living person on this planet."[84]

UFOs AND ETs, "THE WORLD'S REALITY"

It is hard to deny what appear to be real UFOs and ETs when one reviews the evidence. There are over 12,000 reports of UFOs that were reviewed by Project Bluebook since 1947. Although a majority of the reported objects were identified as natural or man-made, there are a significant number of reports that have no apparent earthly explanation.[85]

The belief in UFOs and ETs is growing; they are becoming accepted as an established fact. The current belief in UFOs was not even a consideration fifty years ago. Not only is there a growing acceptance by the mass populace, but there is also an acceptance by governmental agencies. The Federal Emergency Management Agency (FEMA) has a training manual that includes UFO situations. Chapter 13, titled "Every Attack and UFO Potential," refers to the "very real threat posed by Unidentified Flying Objects (UFOs) whether they exist or not" (*Fire Officers Guide to Disaster Control*, 1993 Manual, Second Edition (1992) by William M. Kramer and Charles W. Bahme).

This confirms that the government accepts UFOs. The existence of what appears to be UFOs can hardly be questioned in this day and time. "As Temple University history professor and UFO expert, David Jacob, puts it, UFO's existence is so well established that it is no longer a matter to prove as was the case in the 1950s and 1960s."[86]

ANCIENT VISITORS OR ASTRONAUTS?

ANCIENT WRITINGS

Although the UFO phenomena and the belief in ETs have grown rapidly over the last fifty years, there is evidence that "they" visited our planet thousands of years ago. We have ancient records of some type of alien visitation from the Sumerians in the third millennium B.C.

The history of Sumer has been reconstructed from thousands of clay tablets telling of the "gods" that came down to earth from the heavens. Popular authors have interpreted these texts as "ancient astronauts" who flew to earth in spaceships and were worshipped as "gods."[87]

Not only do we have written records of ancient visitors referred to as "gods," we also have archaeological accomplishments that are beyond our ability to duplicate in this day and time, such as the Great Pyramid of Giza. Even with our current technology, scientists have not been able to duplicate the architectural achievements of ancient Egypt.[88] There are other examples of ancient supernatural feats that cannot be accounted for by human beings.

How do we interpret or understand ETs from past paintings, which have striking similarities to current day descriptions as reported by abductees? What kind of beings lived on this planet thousands of years ago that were more advanced technologically than our current scientists?[89]

Could these ancient visitors be supernatural beings? What about human beings with extraordinary intelligence and strength? Some of the evidence points to both human and supernatural.

MEN AND "GODS": JOINING OF SUPERNATURAL WITH NATURAL

Is it really possible for supernatural beings to have sexual intercourse with humans? To answer this question, we again turn to the only true point of reference, God's Word.

BIBLICAL VIEWPOINT

Genesis 6:2 says, "... the sons of God saw that the daughters of men were beautiful; and they took wives for themselves, whomever they chose." These "sons of God" were supernatural beings. The "sons of God" is most likely a reference to angels. Job 1:6 says, "... the sons of God came to present themselves before the LORD, and Satan also came among them." Satan is the fallen archangel Lucifer who is the leader of the other fallen angels. In Matthew 25:41, Jesus makes reference to "... the eternal fire which has been prepared for the devil and his angels ..."

It is clear that these were not "beings" or angels who were following God's will. Consider what kinds of offspring were produced as a result of this sexual union between fallen angels and human beings. Genesis 6:5, states: "Then the LORD saw that the wickedness of man was great on the earth, and that every intent of the thoughts of his heart was only evil continually." The offspring of this intermarriage were called the Nephilim. The word "Nephilim" actually comes from the root "naphal," meaning "fallen ones."[90]

The Nephilim were the offspring between humans and demonic beings, referred to as fallen angels. This would not only account for the extreme wickedness of humanity, but it would also account for the supernatural strength and intelligence necessary to accomplish feats, such as the building of the Great Pyramid of Giza. It could also be the origin of myths involving this kind of union between supernatural beings (referred to as "gods") and human beings. Remember, myths are often distortions of reality.

MYTHOLOGICAL VIEWPOINT

Greek and Roman mythology also gives an account of this intermarrying between "gods" and humans. The Titans were the giant offspring of the gods and their human wives. "According to mythology, they also assisted in the building of the magnificent monuments of Greece … According to numerous authors, 'these mighty men' of the golden age were the 'third party' who assisted mankind in the building of the monuments of Egypt, Stonehenge, the Americas, and the Far East."[91]

A copy of the Genesis Apocryphon, which dated back to the second century B.C., was discovered at Qumran in 1947. This document gave further evidence that celestial beings from the skies had landed on planet Earth and mated with earth women and begat giants.[92]

In ancient times, these supernatural beings were referred to as "gods." In our day, they are referred to as "aliens" or "ETs." We have briefly reviewed the following accounts for UFOs and ETs in regards to ancient writings, archaeological evidence, and mythological accounts. Now we will briefly look at their origin from a scientific framework.

SCIENCE IN THE NEW AGE: HOW MANY DIMENSIONS?

SCIENTIFIC VIEWPOINT

Many scientists believe in extraterrestrial life and UFOs. Although there is much evidence for the existence of UFOs and ETs, their origin is very controversial even among experienced UFO investigators. The common view is the "extraterrestrial hypothesis" (ETH). This is the belief that ETs come from another star system. However, in recent years, a number of researchers have challenged this hypothesis as a result of well-documented accounts of UFOs defying physics.[93]

UFOs have been tracked on radar traveling at over 25,000 miles per hour within our atmosphere. Yet, unlike physical objects, they do not cause sonic booms and they do not burn up. They have been known to make right angle turns at over 15,000 miles per hour, something no physical object could endure. And despite visual confirmation, UFOs often fail to show up on photographic film or radar devices, although some do show up.[94]

If UFOs are not permanent constructions of matter and if they do not travel by conventional means from one solar system to another, what are they? If the extraterrestrial hypothesis is rejected, what is the alternative?

Even if we consider the possibility that UFOs are constructed from some other form of hardware, where do they hide when not visible to the human eyes? In 1950, nuclear physicist Enrico Fermi raised some interesting questions. " 'If extraterrestrials are commonplace,' he asked, 'where are they? Should their presence not be obvious?' This question became known as the Fermi Paradox" (*Scientific American*, July 2000, "Where are they?" Ian Crawford). These are questions asked from the standpoint of a three dimensional universe.

Jacques Vallee is a noted scientist and UFO researcher with a background in astrophysics and computer science. He offers an alternative explanation.

> I believe that the UFO phenomenon represents evidence for other dimensions beyond space-time; the UFOs may not come from ordinary space but from a multiverse which is all around us ... If they are not spacecraft, what else could UFO's be? ... I believe there is a system around us that transcends time and space. Other researchers have reached the same conclusion.[95]

Once we go beyond our three-dimensional existence, we move into hyperspace. These dimensions are beyond our perception of reality and may be more in line with a multiverse or parallel universe. In other words, a being in hyperspace or in a dimension beyond our three dimensional existence would have capabilities and rules of their own geometry, which is beyond our understanding. (See Appendix B, The UFO Grand Deception for further elaboration, especially "Flatlands.")

We live in a three-dimensional world with a fourth dimension representing time. Einstein's theory of relativity demonstrates that time, space, and motion interact. In other words, time is not a constant. We now know from particle physics that we live in a universe of at least ten dimensions.[96]

Given the fact that UFOs defy physics and the "nuts and bolts" descriptions, we can begin to look at dimensionality as a way to understand the UFO phenomenon. "With such a framework, UFOs can be viewed as an inter-dimensional phenomenon that can materialize and interact with us within our space-time domain."[97] For additional information on UFOs and quantum physics, see Appendix B, The UFO Grand Deception.

We can conclude that UFOs are not what they appear to be, i.e., a spacecraft carrying aliens from another planet or star system. There is evidence of intermarriage between supernatural beings and human beings. This can be seen in the biblical account in Genesis 6. It is symbolized in mythological accounts and further confirmed by archaeological evidence and ancient writings. The scientific hypothesis of dimensionality—UFOs coming from a dimension beyond our three-dimensional world—fits with the biblical account of supernatural beings (sons of god) making contact with human beings. The inter-dimensional phenomenon explains how supernatural beings can be invisible one minute and then materialize, making contact with human beings.

GRAND DELUSION: NEW AGE RAPTURE

NEW AGE RAPTURE VIEW

Jesus compared His return to the days of Noah. He said, "For the coming of the Son of Man will be just like the days of Noah" (Matthew 24:37). The "days of Noah" is a reference to the condition of the world just after the "sons of god" married the "daughters of men" (Genesis 6:1-5). This is a reference to the surprise element and also to the wickedness of the world in Noah's day. The condition of the world during the Tribulation Period will be like in Noah's day, wicked. During the Tribulation Period, there may be another visitation by fallen angels, only this time, they could be updated with contemporary names like "aliens" or "extraterrestrials" instead of "gods."

The New Age concept of a Rapture event is very widespread. Some people have never heard of the Rapture outside of the New Age concept of it. There are various New Age concepts of the Rapture. Some include a UFO evacuation of people. Other authors believe in "high vibrations" that will cause some people to literally walk into heaven in their same form. (See Appendix B, The UFO Grand Deception, for other examples of a counterfeit Rapture). When the real Rapture happens, there will be plenty of explanations as to what happened. The UFO/ET belief system is in place to provide for a "deluding influence," as referred to in 2 Thessalonians 2:11.

This chapter addressed two prophetic segments of time and events. The first part covered the events that move us closer to the Rapture. The second part covered a potential post-Rapture lie that could be used to explain away the Rapture.

Chapter Eight will cover the Tribulation Period. It describes events and judgments during that period. This will be a worldwide judgment. According to the Bible, there are only two worldwide judgments. The first was the great flood in Noah's day. The second is the seven-year Tribulation Period.

Jesus described this period of time in the following way: "For then there will be a great tribulation, such as has not occurred since the beginning of the world until now, nor ever will. Unless those days had been cut short, no life would have been saved ..." (Matthew 24:21-22).

Chapter Eight

Apocalypse / Last Days

This final chapter will cover the future Tribulation Period, the most horrifying days in the history of mankind. This chapter begins with a world in total shock following the Rapture of the Church, which consists of the true believers in Jesus Christ, and will then proceed to cover the main events of this seven-year Tribulation Period.

RAPTURE SHOCK

In the days following the Rapture, the mass disappearance of millions of people will leave the world in a state of chaos. An explanation for this event will be demanded as people desperately seek answers.

The One World stage will already have been set in place preceding the Rapture, or it will be close. Satan and his hierarchy of fallen angels will be working through human experts to provide one or more explanations. One possible scenario is that preceding the Rapture, there will be an open alien contact. If this were to happen, it would cause a great "apostasy" to help explain away the Rapture as a mass alien abduction. It is also possible that open alien contact could happen after the Rapture during the Tribulation Period. This would create a world environment similar to Noah's day after the "sons of God married the daughters of men."

As discussed in the previous chapter, abduction by aliens is a possible explanation. Satan has used the New Age philosophy and the New Age prophets to pave the way for the Rapture.

A number of other explanations may also be given. The people left behind will be desperate for an explanation. People will be in a state of shock, many having lost their whole families, and will be willing to believe anything. The ones who have been exposed to the gospel but did not accept it will be spiritually blinded. They will believe a lie.

> ... because they did not receive the love of the truth so as to be saved. For this reason God will send upon them a deluding influence so that they will believe what is false ... (2 Thessalonians 2:10-11)

PENTECOST REVERSAL

When God dealt with the nation of Israel, there was a correlation between events, holy days, and the number of years prophesied. The prophecies in the Old Testament were very specific in every way, including length of time. For example, Judah's seventy-year captivity under Babylon was predicted in Jeremiah 25:11. It says, "This whole land will be a desolation and a horror, and these nations shall serve the king of Babylon seventy years." Daniel referred to the Book of Jeremiah near the end of the seventy-year captivity. He knew when the captivity would end since the exact number of years was predicted (Daniel 9:2).

Another example of length of time is the seventy-weeks prophecy in Daniel 9:24-27 that symbolized or represented 490 years. One week represents seven years; 7 x 7 = 49 years. In this prophecy, there was an exact number of years decreed for the nation of Israel comprising three segments of time. The first segment of time was seven weeks, or forty-nine years, beginning with the decree to rebuild Jerusalem under Artaxerxes in the year 444 B.C. and lasting until the rebuilding of Jerusalem was completed. The second segment of time was sixty-two weeks, or 434 years (7 x 62 - 434 years) (Daniel 9:25). This covered the period of time between the completion of the rebuilding of Jerusalem until the Triumphal Entry, just before Christ was crucified, or "cut off," in A.D. 33 (Daniel 9:26). The remaining one week, or seven years, is the Tribulation Period.

Jesus died during Passover, which was in observance of the Israelites being freed from Egypt. The final plague before the Egyptians freed the Israelites was the death of the firstborn of both man and beast. The Israelites were protected, or "passed over," by the death angel when the blood of a lamb had been applied to the doorposts (Exodus 12:21-23). Jesus' death occurred simultaneously with the celebration of that event.

He was the ultimate sacrificial Lamb. His crucifixion could have occurred at any time during the year, but God chose the Passover celebration.

The first day of Pentecost following the death of our Lord was the start of the Church. This event was marked by the outpouring of the Holy Spirit (Acts 2:1-21) Who now seals and indwells every true believer in Jesus Christ (Ephesians 1:13-14). (See Ephesians 4:30 and Romans 8:9.)

When the Rapture occurs, believers in Jesus Christ who are alive will "meet the Lord in the air ..." (1 Thessalonians 4:17). Study Ephesians 5:25-32 for more understanding of the relationship of Christ and the Church.

The Church was established by the outpouring of the Holy Spirit at Pentecost (Acts 2:1-4). The Church will be Raptured (1 Thessalonians 4:16-17), and the Holy Spirit will be removed from the earth (2 Thessalonians 2:7). It will be, in essence, a reversal of Pentecost.

Pentecost comes during May or June.[1] The calendar parallels the Feast of Pentecost with "early figs ripening." Matthew 24:32 relates the parable of the fig tree, "... when its branch has already become tender and puts forth its leaves, you know that summer is near."

As mentioned in Chapter One, the fig tree symbolizes Israel. Putting forth its leaves immediately before it ripens signifies that the return of Christ will occur near the time when Israel once again becomes a nation. That happened in 1948. Verse 34 continues, "... this generation will not pass away until all these things take place."

In summary, Israel is symbolized by a fig tree. The putting forth of its leaves in the spring signifies the closeness of summer (Matthew 24:32), the time when the fig tree ripens. Pentecost was in the early summer when the early figs ripen. Could the Rapture happen at the time of Pentecost (May or June) in a year not too far away? Or could it possibly occur at the Feast of Trumpets in the late summer or early fall? Perhaps it could occur this year or within the next few years. It is something to consider! Another name for Pentecost on the Jewish calendar is "First Fruits."

OVERVIEW OF THE AGES

To see the Tribulation Period in its historical context, the following material will briefly review historical world empires and prophetic time periods. The historical world empires are referred to as the "Times of the Gentiles" (see Chapter One). The seventy weeks in Daniel is a prophecy concerning Israel's time line (see Chapter Three).

TIMES OF THE GENTILES: BEGAN IN 606 B.C.
WITH THE CAPTIVITY OF JUDAH

Daniel Chapter 2 relates that King Nebuchadnezzar, the Babylonian king, had a dream. He called for his wise men to tell him the dream and the interpretation, but they could not. After Daniel prayed, "… the mystery was revealed to Daniel in a night vision …" (v. 19). Daniel then went before the king and told him the dream and its interpretation.

Daniel related that the king saw in his dream an image of a man, depicting four world empires. The first empire was the Babylonian Empire, represented by the head of gold. This empire began in 626 B.C. [Although the Babylonian Empire began in 626 B.C., the "Times of the Gentiles" started with Nebuchadnezzar's reign around 606 B.C.] The second empire was the Medo-Persian Empire, represented by the chest and arms made of silver. It began in 539 B.C. The third empire was Greece, represented by the belly and thighs made of bronze. It began in 330 B.C. The fourth empire was the Roman Empire, represented by the legs of iron and feet of iron and clay. It began its rise in 242 B.C. Jerusalem later fell in 68 B.C.

The succeeding empires overtook each of the first three empires. Rome, the fourth empire, was never succeeded by another empire. The iron legs represented the divided Roman Empire. The capital of the Eastern Roman Empire was Constantinople. Rome was the capital of the Western Roman Empire. "Rome held sway when Jesus was born in Bethlehem and when He was crucified."[2]

The feet and toes are made of iron like the legs, but the iron is mixed with clay. The ten toes in Daniel 2:40-43 parallel the ten horns in Daniel 7:7 and Revelation 13:1. They are identified as "ten kings" in Daniel 7:24.

We know that the ten toes represent a revived form of the Roman Empire, since the final Roman Empire with ten kings has never been destroyed. This revised form of the Roman Empire has yet to be established. "There has never been a period in the Roman Empire when ten kings have sat simultaneously."[3]

"By the time Christ was born, all of western Asia, northern Africa, southern Europe, including a portion of Great Britain, had succumbed to Rome …"[4] A future revived Roman Empire may cover the same geographical areas. The geographical area currently covered by the European Union is similar to that area covered by the Roman Empire in Jesus' day.

As discussed previously, the Church Age was a mystery and was not revealed in the Old Testament. Some of the Old Testament prophecies included both comings of Christ in the same verse. The Church Age is sometimes referred to as a "parenthesis" in time.

One example of an Old Testament prophecy that relats both comings of Christ in the same verse, yet not mentioning the Church Age, is found in Isaiah 61:2. In that verse, "the expression 'To proclaim the year of the Lord's favor' is immediately followed by 'and the day of vengeance of our God.' The 'year of the Lord's favor' refers to the first coming of Christ, and the 'day of vengeance' to His second coming. When quoting this verse in the synagogue at Nazareth (Luke 4:16-21), Christ stopped in the middle of the verse at the end of the description of His first coming."[5] The second half of the verse refers to His Second Coming.

ISRAEL'S CLOCK: DANIEL'S SEVENTY-WEEKS PROPHECY

The "seventy-weeks" prophecy is found in Daniel 9:24-27. This prophecy is given specifically to the Jewish people and the nation of Israel and refers to a Jewish time line in terms of 360-day Jewish years. The angel Gabriel spoke to Daniel, "Seventy weeks have been decreed for your people and your holy city ..." (v. 24). The reference to "your people" and "your holy city" is a reference to the Israelites and Jerusalem. This is in contrast to "Times of the Gentiles," which referred to succeeding world empires.

Seventy weeks represent 490 years. The Jewish time clock started in 444 B.C. at the "decree to restore and rebuild Jerusalem" issued under Artaxerxes (vv. 25-26). The crucifixion, when the Messiah is "cut off," is the conclusion of the sixty-nine weeks, or 483 years. Now insert the parenthetical Church Age, that began at Pentecost and ends with the Rapture of the Church prior to the Tribulation Period. The remaining one week, or seven years, represents the Tribulation Period. (For more on the explanation of "weeks," see Chapter Three, "Daniel's Seventy-Weeks.")

PROPHETIC CLOCKS

The Lord deals with Israel and the Church differently. Missler and Eastman state: "It seems that the Lord deals with Israel and the Church mutually exclusively. A chess clock, with its two interlocked representations, is an illustrative example; one clock is stopped while the other is running."[6]

Prophetically, Israel was given precise prophecies by way of a succession of world empires or predictions in terms of years (seventy years captivity in the book of Jeremiah and seventy weeks in Daniel) ... We are given signs that precede the Second Coming (Matthew 24; Mark 13; Luke 21), but not an exact date. Matthew 24:36 says, "But of that day and hour no one knows ... but the Father alone."

By contrast, the Rapture is a signless event. It could happen at any point in history, but it does precede the Tribulation Period. As the Second Coming draws closer, we know the Rapture draws even closer, at least seven years prior to the Second Coming.

Regarding the Church age, Dwight Pentecost states: "The concept must stand that this whole age with its program was not revealed in the Old Testament, but constitutes a new program and new line of revelation in this present age."[7] In many ways, biblical prophecy in the Church Age is like a puzzle. The pieces of the puzzle include the signs preceding the Second Coming, coupled with current events. As the time gets closer, the picture nears completion.

TIME GAP

According to Scripture, the Church Age began at Pentecost, and the consummation of the Church Age will occur at the Rapture. The event that restarts Israel's prophetic clock will be a covenant between Israel and the Antichrist (Daniel 9:27). That covenant will start the seven-year Tribulation Period, also known as Daniel's seventieth week.

What the Bible doesn't reveal is the time interval between the Rapture and the beginning of the Tribulation Period. The assumption that the Rapture begins the Tribulation Period is a misconception. It is the signing of the covenant between Israel and the Antichrist that marks the beginning of the Tribulation Period. The length of time between the Rapture and the signing of the covenant is not given.[8]

The Rapture will occur prior to the beginning of the Tribulation Period. In reference to the Antichrist, the Bible says he is being "restrained." Second Thessalonians 2:7-8 says, "... he who now restrains will do so until he is taken out of the way. Then that lawless one will be revealed ..."

The only One with the power to restrain the Antichrist is the Holy Spirit. When the Rapture occurs, the Holy Spirit will be "taken out of the way." His restraint will be removed following the Rapture, allowing the

Antichrist to be revealed, not before that time.

There are some scholars who believe the Rapture will happen in the middle of the Tribulation Period prior to the Great Tribulation (the last three and one-half years). This author believes the Rapture will happen prior to the seven-year Tribulation Period for a number of reasons. Space doesn't allow them to be listed. Whether the correct interpretation of Scripture is pre-tribulation Rapture (prior to the beginning of the seven-year tribulation) or mid-tribulation Rapture, it will happen prior to the horrible judgments that will occur in the last half of the Tribulation Period—the "Great Tribulation."

"There is some passage of time between the revelation of antichrist and the beginning of the tribulation period ... 'Rome wasn't built in a day.' It was true in ancient times. It will also apply to the revived Roman Empire under antichrist."[9]

A global disturbance of some type—war, environmental destruction, or Rapture—will most likely pave the way for the Antichrist to sign a peace plan (Daniel 9:27). Other causes are also possible. For example, terrorism, the threat of war, and pressure by allies led to peace treaty negotiations during the late 1990s and into the year 2000 between Israel and Palestine and between Israel and Syria. We also have the possibility of the destruction of Damascus that would fulfill the prophecy of Isaiah 17. It is very likely that these are preliminary to the seven-year peace covenant to be signed by Israel and the Antichrist.

The first half of the Tribulation will most likely be characterized by peace, at least in comparison to the Great Tribulation of the second half. The Bible says, "While they are saying, 'Peace and safety!' then destruction will come upon them suddenly like labor pangs upon a woman with child, and they shall not escape" (1 Thessalonians 5:3).

RIGHT AT THE DOOR

How close is mankind to the final seven-year countdown known as the Tribulation Period? Very close! We cannot know the day or the hour (Matthew 24:36), but we are given enough signs to know the season.

The three remaining elements of the last days are the global economy, the global government, and the global religion.[10] Israel became a nation in 1948. Within one generation of that point in time, the three remaining elements will occur. Chapters Four, Five, and Six reviewed the formation of these three elements, particularly the movement toward a one world religion.

The three global elements of economy, government, and religion do not have to be established prior to the Rapture, but they will be in place during the Tribulation Period. Mankind is currently moving toward a One World Unification.

The symbolic interpretation of the Book of Revelation dominated until 1945. After 1945, the results of a nuclear holocaust could be envisioned. Prior to 1945, the descriptions in the Apocalypse were beyond comprehension. It could not be envisioned apart from a supernatural intervention.[11]

Throughout the history of the Church and up until the 1950s and 1960s, the symbolism of the Book of Revelation could not be understood. It was a mysterious book of symbols. Daniel, after receiving and recording a revelation about the end times in Daniel 12, responded: "As for me, I heard but could not understand; so I said, 'My Lord, what will be the outcome of these events?' He said, 'Go your way, Daniel, for these words are concealed and sealed up until the end time' " (Daniel 12:8-9).

John recorded his vision in the Book of Revelation. He used everyday words from his era to describe the events that were revealed to him. Planes, helicopters, guns, and bombs were unknown in John's day. He described what he saw as a time traveler. "John was a first-century man trying to describe a twenty-first century war."[12]

Our current generation is the only generation since the time of Christ that is capable of fulfilling one of the prophecies found in Revelation 9:16. This prophecy refers to the number of soldiers invading Israel from the east (China). "The number of the armies of the horsemen was two hundred million ..." (Revelation 9:16). Hal Lindsay comments:

> When John made the prophecy of 200 million Asian solders invading Israel to take on the armies of the west, which will be led by the revived Roman Empire, there were not 200 million people in the world. China can now raise an army of 352 million soldiers.[13]

Only in this generation, since Israel became a nation, are we able to understand prophecy. Daniel 12:9 has come true: "... these words are concealed and sealed up until the end time." What was concealed is now being revealed in these last days.

The first three chapters of Revelation cover the Church age. According to Dwight Pentecost, "Chapters one through three present the development of the church in this present age."[14] The "church" is not mentioned from Chapter 4 through Chapter 21, which includes the entire Tribulation Period and the Second Coming of Christ. It is only mentioned again in Chapter 22, the last chapter of Revelation.

The first three chapters address the churches. In Revelation 3:22 Jesus says, "He who has an ear, let him hear what the Spirit says to the churches." This is the last mention of the word "churches" in the book of Revelation until Chapter 22, the last chapter, where the word "churches" is mentioned again. It serves as the closing of His letter to the churches with an appeal to come and hear. This is evident in Revelation 22:16-17, which says, " 'I, Jesus, have sent My angel to testify to you these things for the churches.' … The Spirit and the bride say, 'Come.' " Jesus addressed the churches in Revelation 3:22 and closed His address in Revelation 22:16-17.

Revelation 3 concludes with one last invitation to people prior to the Rapture. "Behold, I stand at the door and knock; if anyone hears My voice and opens the door, I will come in to him and will dine with him, and he with Me" (Revelation 3:20).

THE LONGEST SEVEN YEARS IN HISTORY:
THE TRIBULATION PERIOD

The Tribulation Period has been referred to as "Jacob's trouble" or "Jacob's distress" (Jeremiah 30:5-7) and the "day of the Lord" (1 Thessalonians 5:2). This seven-year time period will be a judgment on the whole world.

Israel's prophetic time clock will begin when the Antichrist signs a peace agreement with Israel (Daniel 9:27). God will turn His attention back to Israel as the seventieth week of Daniel or the seven-year Tribulation Period countdown begins.

CHARACTERS, PHRASES, AND TERMS

There are several characters who will play major roles during the period of time called the Tribulation Period. The following reviews some of these people and their characteristics.

ANTICHRIST

The Antichrist is a key player and Satan's pawn or man of the day. Scripture gives him three common names:

1. Antichrist (1 John 2:18),
2. Man of lawlessness, man of sin, or son of perdition (2 Thessalonians 2:3, 8), and
3. Beast (Revelation 13:1, 17-18; Daniel 7:19).

OUT OF THE SEA

The Antichrist comes out of the Gentile nations and will be a Gentile leader. Revelation 13:1 says: "… Then I saw a beast coming up out of the sea, having ten horns …" "John sees this beast coming up 'out of the sea.' … John didn't call it a beast because it was a Gentile but, rather, because it comes up out of the sea of nations. In Daniel Chapter 7, the prophet records a dream that he had in which he saw the rise and fall of four gentile world empires. Each was characterized as a beast coming from the sea of nations"[15] (see Daniel 7:1-7).

MAN OF SIN

In 2 Thessalonians 2:3, the Antichrist is described as the "man of sin … the son of perdition." This man is evil to the core of his being. He will be characterized as follows.

Daniel 7

1. He will utter great boasts (v. 8).
2. He will persecute and wage war against Christians (v. 21).
3. He will make changes in time and in the law (v. 25).
4. He will be destroyed forever (v. 26).

Daniel 11

1. He will "exalt" himself against every god (v. 36).
2. He will speak "monstrous" things against the "God of gods" (v. 36).
3. He will rely on his military strength (v. 38).
4. He will be a merciless conqueror (vv. 39-42).
5. He will "gain control" over the world's economy (v. 43).
6. He will come to his end between "the seas and the beautiful Holy Mountain" (v. 45).[16]

Revelation 13
1. He will be arrogant and blasphemous (vv. 5-6).
2. He will war against the saints (Christians) (v. 7).
3. He will demand worship or impose death on non-worshippers (v. 15).

Other references
1. He will be a covenant-breaker (Daniel 9:27).
2. He will be a "man of lawlessness" (2 Thessalonians 2:3).

In addition to the above, the Antichrist will be head over the revived Roman Empire consisting of ten nations or regions (Daniel 2:40-43; 7:20-21, 23-24).

FALSE PROPHET: LOOKS LIKE A LAMB, TALKS LIKE A DRAGON

The false prophet, described as "another beast" in Revelation 13, will be the Antichrist's right-hand man. "Then I saw another beast coming up out of the earth; and he had two horns like a lamb and he spoke as a dragon" (Revelation 13:11). He is described as a "beast" and a "lamb with two horns." He is also referred to as the "false prophet" (Revelation 16:13; 19:20; 20:10).

OUT OF THE EARTH
The false prophet will come "out of the earth" (Revelation 13:11), whereas the Antichrist will come "out of the sea" (Revelation 13:1). The sea of nations is a reference to the whole earth or the Gentile nations. The word "earth" (land) is representative of Israel. The word "land" "with the definite article and not otherwise defined always refers to Israel."[17]

The false prophet will probably be a Jew, according to some commentators. He is described as a "lamb" that points the way to the first beast, the Antichrist (Revelation 13:12).

THE MAN BEHIND THE MAN
The role of the false prophet will be to "make the earth and those who dwell in it to worship the first beast ..." (Revelation 13:12). Just as the Antichrist will have a role that is more political in nature, the false

prophet will have a role that is more religious in nature. It could be paralleled, in a demonic sense, to the Holy Spirit's role in pointing people toward Jesus.

The false prophet will derive power and authority from both Satan (the dragon) and the Antichrist (Revelation 13:4, 12). He will have the ability to perform great signs and miracles (v. 13). "And he deceives those who dwell on the earth because of the signs ..." (v. 14). Remember, "... Satan disguises himself as an angel of light ..." (2 Corinthians 11:14).

MIRACLES AND IMAGES

The false prophet will have the power to perform miracles and great signs, "so that he even makes fire come down out of heaven to the earth in the presence of men" (Revelation 13:13). He will be empowered by Satan, along with the Antichrist.

During the Tribulation Period the Antichrist will be slain and then brought back to life (Revelation 13:3). As a result of this miracle, the whole earth will follow after him. This will occur around the middle of the Tribulation Period. Through Satan's power, the Antichrist will be healed and brought back to life. It is questionable whether Satan will have that kind of power or whether possibly a great deception will be involved.

The Muslims believe that their messiah will reign for seven years after signing a peace covenant with Israel and then die (see Chapter Seven). This is a perfect parallel to the Antichrist, the false messiah. He will do likewise and then die. When he appears to be resurrected, the whole world follows him. This will certainly be true for the Muslims. It fits their prophecy for the real messiah.

In Chapter Seven, we discussed aliens and "their incredible mastery over the laws of physics and the seemingly supernatural powers they possess. The ability to perform 'signs and wonders' and provide answers for mankind's problems are characteristics shared by the Antichrist as well. He will have a global plan that is so incredible that he will be embraced as a technological savior." [18]

As Christ died and was resurrected, so the great counterfeiter, the Antichrist, will be or will appear to be slain and resurrected. Jesus' death and resurrection are the foundational stones for Christianity. The Antichrist's death and resurrection, whether real or through supernatural deception, establishes or gives power to the false world religion. "... and the whole earth was amazed and followed after the beast" (Revelation 13:3).

Considering the supernatural characteristics of the Antichrist, where will he say he got his power? If he says God, the secular scientific community would reject him. If he says from demonic forces, many others would also reject him. Contemporary Christian authors Missler and Eastman "believe it is very likely that the coming world leader will boast of a connection with the powerful god-like alien entities who have, it is believed, overcome the problems of poverty, famine, disease, war, and the pain of cultural and religious division."[19]

The whole UFO-alien belief system that has been established may very well come into the picture. If UFOs are the delusion or the false explanation for the Rapture, the people left behind will have a belief system that paves the way for the Antichrist. The false prophet will point the way to the Antichrist. He will make an image of the Antichrist whose "fatal wound was healed" (Revelation 13:14). He will be given the power to give breath to the image and the power to speak. He will require worship of the image and death to those who refuse to worship the image (Revelation 13:15).

Remember Daniel Chapter 3? Nebuchadnezzar made an extremely large golden image of himself and required everyone to worship it (Daniel 3:1-6). He made the same requirements as the Antichrist, death to those who refuse to worship his image.

An interesting parallel can be drawn between these passages. During the Babylonian Empire, a great image of the king was made with a mandatory worship requirement. During the Tribulation, the world ruler, the Antichrist, does the same thing. The Babylonian Empire was characterized by the occult (Daniel 2:2). The new world religion will be characterized by the occult (Revelation 9:20-21).

The only difference is the nature of the images built for worship. The false prophet gives life to the image. What does this mean? How can life be given to an inanimate object? How can the whole world worship it? Some writers suggest that it will be a very high-tech image that uses television to provide one-way communication to the whole world, or that the image may exist as an electronic tracking device that works in conjunction with an interactive internet program.

THE GOOD GUYS: THE TWO WITNESSES

Two men from God, His witnesses, will come on the scene. "And I will grant authority to my two witnesses, and they will prophesy for twelve hundred and sixty days, clothed in sackcloth" (Revelation 11:3).

No one knows the exact identity of the two witnesses. Some scholars believe "that they are Moses and Elijah, because of the similarity of judgment inflicted to those pronounced by Elijah and Moses, namely fire from heaven, turning water into blood, and smiting the earth with plagues."[20]

The two witnesses will prophesy for the last three and one-half years of the Tribulation Period. They will have the power to project fire out of their mouth to destroy anyone trying to harm them (Revelation 11:5). They will have the power to stop rain like Elijah and to turn water into blood like Moses (v. 6). These two witnesses will have the following characteristics:

1. They will be sent by God to prophesy (Revelation 11:3).
2. The period of time they will prophesy is three and one-half years (v. 3).
3. They will most likely be prophets of doom prophesying the coming of Jesus and God's judgment. They will wear sackcloth like John the Baptist (v. 3)
4. They will have supernatural powers (v. 5)
5. They will be immune to death until their mission is accomplished (v. 7)
6. They will be killed by the Antichrist after their mission is accomplished (v. 7)
7. Their bodies will be in the streets of Jerusalem for three and a half days (vv. 8-9),
8. People will rejoice over their death (v. 10)
9. They will be resurrected by God after three and a half days (v. 11).
10. They will ascend into heaven (v. 12).

These two witnesses will have supernatural powers from God. There will be a display of the miraculous. They will be able to project fire, turn water to blood, and smite the earth with every plague (Revelation 11:6).

We have seen Satan's powers in performing miracles though the

Antichrist and the false prophet. Through the two witnesses, God's miraculous power will be exhibited. It will be similar to the display of miracles when Moses led the Israelites out of Egypt. Both Moses and the sorcerers produced miracles (Exodus 7:10-12). "… Aaron's staff swallowed up their staffs" (v. 12). God delivered Israel from Egypt, and He will once again turn His attention to Israel. Romans 11:1 says, "I say then, God has not rejected His people, has He? May it never be!"

God will send His two witnesses to prophesy in the interlude between the sixth and seventh trumpet judgments. His representatives will be sent just prior to the most horrible judgments of mankind, the bowl judgments.

A MULTITUDE OF JEWISH EVANGELISTS: SEALING OF 144,000 JEWS FOR JESUS

As the world enters into a time of horrendous judgment, God will appoint and seal 12,000 Jews from each of the twelve tribes of Israel (Revelation 7:3-8). No one knows the exact time within the seven-year Tribulation Period when God will seal His "bond-servants." It is apparently before the time of the Great Tribulation (last three and one-half years) and prior to the trumpet and bowl judgments. Revelation 7:2-3 says, "And I saw another angel ascending from the rising of the sun, having the seal of the living God; and he cried out with a loud voice to the four angels to whom it was granted to harm the earth and the sea, saying, 'Do not harm the earth or the sea or the trees until we have sealed the bond-servants of our God on their foreheads.'"

According to Mark 13:10, "The gospel must first be preached to all the nations." Many prophecy scholars expect the worldwide spread of the gospel to occur during the tribulation.[21] These Jewish evangelists will spread the gospel across the globe in what will truly be a "Jews for Jesus" revival as the world has never seen. This seal of the 144,000 Jews will happen in the interlude between the sixth and seventh seal judgments. The Lord will seal His representatives just prior to the trumpet judgments.

Due to modern means of communication, the gospel can be spread much more quickly and can reach more people than ever before. An example is one of Billy Graham's last messages. "It was carried to more countries simultaneously by video than ever before. One reporter estimated that the evangelist preached the gospel that day to 281 million people. Even if that estimate was half right, that is an astonishing number."[22] The actual estimate is probably much higher in 2008 as a result of the widespread use of the Internet.

ON THE STARTING BLOCK

God's time clock is precise. He allotted 490 years (70 x 7 weeks) according to the seventy-week prophecy of Daniel 9:24-27 (see Chapter Three, "Daniel's Seventy Weeks"). The first 483 years took us from 444 B.C. to the time of Jesus' crucifixion, when Israel's prophetic clock stopped. Upon Jesus' triumphal entry into Jerusalem, "… He saw the city and wept over it, saying, 'If you had known in this day, even you, the things which make for peace! But now they have been hidden from your eyes' " (Luke 19:41-42). He goes on to prophesy the destruction of Jerusalem, which occurred in A.D. 70, about forty years later, because they did not recognize the time of their visitation (Luke 19:44). The time of the Jews' visitation—the coming of their Messiah—was prophesied in Daniel's Seventy Weeks (Daniel 9:24-27).

The nation of Israel as a whole has experienced a partial spiritual blindness (Romans 11:8) until the "fullness of the Gentiles has come in" (v. 25), or until the nation of Israel turns to Him. At some point during the Tribulation Period, this "partial hardening" will be removed and "all Israel will be saved" (Romans 11:25-26). Israel was set aside because they, for the most part, rejected the Messiah, but Israel has not been rejected by God (Romans 11:1). This interlude or "parenthesis" in Israel's prophetic time clock lasts from the crucifixion of Christ to the beginning of the Tribulation Period.

This prophetic clock stopped after 483 years, the sixty-ninth week in Daniel 9:26, and it will restart when the Antichrist signs a peace covenant with Israel for the final seven years or seventieth week (Daniel 9:27).

The Tribulation Period is divided into twenty-one judgments: seven seal judgments, seven trumpet judgments, and seven bowl judgments. Each succeeding set of judgments is more destructive than the previous one.[23]

Many scholars assume that the Book of Revelation covers the whole seven-year Tribulation Period. In reality, the Book never refers to a seven-year period of time but frequently makes reference to a forty-two month (three and one-half years) period of time (Revelation 11:2; 13:5).

The seven-year period of time is drawn from Daniel 9:27 and starts with the signing of the covenant between the Antichrist and Israel. Revelation 6 and the chapters following frequently make reference to the last three and one-half years called the "Great Tribulation," as mentioned in Revelation 7:14. There are good reasons to conclude that the judgments are generally compacted within the last three and one-half years before Christ returns (Walvoord and Zuck, *Bible Knowledge Commentary, New Testament*, p. 947).

We know the Book of Revelation does cover the final forty-two-month Great Tribulation period, and, based on Daniel 9:27, we know that the time span of the entire Tribulation Period is seven years. With the exception of the first seal judgment, a very likely implication involves all three sets of judgments appearing in the final three and one-half years, with peace characterizing the first three and one-half years. This conclusion, in part, can be supported by Daniel 9:27 where the man of lawlessness, the Antichrist, breaks his covenant with Israel in the middle of the seventieth week. This week refers to the final seven-year period.

Also, 1 Thessalonians 5:2 makes reference to the "day of the Lord" (a reference to judgment) that "... will come upon them suddenly like birth pangs upon a woman with a child, and they will not escape." This happens while people are saying "Peace and safety!" (v. 3).

JUDGMENT OF THE SEVENS

The Book of Revelation details twenty-one judgments, three sets of seven each, that will occur during the Tribulation Period. These three sets are progressive. They are the seal judgments, the trumpet judgments, and the bowl judgments. Each set is more severe than the previous one. The seals are the mildest, and the bowls are the most severe.

The first set of judgments is called the "seal judgments" and is found in Revelation 5, 6, and 8. The seven seals are introduced as a symbolic presentation to John, who authored the Book of Revelation under divine inspiration. The symbolic presentation involves a "strong angel" holding a scroll, or rolled up parchment, with seven seals. The scroll has "seven seals affixed to the side in such a way that if unrolled the seven seals would need to be broken one by one" (Walvoord and Zuck, N.T., p. 954). Each seal represented a new judgment. The four horsemen are considered the first four seals (Revelation 6:2-8).

The word "seal" is also used in the Book of Revelation when it speaks of the sealing of the 144,000 Israelites "from every tribe of the sons of Israel" (12,000 from each tribe) (Revelation 7:4). This is a seal of protection from God that will be placed on their foreheads (Revelation 7:3-4). The seal may or may not be visible, but will mark them as belonging to God. They will be saved by God and will most likely serve as missionaries or evangelists to spread the Gospel.

The second set of judgments is referred to as the "trumpet judgments." The presentation of these seven trumpet judgments will also be done in a symbolic fashion. There were seven angels, each holding a trumpet. The sounding of the trumpet was like an announcement of the upcoming judgment (Revelation 8-9).

The final seven judgments are referred to as the "bowl judgments." They are introduced in Revelation 16:1. Again, we have seven angels, each holding a bowl. The bowls being poured out are a representation of God's wrath being poured out "into the earth."

The series of the three sevens are actually included in one series of seven. The seven trumpets are included under the seventh seal, and the seven bowls are under the seventh trumpet. "We have in fact a series in three movements" (Walvoord and Zuck, N.T., p. 951).

The three sets of judgments overlap each other. The trumpets and bowls are very similar, but not identical. The bowl judgments are the most severe of the three sets. For a diagrammatic representation, see Chart 11, "Interrelationships of Seal, Trumpet, and Bowl Judgments."

We are close to the time of the Rapture, which will open the door to the Tribulation Period. "Zola Levitt put it beautifully in a television broadcast. He said, 'We are pushing out the membrane of time that separates the Church Age from the beginning of the Tribulation.' "[24]

ONE WHITE HORSE / ONE "BAD NEWS" RIDER
[FIRST SEAL]

The first seal is opened, "I looked, and behold, a white horse, and he who sat on it had a bow; and a crown was given to him, and he went out conquering and to conquer" (Revelation 6:2). Riders of white horses usually symbolize victory. Christ is portrayed as riding a white horse at the Second Coming (Revelation 19). This rider does not represent Christ. The first seal symbolizes the beginning of the Tribulation, not the end.

According to Walvoord and Zuck, "This ruler has a bow without

CHART 11

Interrelationships of Seal, Trumpet, and Bowl Judgments

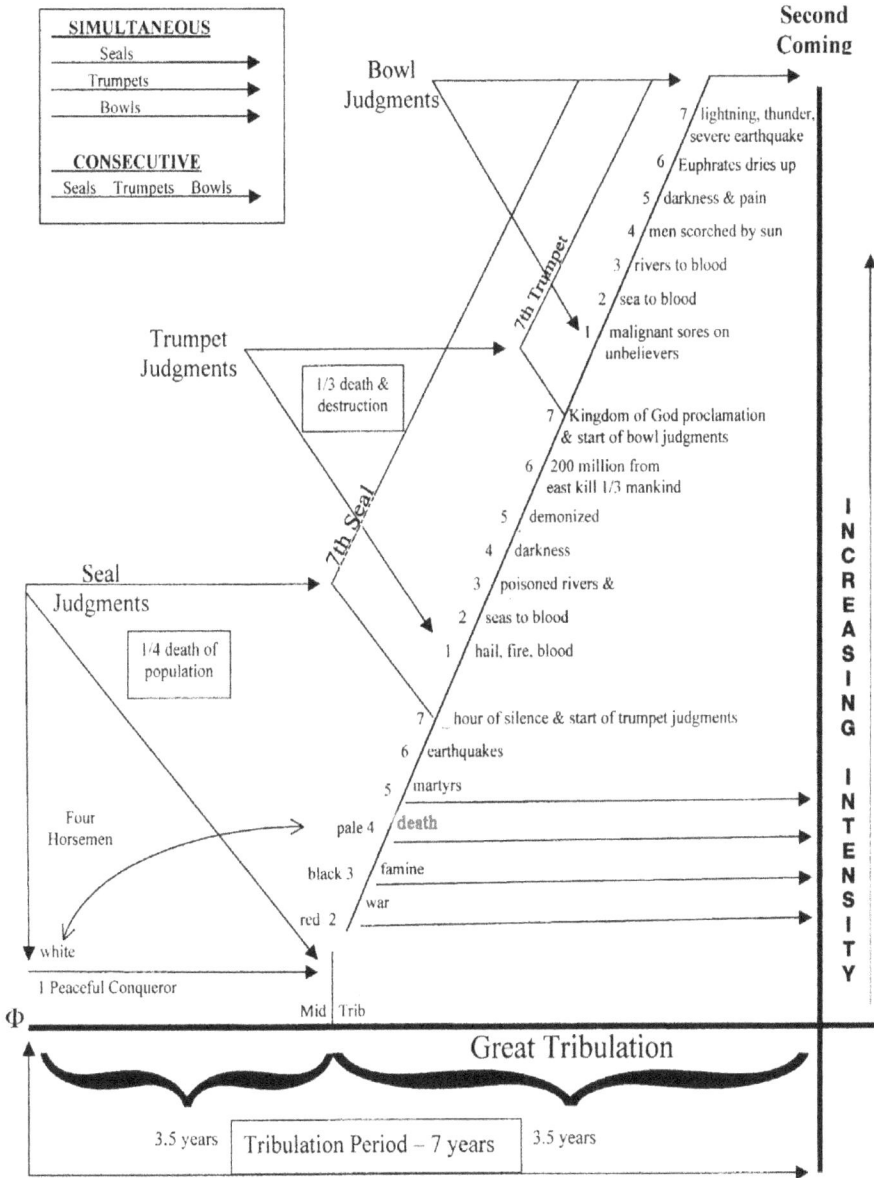

Second Coming

SIMULTANEOUS

Seals →
Trumpets →
Bowls →

CONSECUTIVE

Seals Trumpets Bowls →

Bowl Judgments

7 / lightning, thunder, severe earthquake
6 / Euphrates dries up
5 / darkness & pain
4 / men scorched by sun
3 / rivers to blood
2 / sea to blood
1 / malignant sores on unbelievers

7th Trumpet

Trumpet Judgments

1/3 death & destruction

7 / Kingdom of God proclamation & start of bowl judgments
6 / 200 million from east kill 1/3 mankind
5 / demonized
4 / darkness
3 / poisoned rivers &
2 / seas to blood
1 / hail, fire, blood

7th Seal

Seal Judgments

1/4 death of population

7 / hour of silence & start of trumpet judgments
6 / earthquakes
5 / martyrs
pale 4 / death
black 3 / famine
red 2 / war

Four Horsemen

white
1 Peaceful Conqueror

Mid | Trib

Φ

INCREASING INTENSITY

Great Tribulation

3.5 years | Tribulation Period – 7 years | 3.5 years

Φ Timeline not drawn to scale

an arrow, indicating that the world government which he establishes is accomplished without warfare."[25] The Church will already have been raptured at the time of this rider. Satan's counterfeit Christ, the Antichrist, will come on the scene, symbolically riding on a white horse, and will sign a covenant with Israel (Daniel 9:27). **He is the counterfeit Christ.** The restraining influence of the Holy Spirit through the Church of born again believers will be removed. The deception begins!

THE ULTIMATE POLITICIAN

If you haven't previously trusted politicians, this will not be the time to start. This man is no fool. He will have the ability and charisma to put to shame the most beloved and adored leaders throughout history. The Antichrist will gain the world's adoration by bringing peace to the earth during the first half of the Tribulation Period. Riding a white horse is the symbol of a conqueror.[26] According to the original Hebrew text, Daniel predicted, "and by means of peace, he will destroy many ..."[27]

The first three and a half years preceding the Great Tribulation will be characterized as a relative time of peace.[28] As a result of the signed covenant with the Antichrist, Israel will be at peace and will feel secure. Israel is referred to in Ezekiel 38:11 as a "land of unwalled villages." Another reference that characterizes the Tribulation Period during the first half is found in 1 Thessalonians 5:3: "While they are saying, 'Peace and safety!' then destruction will come upon them suddenly like labor pains upon a woman with child, and they will not escape." This is a reference to the world just prior to the Great Tribulation when the trumpet and bowl judgments begin.

The Antichrist will be conquering nations through this period of time, without war but with the threat of war, as symbolized by a bow but no arrow. This bow could very likely be the threat of nuclear war. As leader of a ten-nation Revived Roman Empire, he would have a nuclear arsenal at his disposal that would intimidate any other nation. Besides, he is a man of peace. He walks softly, but carries a big stick. "The crown identifies him as one who will eventually be accepted as king of the world."[29]

A TEMPLE REBUILT

A prophecy that must be fulfilled by the time of the Tribulation Period is the rebuilding of the Jewish temple. It must be rebuilt in Jerusalem in order for the Antichrist to desecrate it halfway through the Tribulation Period. Temple sacrifices will resume (Daniel 9:27).

The existence of a Jewish temple is further confirmed in Revelation 11:1-2, which states: "… Get up and measure the temple of God and the altar, and those who worship in it … for it has been given to the nations; and they will tread under foot the holy city for forty-two months."

Prophecy teachers who interpret Scripture literally agree that a Jewish temple in Israel must be rebuilt. Historically, Israel has had two temples. The first temple was built under Solomon's rule and destroyed by the Babylonians in 586 B.C. The second temple began in 535 B.C. and was completed in 516 B.C. It was renovated by Herod the Great starting in 19 B.C. and was finally destroyed by the Romans in A.D. 70. "That there will be a third temple is predicted by the prophet Daniel, the apostles Paul and John, and none other than the Lord Jesus Himself."[30] (Daniel 9:27; Matthew 24:15; 2 Thessalonians 2:3-4; Revelation 11:1-2).

Currently, Gershom Solomon heads the Temple Mount Faithful movement, an organization dedicated to rebuilding the Temple. This is a man who definitely believes in a coming Messiah. Solomon is not the only individual who is actively pursuing a rebuilt temple. "Many plans are being made for a rebuilt temple, and many diverse groups in Israel are preparing for it."[31]

The Messiah is coming back, and His name is Jesus Christ. But a counterfeit messiah, the Antichrist, will precede Him. The counterfeit messiah will desecrate the temple in the middle of the Tribulation Period and will break his covenant with Israel (Daniel 9:27).

The Sanhedrin was a council of seventy-one Jewish sages who constituted the Supreme Court and legislative body in Judea during the Roman period. Historically, the Sanhedrin commanded universal authority among Jews. It functioned for 400 years after the destruction of the temple in A.D. 70. It was disbanded for the next 1,500 years. Although the Jews made attempts to reestablish it over the years, they were never successful until 2004 when the new Sanhedrin was re-established.[32] "In the year 2005, the Sanhedrin made the decision to rebuild the temple. All of the furniture and furnishings are already in place."[33]

It is interesting to note that it was not until the present generation that the Jews re-established the Sanhedrin and made the decision to rebuild the third temple. The Jews believe this temple will be the

Messianic Temple, but it is not. This temple will be desecrated by the Antichrist during the Tribulation Period. There will be a Messianic Temple, but it will follow the Second Coming of Christ.

According to Bible prophecy, this temple will be in place during the Tribulation Period. The nation of Israel will have their temple for the first time since A.D. 70. The Antichrist will desecrate this temple. He will seat himself in the temple and displays himself as God. He will blaspheme God, build an image of himself to be worshipped, and then break his covenant with Israel (2 Thessalonians 2:4; Revelation 13:6; Daniel 9:27).

THE OTHER SIDE OF THE CURTAIN:
A SUPERNATURAL WAR

And there was war in heaven, Michael and his angels waging war with the dragon. And the dragon and his angels waged war, and they were not strong enough, and there was no longer a place found for them in heaven. And the great dragon was thrown down, the serpent of old who is called the devil and Satan, who deceives the whole world; he was thrown down to the earth, and his angels were thrown down with him. (Revelation 12:7-9)

Good and evil will have a preliminary showdown, but this battle is not Armageddon, the final battle of the Tribulation Period that will be brought to an abrupt end with the Second Coming of Christ (Revelation 19). This battle between Michael and the dragon, along with their angels, will be fought in heaven.

This war in heaven will set the stage for the Great Tribulation period, the final three and a half years. "Here (Revelation 12:8-9) he [Satan] will be cast out of heaven in the middle of the tribulation."[34] This will literally result in a hell on earth through wars and judgments. The time of peace that was enjoyed in the first three and a half years will come to an abrupt end.

Prior to this war in heaven, mankind has struggled or given into invisible supernatural demonic forces. The Ephesians 6:12 states: "For our struggle is not against flesh and blood, but against the rulers, against the powers, against the world forces of this darkness, against the spiritual forces of wickedness in the heavenly places" (Ephesians 6:12). "The cosmic (spiritual) battle is going to become increasingly visible."[35]

THE UFO / ET CONNECTION

The previous chapter and the related Appendix discuss UFOs, extra-terrestrials, alien abductions, and hybrids. As stated earlier, there is documentation and evidence supporting the UFO/alien existence and their interaction with mankind. The problem is the interpretation and the implication drawn from the evidence. The nonbiblical worldview generally supports the view that UFOs and ETs are a result of visitations from life on other planets. This worldview disregards the biblical view of demonic deception.

The UFO movement falls under the umbrella of the New Age Movement. The belief in UFOs and ETs is one of many beliefs that fits into the New Age Movement philosophy.

The New Age Movement becomes evident when what was tradition-ally considered evil merges with good. One key belief system of the New Age is "all is one" or *monism*.[36] With monism, we have the elimination of evil and the disregard of a dualistic world system that is built on the biblical base of two kingdoms. One kingdom is God's—good, and one is Satan's—evil.

The biblical worldview puts aliens, UFOs, ETs, and abductions as coming from one of the two kingdoms. As pointed out earlier, the evi-dence points toward a demonic deception.

One natural human tendency is a desire to believe in UFOs as visitors from other planets, provided they're friendly. "As Pastor Joe Focht of Calvary Chapel of Philadelphia has said, 'If I wasn't a Christian, I'd prob-ably believe we were placed on earth by aliens.' ... He says people want to believe in ancient astronauts because it absolves them of their responsi-bility to their Creator. It gives them an out, and most people will take it every time."[37]

John Mack, a well-known psychiatrist, has done extensive research in the area of alien abduction and the hybridization program. He states:

It is difficult to ignore the fact that the UFO abduction phenomenon is taking place ... abductions seem to be concerned primarily with two relat-ed projects: changing human consciousness to prevent the destruction of the earth's life, and a joining of two species for the creation of a new evolu-tionary form.[38]

In light of our interpretation of Genesis 6:2, where the "sons of God" married the "daughters of men" as a union of fallen angels with humans, a hybridization program is not unrealistic. "John Mack, M.D., and other researches believe that one of the primary purposes for the alleged alien abductions is the production of hybrid (half-alien, half-human) offspring."[39]

Hebrews 13:2 says: "Do not neglect to show hospitality to strangers, for by this some have entertained angels without knowing it." This is a reference to good angels who evidently appear as human beings. If we have entertained good angels without knowing it, is it also possible that some humans have had contact with fallen angels or hybrids without knowing it?

The result of the ungodly union of fallen angels with humans in Genesis 6:2 was a powerful hybrid offspring called the "Nephilim," who corrupted, harassed, and even killed mankind. "Now at the end of the twentieth century, we have the return of 'alien' entities with apparent supernatural powers."[40] Many Christians can accept the idea of a union between humans and fallen angels in Noah's day, but recoil at the thought of a reoccurrence today.[41]

When we look at Revelation 12:9, we see that Satan and his fallen angels were "thrown down to the earth." We know that world events during the Tribulation Period, especially the last half, will be energized by Satan. "As we approach the end times, the interest in extraterrestrial life and UFO phenomena has reached an all-time high. The prevailing view that they are our highly evolved ancestors ... has prepared the world to receive them as our technological saviors. The stage is set for the worship and reverence of alien entities."[42] It is very likely that the "alien entities" or "space brothers" will be considered "gods" during the Tribulation Period.

The Book of Daniel is also relevant here. The image in Daniel 2 is prophetic of the "Times of the Gentiles." It covers history starting with the Babylonian Empire and concluding with the end of the Tribulation Period. The ten toes represent ten kings (Daniel 2:40-42), which represent the revived Roman Empire under the authority of ten rulers (as understood by many commentators).

When we consider aliens and hybrids in the end times, we find an interesting prophecy in the Book of Daniel in regards to the ten toes. Consider the following passage: "And in that you saw the iron mixed with common clay, they will combine with one another in the seed of men; but they will not adhere to one another, even as iron does not combine with pottery" (Daniel 2:43).

Notice that the text switched to the use of a personal pronoun, "… they will combine with one another in the seed of men …" This is extremely suggestive. Missler and Eastman give their interpretation of this passage; they ask the question, "What (or who) is combining with the seed of men? Who are the non-seed?" They believe the significance of Daniel's passage is staggering. They view aliens, and the hybrid offspring of aliens, as part of a new world empire, one in which UFO incidents are part of a political agenda.[43]

What then are the implications concerning the Antichrist? "Surprisingly, a number of prominent Bible teachers—Hal Lindsey and Dave Hunt as examples—have publicly stated their view is that this leader will either be an alien, or he will boast of alien connections!"[44] There are many clues in the Bible that connect the coming world leader to Satan and his alien forces.

Paul's Epistle to Timothy becomes very relevant in the end times. "But the Spirit explicitly says that in later times some will fall away from the faith, paying attention to deceitful spirits and doctrines of demons" (1 Timothy 4:1).

A RED HORSE WARRIOR
[SECOND SEAL]

The opening of the second seal reveals a red horse, which represents war. Revelation 6:3-4 says, "When he broke the second seal, I heard the second living creature saying, 'Come.' And another, a red horse, went out; and to him who sat on it, it was granted to take peace from the earth, and that men should slay one another; and a great sword was given to him."

This is a picture of political power with the rider as the world ruler.[45] This second seal opens a time of war. "While they are saying, 'Peace and safety!' then destruction will come upon them suddenly like birth pains upon a woman with child …" (1 Thessalonians 5:3).

BROKEN COVENANT

The first seal will parallel the signing of a covenant between the Antichrist and Israel. The second seal shatters that covenant (Daniel

9:27; Revelation 6:3-4). The man of peace who characterizes the first half of the Tribulation Period will show his true colors at mid Tribulation—a man of war, a covenant breaker, and a blasphemer. He will no longer be "under cover." Satan will use him in a direct way.

THE RUSSIAN CONFEDERACY INVASION

This invasion of Israel will most likely occur at mid-tribulation with the opening of the second seal, a red horse of war. This will occur while Israel is at peace. Israel is characterized as "living securely" and as a land of "unwalled villages" (Ezekiel 38:8-11). This invasion will be led by Russia. John Walvoord, a well-known theologian, author, and an expert in the area of Bible prophecy, describes the root words for modern-day Russia. From a human standpoint, one has to ask why would Russia lead a host of Islamic countries to invade Israel? Up until the last six years, this question could not be answered.

Two things must occur in regard to Israel prior to the war of Gog and Magog (Russian invasion of Israel). The first, as previously mentioned, is a period of peace and security. The second is a significant buildup of wealth (Ezekiel 38:3, 11-13).[46] This next section deals with Israel's newly acquired wealth.

OIL IN ISRAEL

In 1981, Reverend James Spillman, pastor of a church in Clawson, Michigan, preached a sermon based on his book, *The Great Treasure Hunt*. According to Spillman's book, Gog and Magog will lead the armies of the world "to take a spoil." He asks the question, "What could Israel possibly possess in the last days that would make it a prize for conquest that the world's armies would meet there to fight for the spoils? ... Countries don't invade neighbors for pomegranates and olive oil, but they do go to war over another kind of oil. Petroleum ... The problem is that Israel is an oil poor country."[47]

Prior to the beginning of the twenty-first century, the only other incentive for a Russian-led invasion of Israel would be anti-Semitism. That might be enough incentive for the Muslim countries that are involved in the Russian invasion, but it would not be enough incentive for Russia, which is primarily an atheistic country. Putin, the former prime minister, has made agreements with Islamic countries as long as they keep their religion to themselves.

Since 2004, there has been a "gusher" of headlines about oil in Israel, which had only just begun to flow.[48] The following is a sample of those headlines:

Israel Strikes Black Gold
Arutz Sheva, May 4, 2004

Oil Baron Seeks Gusher from God in Israel
Reuters, April 4, 2005

His Mission: Seek and Ye Shall Find Oil
USA TODAY, May 19, 2005

Moses' Oily Blessing: Will Israel Find Oil?
The Economist, June 18, 2005

Is Israel sitting on an Enormous Oil Reserve?[49]
WorldNet Daily, September 21, 2005

Gas Deposits off Israel and Gaza
Open Visions of Joint Ventures
The New York Times, September 15, 2000

Arafat Hails Big Gas Find Off the Coast of Gaza Strip
The New York Times, September 28, 2000

Reporter William Orme wrote: "Drilling deep below the seas off Israel and the Gaza Strip, foreign energy companies are discovering gas reserves that lift the Palestine economy and give Israel its first taste of energy and independence. ... The Palestinians and Israelis will both profit if they can work together in a high stakes relationship."[50]

Experts had calculated that Israel had "some three to five trillion cubic feet of proven gas reserves," and, according to Yehezkel Druckman, Israel's petroleum commissioner, "there may be more." At the current prices, Orme reported, "the value of the strike was estimated [at] $2 billion to $6 billion, depending on pressure, quantity, and other variables."[51]

Behind many of these large oil and gas discoveries, there is a group of Christian businessmen, geologists, and at least one Orthodox Jew who started oil explorations in Israel based on the Old Testament prophecies. According to Philip Mandelker, Zion Oil's lawyer, there are at least six companies "whose founders were originally inspired to start drilling because of the Old Testament passages."[52]

John Brown, a born-again Christian, and Tovia Luskin, an Orthodox Jew, both started oil companies in Israel based on "Old Testament passages describing God's ancient promise to unlock enormous wealth and treasures in the last days."[53] The following is a list of the passages of God's promises for the last days to prosper Israel. These passages motivated both men toward oil exploration. The list will include the Bible reference and the relevant phrase therein that pertains to oil.

In context, these references are from the blessings that Jacob gave to each of his twelve sons just prior to his death. The references also include the blessings given by Moses to each of the twelve tribes, the descendants of Jacob's twelve sons.

Genesis 49:25 — "blessings of the deep that lies beneath." This is part of a prophecy that Jacob made to Joseph, one of his twelve sons.

Deuteronomy 33:13 — "And from the deep lying beneath." This concerns the blessings of Moses in reference to Joseph's blessing.

Deuteronomy 33:19 — "hidden treasures of the sand." This is in reference to the blessings of Moses to two of the twelve tribes/sons of Jacob—Zebulan and Issachar.

Deuteronomy 33:24 — "And may he dip his foot in oil." The blessings of Moses in reference to the descendants of Asher, one of the twelve sons of Jacob.

In November 2002, an interesting headline flashed across the newswire: "Israel Geologist Drills for Oil Based on Biblical Guidance." This geologist was Tovia Luskin, an Orthodox Jew, born and raised in Russia. He became so convinced by studying the Bible that there was black gold buried under the sands of the Jewish state that he moved to Israel, conducted extensive research, launched a limited partnership called Givot Olam, and came to the conclusion that "there are 65 million barrels of oil in central Israel alone."[54]

Luskin was proved wrong. A year later, Luskin and his colleagues discovered oil at their Meged-4 drilling site, but it was not 65 million barrels but 100 million barrels.[55] A few months later, new testing revealed that the Givot Olam site contained not 100 million barrels but upward of a billion barrels. This led the *Associated Press* to report, "An Israeli oil company has made the largest oil find in the history of the country."[56]

According to the London-based *Economist*, Luskin was not the only businessman who believed the Bible concerning the existence of oil in Israel. "In the 1980s, John Brown, a Catholic Texan cutting-tools executive, and Tovia Luskin, a Russian geophysicist and career oil man, both had religious epiphanies. Mr. Brown became a born-again Christian, while Mr. Luskin joined the Orthodox Jewish Lubavitch movement. Soon after, each found inspiration in Chapter 33 of the book of Deuteronomy."[57] It is in Chapter 33 that Moses, nearing death, left each tribe with a blessing.

John Brown founded Zion Oil in 2000. Gene Soltero, president and CEO of Zion Oil, was interviewed by author Joel Rosenberg in August 2005. According to the interview, Soltero had joined Zion Oil shortly after Brown founded it in 2000. Soltero had worked in the oil-and-gas business for more than four decades. He then joined Zion Oil because he was intrigued by Brown's perspective concerning Israel and oil.[58]

According to the interview, Brown's interest began in 1981 after he heard Reverend James Spillman's sermon, which was based on his book, *The Great Treasure Hunt*. As mentioned previously, the sermon and book made a case for the coming Russian invasion of Israel. It was based on Old Testament prophecies found in Genesis and Deuteronomy concerning oil in Israel.

Brown was electrified by the sermon and, as a result, spent the next twenty years studying the Scriptures laid out by Spillman, learning about the oil and gas business, traveling to Israel, researching, making contacts, and praying for guidance.[59] By April 2000, Brown launched Zion Oil with the assistance of an Israeli lawyer named Philip Mandelker.[60]

Prior to hearing Spillman's sermon, Brown had a spiritual conversion experience. By the late 1970s, Brown was rising through the ranks of Valeron, a manufacturer of cutting tools that was later acquired by General Telephone and Electronics in 1984. Brown was married with four children. The only problem was his drinking. His formerly social drinking eventually unraveled into blackouts and four unsuccessful tours through local rehab centers.[61] In 1981, as his alcoholism progressed, his marriage began to dissolve, and he moved into a one-bedroom apartment. The mover Brown hired, a laid-off autoworker, "began preaching Christ's salvation as he unpacked Brown's belongings. He invited Brown to accept Jesus into his heart. Brown says he wept uncontrollably at the young man's words and, at the age of 41, became a born-again Christian."[62] This was in 1981. It was a few months later, in the same year, that Brown heard Spillman's sermon.

On a follow up with Soltero, Rosenberg learned that Zion Oil was originally awarded and licensed by the government of Israel to explore 28,800 acres in northern Israel, but "were recently awarded an expanded contract for 219,000 acres in northern Israel." Soltero said, "We've been drilling for the past several months, and the initial results are very exciting. For legal reasons I can't say more right now. But let's just say it's possible that your novels [Rosenberg's novels, *The Last Jihad, The Last Days*] have vastly understated how much oil is out there[63] [brackets by author].

Soltero described where Zion Oil had been drilling for the past several months. The site was only a few miles from the Jezreel Valley and the ancient city of Megiddo, under Armageddon. Rosenberg confirmed that both oil and natural gas are under the region the Bible refers to as Armageddon.[64]

Brown recruited a man named Perry, "a solid old-school oil driller." He was recruited in Israel where he was doing consulting work for Delek, an Israeli energy conglomerate. "Perry has brought in wells in hard-scrabble places like Siberia and the Republic of Georgia. He signed on after reviewing Zion's seismic data, not its Bible-based mission statement" (Conde Nast Portfolio, October 2007, p. 94). Brown's mission is biblically based, but according to Perry, "the operations are done by experienced oil professionals, not the guy preaching salvation on the street corner" (Ibid, p. 94).

According to seismic data, Israel's oil is most likely to be found at the Permian level, which is more than 18,000 feet in depth (Ibid, p. 98). "This gives some credence to Zion Oil's quest. By next spring, the company plans to break ground on a second well, which will be drilled to a depth of more than 18,000 feet, reaching the Permian level" (Ibid, p. 98).

Israel has also become very wealthy. With a population of only seven million people, Israel is now home to 6,600 millionaires. "Of the 500 wealthiest people in the world, six are now Israeli …"[65] It has also become technologically advanced and wealthy. Israel has made extraordinary "economic gains since 1948[66] and has become dramatically wealthier than any of its immediate neighbors."[67]

In one generation, Israel has skyrocketed in abundance and wealth, as prophesied in Chapter 38 of Ezekiel. God is speaking to the future dictator of Russia, or perhaps the present one, in Ezekiel 38:3, 8, 11-13. The last part of the passage says, "... Have you come to capture spoil? Have you assembled your company to seize plunder, to carry away silver and gold, to take away cattle and goods, to capture great spoil?" (v. 13). This is a reference to the Russian invasion (vv. 2-6) against Israel (v. 8). It is true that supernatural forces will underlie this invasion. When viewed from a human standpoint, Russia and its allies have an incentive to invade Israel today. This wasn't the case twenty years ago, or even ten years ago.

The Russian invasion of Israel is led by Gog. "Gog" refers to a leader and "Magog" refers to the territory from which he comes. According to Genesis 10:2 and 1 Chronicles 1:5, Magog is one of Japheth's sons. Japheth's father was Noah. Gog is referred to as the "chief prince of Mesheck and Tubal" (Ezekiel 38:2). "Chief prince" is translated in the *New American Standard Bible* as "prince of Rosh." "Rosh" is the root for "Russia." This seems to be the land referred to in Scripture as "the land north of Israel."[68]

"Gog" refers to the leader of this invasion. "Magog," as we have indicated, is a reference to what is modern-day Russia. The country of Russia will invade with an alliance or confederation of nations or regions. This confederacy, allied with Russia, according to Ezekiel 38:5-6, consists of Persia, Cush, Put, Gomer, and "Beth-Togarmah from the far north with all its troops."

The current names for these nations or regions include: Iran (Persia); Black African Nations (Cush); North African nations such as Libya, Algeria, Tunisia, Morocco, Mauritania, Sudan, and Northern Ethiopia (Put); Turkey (Gomer); and people to the north of Caucasus Mountains and eastward (Beth-togarmah from the far north). This rather large confederation has one thing in common. They are primarily Islamic. Muslims regard Jerusalem as the third holiest site in Islam and they detest the Jewish nation of Israel. Muslims refer to Israel as the "Zionist nation." As a side note, it is of interest to note that Russia not only leads an Islamic Confederacy, but it is rapidly moving toward becoming an Islamic nation. By mid-century, the Russian Federation will be majority Muslim. Of the

10 million people in Moscow, 2.5 million are Muslim. This is a quarter of the population. Ethnic Russians are in net population decline. In contrast, the Muslim population has increased by 40% in the last 15 years. Seven out of ten Russian pregnancies are aborted; by contrast, in Muslim communities, the fertility rate is 10 babies per woman. If a Muslim military coup occurs, Russia will become another Muslim nuclear power (the first with a permanent seat on the U.N. Security Council)" (*The Toronto Star*, SteynOnline.com, *National Review,* Dec. 18, 2006).

Russia and the Muslim Confederacy will invade Israel during a time of peace. Israel is not currently experiencing a time of peace. The Bible does not give a time period for this invasion, but we know that it happens when Israel is "at rest" and feels secure "without walls or gates" (Ezekiel 38:8, 11). This invasion will most likely take place at the opening of the second seal toward the middle of the Tribulation Period.

At the middle of the Tribulation, the Antichrist will set himself up in the rebuilt Jewish Temple and declare himself to be God. According to 2 Thessalonians 2:4 (NIV), "He will oppose and will exalt himself over everything that is called God or is worshiped, so that he sets himself up in God's temple, proclaiming himself to be God." He will also stop temple sacrifices (Daniel 9:27). He will set himself up to be worshipped in the temple. This event is called the "abomination that causes desolation" predicted by the prophet Daniel. "This will be the sign that immediately precedes the Russian-led Islamic invasion of Israel." [69]

When the Antichrist desecrates the temple and sets himself up to be worshipped, the Jews will then reject him. The Antichrist will break his peace covenant as the Russian-Muslim invasion begins. Up until that time, Israel will have had the protection and backing of the Antichrist and the European Union (revived Roman Empire). Once Russia and the Islamic nations detect a weak link in the chain, by way of the chaos in Israel over the desecration of their temple, they will invade Israel (Ezekiel 38).

Prior to this Russian invasion, the Antichrist will rule the Western nations but not the World. There will then be an escalation in power from Western leader to World leader (Revelation 13:7). How will this shift in power take place?

THE BALANCE OF POWER: GOD'S STRATEGY

Ezekiel 38 and 39 show God's wrath against Russia. When Israel was freed from Egyptian captivity under the leadership of Moses, God hardened Pharaoh's heart to pursue the Israelites, so God would be honored through Pharaoh and all his army (Exodus 14:4).

In a similar way, God uses the Russian leader (Gog) to come against Israel. "... Thus says the Lord GOD, 'Behold, I am against you, O Gog, prince of Rosh, Meshech and Tubal. I will turn you about and put hooks into your jaws, and I will bring you out, and all your army, horses and horsemen ...' " (Ezekiel 38:3-4). Verse 16 says, "and you will come up against My people Israel like a cloud to cover the land. It shall come about in the last days that I shall bring you against My land, so that the nations may know Me when I am sanctified through you before their eyes, O Gog."

Russia and its Muslim allies will invade Israel so that the nations will recognize the one true God (v. 16). This invasion will arouse the fury and anger of God (v. 18). The Lord will destroy most of Russia (Ezekiel 38:19–39:6). This is done either directly by supernatural means or indirectly through a nuclear exchange. The end result of Russia's destruction is summed up in Ezekiel 39:7, "My holy name I shall make known in the midst of My people Israel; and I shall not let My holy name be profaned anymore. And the nations will know that I am the LORD, the Holy One in Israel."

THE VACUUM: A POWER SHIFT

The destruction of Russia will be so great that it will take seven months for the Israelites to finish burying the dead in order to cleanse the land (Ezekiel 39:12). After Russia is overthrown, the Federated States of Europe, under the Antichrist, will move into the vacuum, with the Antichrist assuming the role of world leader. "Then there will be one world government, one world religion (worship of the Antichrist), one world dictator with no competition from the 'king of the North.' "[70]

When Russia is destroyed, many Jews will turn to God. "And the house of Israel will know that I am the LORD their God from that day onward" (Ezekiel 39:22).

RUSSIAN UPDATE

When reading Chapter 38 of Ezekiel, we know that the Russian leader, Gog, will probably be a powerful military leader. In 1998, Hal Lindsay authored the book, *Planet Earth: The Final Chapter*. He said,

"There is every probability that the next president of Russia will be a military strongman who will be bent upon re-establishing Russia's former super-power status ... I believe that the military strongman must come before the events of Ezekiel take place."[71]

This has occurred quickly. On Friday, December 31, 1999, President Boris Yeltsin abruptly resigned, and Prime Minister Vladmir Putin was his chosen successor. The *Dallas Morning News* reported on January 1, 2000.[72]

> After the announcement, Mr. Putin—a former spy who was named prime minister five months ago—took control of Russia's formidable nuclear arsenal and announced that there would be no change in the nation's foreign policy objectives.[72] Mr. Putin launched the war in Chechnya after his August appointment as premier, his popularity soared among the public hungry for a strongman ... "With his law-and-order stance, Mr. Putin, a KGB spy for 16 years, seems less the heir to Mr. Yeltsin than to Mr. Primokov, another longtime KGB operative ..."[73]

Lindsey seems to have been right on target. Mr. Putin launched the war on Chechnya, he is considered a "strongman," he took control of Russia's nuclear arsenal, and he was formerly a spy and a KGB agent. Mr. Putin may very well be "Gog" of Ezekiel 38. Putin's term in office ended in 2008. After promoting Dmitry Medvedev to be his successor, Medvedev won the presidential election and was sworn in on May 7, 2008. Two hours later, Medvedev nominated Putin as prime minister. Putin may very well continue his "strongman" role through Medvedev. In time it will become obvious who Russia's real leader is.

WAR, FAMINE, POVERTY

War takes a heavy toll. Nuclear war will most likely characterize the Great Tribulation period. The toll it will take on mankind is unimaginable. In the gospel of Matthew, Jesus said, "For then there will be a great tribulation, such as has not occurred since the beginning of the world until now, nor ever will" (Matthew 24:21).

Prior to 1945, the symbolic interpretation dominated the Book of Revelation. After 1945, the results of a nuclear holocaust could be envisioned. Calvin and Luther saw Revelation as a book of symbols and confusing images. Today, the things described in prophecy take on substance.[74]

The description of the destruction of Russia in Ezekiel 38:19-22, could be describing the effects of a nuclear explosion. Although God initiates the invasion of Israel and causes the destruction of Russia, He may accomplish this supernaturally or through a nuclear weapon such as Israel's neutron bomb. "The Israeli defense forces have highly developed battlefield nukes called 'neutron bombs.' They are nicknamed 'dial a nuke' in reference to the precision with which they can be programmed just before being deployed … And they only destroy living flesh."[75]

The effects of the neutron bomb would match the description found in Zechariah 14:12. "Now this will be the plague with which the LORD will strike all the peoples who have gone to war against Jerusalem; their flesh will rot while they stand on their feet, and their eyes will rot in their sockets, and their tongue will rot in their mouth." Hebrews 10:31 warns, "It is a terrifying thing to fall into the hands of the living God." God's Word is true, as will be demonstrated during the Great Tribulation.

THE BLACK HORSE: STARVATION AND POVERTY
[THIRD SEAL]

The breaking of the third seal reveals a black horse. The rider has a pair of scales in his hands (Revelation 6:5). War, famine, and poverty have traditionally gone hand in hand. Revelation 6:6 says, "And I heard something like a voice in the center of the four living creatures saying, 'A quart of wheat for a denarius, and three quarts of barley for a denarius; and do not damage the oil and the wine.' " A denarius was equivalent to one day's wages for one person. Thus, a day's wages would only pay for your food for that day. This excludes dependents and other expenses. Inflation skyrockets; money loses its value.

THE PALE HORSE: DEADLY RIDER
[FOURTH SEAL]

When the Lamb broke the fourth seal, I heard the voice of the fourth living creature saying, "Come." I looked, and behold, an ashen horse; and he who sat on it had the name Death; and Hades was following with him. Authority was given to them over a fourth of the earth, to kill with sword and with famine and with pestilence and by the wild beasts of the earth. (Revelation 6:7-8)

The fourth seal speaks of the death of the physical body. Hades speaks of the claim for the soul and spirit of men. Death and Hades in this passage refer to unbelievers. John sees a pale horse, which, according to the Greek text, means pale green. The unveiling of the fourth seal reveals a universal destruction of one fourth of the population, as a result of war and famine. This follows as the Antichrist rises in power to dominate the world.[76]

FOUR HORSEMEN: AN OVERVIEW OF THE TRIBULATION PERIOD

The first seal—the white horseman—covers the first half of the Tribulation Period. The next three seals (horsemen) cover the last half, the Great Tribulation Period. The judgments—seals, trumpets, and bowls—cannot be viewed only in a consecutive manner.

They build on, and overlap, each other. For example, the second seal is the red horse that represents war. This seal, meaning war, continues throughout the remainder of the Tribulation Period and coincides with the other judgments.

The judgments can be viewed simultaneously, consecutively, and telescopically as Chart 11, "Interrelationships Of Seal, Trumpet, and Bowl Judgments," illustrates. For a detailed listing and description of the seal, trumpet, and bowl judgments with references, see Appendix C: List of Tribulation Judgments (Seals, Trumpets, and Bowls).

BLOOD OF THE MARTYRS [FIFTH SEAL]

When the Lamb broke the fifth seal, I saw underneath the altar the souls of those who had been slain because of the word of God, and because of the testimony which they had maintained; and they cried out with a loud voice, saying, "How long, O Lord, holy and true, will you refrain from judging and avenging our blood on those who dwell on the earth?" (Revelation 6:9-10)

The breaking of the fifth seal gives us a picture in heaven through John's eyes. It is a picture of the souls of the slain martyrs who died because of their faithfulness to the gospel of Jesus Christ. They ask how long God will refrain from judging and avenging their blood. "There comes a time when mercy has run its full course and God must execute judgment, so those people cry out that God might avenge them." [77]

The Antichrist engages in a mass killing of Christians. Everyone who accepts Christ during this period becomes the target of his fury.

CONVULSIONS OF PLANET EARTH
[SIXTH SEAL]

I looked when He broke the sixth seal, and there was a great earthquake; and the sun became black as sackcloth made of hair, and the whole moon became like blood ... The sky was split apart like a scroll when it is rolled up, and every mountain and island were moved ... the commanders and the rich and the strong and every slave and free man ... said to the mountains and to the rocks, "Fall on us and hide us from the presence of Him who sits on the throne, and from the wrath of the Lamb." (Revelation 6:12-16)

The opening of the sixth seal may signify a condition where world anarchy reigns. [78] This convulsing of the planet may result from a nuclear counter attack against Russia and its Muslim allies by the Antichrist. Revelations 6:14 says, "The sky was split apart like a scroll ..." This is a description of the atmospheric effect from a nuclear blast. [79]

This sixth seal description reads like a hell on earth. This will not be a good time to be alive. This span of time known as the Great Tribulation, which covers the last half of the Tribulation Period, is mankind's worst nightmare. If you don't know Jesus Christ as your Savior and Lord, now is the time to ask Him into your life. Do it now. Don't wait until after the Rapture. You may run out of time.

ECOLOGICAL HORRORS
[SEVENTH SEAL]
INTRODUCTION OF THE TRUMPET JUDGMENTS

When the Lamb broke the seventh seal, there was silence in heaven for about half an hour. And I saw the seven angels who stand before God, and seven trumpets were given to them. ... The first sounded, and there came hail and fire, mixed with blood, and they were thrown to the earth; and a third of the earth was burned up, and a third of the trees were burned up, and all the green grass was burned up. (Revelation 8:1-2, 7)

An ominous silence in heaven precedes the introduction of the trumpet judgments. The seventh seal also introduces the trumpet judgments, which are sometimes referred to as the judgment of thirds. The seal judgments are sometimes referred to as fourths. The earth is being systematically destroyed because of man's rebellious nature. He is unwilling to repent.

The scene of the seventh seal is in heaven. It is God's response to the prayers of the true believers in Jesus Christ. Revelation 8:4-5 says, "And the smoke of the incense, with prayers of the saints, went up before God out of the angel's hand. Then the angel took the censer and filled it with the fire of the altar, and threw it to the earth; and there followed peals of thunder and sounds and flashes of lightning and an earthquake."

God answers the prayers of the saints in the trumpet and bowl judgments. Each judgment escalates the destruction of the earth, combined with torment and death to mankind. "The seal judgments were rather general. The trumpet judgments are more specific. They are drastic but not universal."[80]

The first four trumpets describe what could be man-made disasters, possibly the result of nuclear warfare. The kind of destruction involved in the first two trumpets include:

First Trumpet Judgment: Hail, fire, blood, and the destruction of one-third of earth, trees, and all grass (Revelation 8:7).

Second Trumpet Judgment: One-third of seas become blood, one-third of sea creatures die, one-third of ships destroyed (Revelation 8:9).

A nuclear blast would cause ice and fire to fall to the earth. The blood is self-explanatory. "The kind of destruction John describes is what today's 'think tanks' theorize will happen if all of these nations let a few of their favorite nukes fly at their favorite enemies."[81]

Third Trumpet Judgment: Refers to a star falling from heaven like a torch on a third of the rivers and springs of waters. The star is called "Wormwood." Many people will die because the waters will be made bitter (Revelation 8:10-11).

Although the actual composition of "Wormwood" is not clear, "the preposition used in Greek is clear that it is of extraterrestrial origin."[82] This may be the result of a comet or meteor. Whatever the nature of the cause, from a human standpoint, it is an awesome judgment of God resulting in the loss of many lives.

Fourth Trumpet Judgment: One-third of the light from the sun, moon, and stars will be blocked out (Revelation 8:12). "Just as the first three trumpets dealt with a third of the earth, so the fourth trumpet dealt with a third of the heavens."[83]

Given the likelihood of a nuclear holocaust prior to the fourth trumpet, it is reasonable to expect what scientists call the "nuclear winter" effect. There is so much debris kicked up into the atmosphere that day turns into night.[84]

There is no way to know exactly how the light from the sun, moon, and stars will be decreased by one-third. We can see a similarity of some of these judgments to the plagues in Egypt. For example, the Lord caused darkness as one of the plagues over the Egyptians (Exodus 10:21-22).

The first four trumpets were primarily against nature (ecological damage). The last three trumpets are more severe and are directed against mankind.[85] "To this point, all the destruction, havoc, and misery that we have witnessed have been essentially man-made. God ordained it in heaven, but he allowed it to take place through natural means."[86]

THE FINAL TRUMPETS: THE DEMONIC TRUMPETS

The three final trumpet judgments are supernatural, demonic, and directed against mankind.

The Fifth Trumpet takes on a supernatural demonic nature against only unbelievers. "Then the fifth angel sounded, and I saw a star from heaven which had fallen to the earth; and the key to the bottomless pit was given to him. He opened the bottomless pit ..." (Revelation 9:1-2).

Walvoord and Zuck provide an interpretation of these two verses. In reference to the "he" in verse 2, and "king" in verse 11, they conclude that the star is probably a personality. The identity of the star probably represents Satan being cast out of heaven (v. 9). The "abyss" is considered the home of the demons (Luke 8:31; Revelation 9:11; 11:7; 17:8; 20:1, 3). In Romans 10:7 (KJV), it is translated "deep."[87]

Out of the pit will come creatures referred to as "locusts," but with a deadly sting like scorpions (Revelation 9:3, 5). These demonic creatures will manifest themselves as locusts. We know these locusts will be demonic beings because of verse 11. "They have as king over them, the angel of the abyss; his name in Hebrew is Abaddon ..." "Abaddon" means "destruction" or "destroyer."

These locusts will be allowed to sting any person who does not have the seal of God on his forehead. They will not be permitted to kill anyone, but they can torment those without God's seal (Revelation 9:4-6). The seal of God on the foreheads of the true believers is God's protection. This protection will extend to all believers. The torment is a judgment on men who reject Christ. The protection includes the 144,000 who are already sealed (see Revelation 7). There is a sense in which all believers are sealed (Ephesians 1:13-14). But at that time there will be a seal on their fore-heads.[88] The seal may be visible or invisible; it may be invisible to humans, but visible in the supernatural realm. Unbelievers will harden their hearts rather than turn to Christ. Revelation 9:6 says: "And in those days men will seek death and will not find it; they will long to die, and death flees from them."

THE ANTICHRIST WOULD LIKE TO SEE YOUR I.D.

During the Tribulation Period, primarily the last three and a half years, the Antichrist will require identification. This identification will allow the person to "buy or sell" (transact business) (Revelation 13:17).

As a result of terrorism, our world is quickly moving at an accelerated pace toward a massive identification process. "With an increasing move toward a cashless society, the introduction of electronic banking, the addition of electronic shopping, worldwide connectivity, and global interdependence, the prophecy of the mark of the beast seems a lot more realistic than it would have even ten years ago."[89]

Furthermore, the increase in terrorism, along with identity theft, has resulted in a movement toward a more secure system of identification. Some of the advances in this area have included: Radio Frequency Identification (RFID), Smart Cards, Biometrics, National I.D. Cards, and the consideration of chip implantation in human beings. President Bush signed a bill in 2005 that was to become effective in May 2008. It would require every citizen of the U.S. to carry a National I.D. Card in order to make certain types of transactions. This National I.D. Card is referred to as the "Real I.D." card. The Department of Homeland Security would like to nationalize a person's identity. The states have rebelled. As of June 2008, all 50 states have been granted extensions until 2011. The outcome of this bill will likely be determined under the next Administration.

As of October 2006, there was a debate in Britain as to whether the government should order every citizen to have a chip implanted with all of the information concerning that person, such as medical records, credit status, etc.[90] The fact that this was even debated confirms the rapid movement toward a world identification system where a person's identity will be marked or implanted within his or her body.

RFID couples radio frequency (RF) identification technology with highly miniaturized computers, which make it possible to identify and track products "at any point along the supply chain."[91] The products contain their own unique information in the form of an imbedded chip.

Biometrics is the use of unique biological data to identify individuals.[92] There are seven leading biometric technologies including: "facial recognition, fingerprint recognition, hand geometry, iris recognition, retina recognition, signature recognition, and speaker recognition."[93] Biometric techniques are being used at certain border crossings, international airport terminals, and various government and corporate work places.[94]

Another example of high-tech security identification is the development of the Smart Card. The Smart Card is a "credit card sized information card that can be used as an access identification card, payment card, medical records card, or a host of other 'intelligent' applications."[95] The Smart Card employs advanced microchip components, which are oftentimes coupled with RFID technologies and/or biometric information.[96]

Iris Recognition is one of the biometric technologies used for identification. On a recent personal and practical note, while in the process of writing this chapter, my wife, an attorney, handed me a computer printout from the web site of the Sheriff's office in Tarrant County, Texas. It said: "The Confinement Bureau books in approximately 32,000 inmates a year. All inmates are centrally located at the Corrections Center where they are booked, photographed, and enrolled by their iris."[97]

These advanced systems of identification are geared toward security and control. **The ultimate system for a secure identification will involve merging one's identification—card, fingerprints, etc.—directly to the individual's body.**

This ultimate form of identification and control, known as the "mark," will be used by the Antichrist during the Tribulation Period. This mark represents "… either the name of the beast [Antichrist] or the number of his name" (Revelation 13:17). This number "… is that of a man; and his number is six hundred and sixty-six" (v. 18). Whatever this mark is, it becomes personalized in two ways. The first is merging the person's identity to his or her body. The second way involves allegiance to and worship of a man—the Antichrist or beast. The person who takes the mark will have the freedom to buy and sell and make daily living transactions.

This will result in more security temporarily, but will also result in a loss of personal freedom. Christians who refuse the mark and "do not worship the image of the beast" will be killed (Revelation 13:15).

Our advanced technological systems of identification are steps toward this ultimate control and allegiance to a one-man dictator. King Nebuchadnezzar of the Babylonian Empire, the first of the four empires represented by the "Times of the Gentiles," made a requirement similar to that of the Antichrist in the Final Empire. He required worship of his image. Refusal to do so resulted in death (see Daniel 3).

Countless attempts have been made to identify what the number 666 means. "Probably the best interpretation is that the number six is one less than the perfect number seven, and the threefold repetition of the six would indicate that for all their pretensions to deity, Satan and the two beasts were just creatures and not the Creator."[98] [Note: The second beast is found in Revelation 13:11-14; 16:13, and is commonly referred to as the False Prophet.]

Just as God will seal His 144,000 Jewish evangelists right after the sixth seal in Revelation 7:4, the Antichrist will also seal his followers. A number of people will be saved during the Tribulation Period, and many will be martyred for their faith.

In this day and age (the Church Age), Christians can conceal their identity. In many cases, it is difficult to discern who really is a true believer in Jesus Christ. During the Great Tribulation, everyone will be marked either by God or by Satan (through the Antichrist). Loyalty is established. Identity will no longer be concealed.

The leader of this worship system, the one world religion, is the False Prophet. According to Dwight Pentecost, the False Prophet is characterized by the following: "He promotes the worship of the first beast (the Antichrist) … He is successful in deceiving the unbelieving world (Revelation 13:14) … he has authority in the economic realm to control all commerce (vv. 16-17); he has a mark that will establish an individual's identity for those who live in that day (v. 18)."[99]

The unholy, satanic trinity will be established, made up of the dragon, the beast, and the false prophet (Revelation 16:13). The place occupied by God the Father in his program is assumed by Satan (represented by the dragon), the place occupied by Christ is assumed by the Antichrist (represented by the first beast), and the Holy Spirit is represented by the False Prophet, who counterfeits the ministry of the Holy Spirit.[100]

Once the Antichrist has established his throne in the Jewish temple and has established an identity system, he can now go after the Jews and the believers in Jesus Christ. "If he's learned anything from history, he's learned this equation: Healthy Economy + Really Big Lie + Weak but Plausible Excuse + Someone Else to Blame = Social Control. It worked for Hitler. It seems to be working even better in the global arena."[101]

THE DEMONIC ASIAN INVASION
[SIXTH TRUMPET]

Then the sixth angel sounded, and I heard a voice from the four horns of the golden altar which is before God, one saying to the sixth angel who had the trumpet, "Release the four angels who are bound at the great river Euphrates." And the four angels, who had been prepared for the hour and day and month and year, were released, so that they would kill a third of mankind. The number of the armies of the horsemen was two hundred million; I heard the number of them. (Revelation 9:13-16)

The opening of the sixth trumpet has a flavor similar to the fifth trumpet. They both involve powerful demons or fallen angels. These four angels are demonic beings, demonstrated by the fact that they were "bound" at the river Euphrates. Good angels aren't bound. The demonic beings are then released to kill one third of mankind.

The river Euphrates was considered a natural boundary between the East and West. According to the Bible, demons are territorial and are assigned areas of authority. They are subject to Satan's authority over the world system. Human affairs are influenced by these territorial demons.[102]

These four demonic beings are the energizing force behind the 200 million-man invasion. This army comes from the East, probably China, and it crosses the river Euphrates on dry ground (Revelation 16:12).

When John wrote the Book of Revelation in the first century AD, a military force that numbered 200 million could not be imagined. Today, the Chinese army, which includes reserves, is well over 300 million.[103] This is evidence of a clear prophetic reference to a future time. This massive invasion is also referred to in the sixth bowl judgment. Time-wise, we are moving rapidly toward Armageddon.

One-third of mankind will be killed during this invasion. The remainder of mankind will refuse to repent of their murders, sorceries, immorality, or thefts (Revelation 9:21). The occult coupled with drug use is the derivative for the translation of "sorceries." It is derived from the word *pharmakeion* which is translated "pharmacies."[104] Participation in the occult and the use of drugs will be at an all-time high.

As of January 2008, the world population was 6.8 billion plus. The fourth seal kills one-fourth of the world population, and the sixth trumpet kills one-third of the remaining population. In other words, the world population is more than cut in half. This does not include deaths that have happened from the other judgments or martyrdom. In less than seven years, the world population would be reduced by at least 3.4 billion people if we were in the Tribulation Period in 2008. It is no wonder that Jesus said, "Unless those days had been cut short, no life would have been saved; but for the sake of the elect those days shall be cut short" (Matthew 24:22).

The Seventh Trumpet: See page 219 for chart and 280 for listing."

THE FINAL STRETCH: GOD'S WRATH ON EARTH – BOWL JUDGMENTS

The bowl judgments are the content of the seventh trumpet judgment. This trumpet judgment [which open opens up the seven bowl judgments] takes us to the end of the seven-year Tribulation Period. God's wrath concludes in the bowl judgments.[105]

These bowl judgments are very similar in nature to the plagues in Egypt. The difference is intensity and scope. The bowls are worldwide. Some of the bowls, like the plagues in Egypt, are inflicted only on the unbelievers.

FIRST BOWL: MALIGNANT SORES

So the first angel went and poured out his bowl on the earth; and it became a loathsome and malignant sore on the people who had the mark of the beast and who worshipped his image. (Revelation 16:2)

Only those who worship the Antichrist receive this "malignant" or cancerous sore; the believers in Jesus are spared this judgment.

SECOND BOWL:
SEA TURNS TO BLOOD / ALL SEA CREATURES DIE

The second angel poured out his bowl into the sea, and it became blood like that of a dead man; and every living thing in the sea died. (Revelation 16:3)

It is horrifying to imagine every sea creature dead and floating to the surface. The stench and disease would be unbearable. Planet earth is dying, not because of a lack of environmental concern. There is a lack of God concern. The rebellious, sinful nature of man is destroying our planet, which was created by God.

THIRD BOWL:
RIVERS AND SPRINGS TURN TO BLOOD

Then the third angel poured out his bowl into the rivers and the springs of waters; and they became blood. ... "for they poured out the blood of saints and prophets, and You have given them blood to drink. They deserve it." And I heard the altar saying, "Yes, O Lord God, the Almighty, true and righteous are Your judgments." (Revelation 16:4-7)

This is another judgment against the unbelievers. "The prayer of the martyred saints in Revelation 6:10 will be abundantly answered. They asked, 'How long, O Lord, holy and true, until You judge and avenge our blood on those who dwell on the earth?' This plague of blood is God's answer."[106] This is a judgment of vengeance on those who spilled the blood of the saints (believers in Jesus Christ).

FOURTH BOWL: MEN SCORCHED WITH HEAT

The fourth angel poured out his bowl on the sun, and the sun was given power to scorch people with fire. They were seared by the intense heat and they cursed the name of God, who had control over these plagues, but they refused to repent and glorify him. (Revelation 16:8-9 NIV)

This judgment literally turns up the heat. Men are scorched and burned by the intense heat. This may be a result of the destruction of the protective ozone layer by environmental destruction or by a supernatural move by God. This judgment is in contrast to the fourth trumpet where light diminishes by one-third. God, our Creator, has total and absolute control over our climate and weather patterns.

In spite of the intense heat and men being scorched with fire, they will not repent. In their rebellion, they will blaspheme the name of God. Not only are they seared by the heat, their hearts are also seared.

FIFTH BOWL: DARKNESS

> Then the fifth angel poured out his bowl on the throne of the beast, and his kingdom became darkened; and they gnawed their tongues because of pain, and they blasphemed the God of heaven because of their pains and their sores; and they did not repent of their deeds. (Revelation 16:10-11)

The first four bowl judgments are worldwide, and the remaining three are localized.[107] The fifth bowl judgment is focused directly toward the Antichrist. This is a special judgment to show the world where the source of their trouble lies. When the Antichrist proclaims himself as God (2 Thessalonians 2:4), he brings on God's wrath. God shows the world who the real God is.[108]

It must have astonished the apostle John when this revelation was disclosed to him—mankind suffering from sores, horrible burns from the sun, and no fresh water. They gnawed their tongues because of pain, but still they blasphemed God and refused to repent.

SIXTH BOWL: EUPHRATES RIVER DRIES UP

> The sixth angel poured out his bowl on the great river, the Euphrates; and its water was dried up, so that the way would be prepared for the kings from the east. And I saw coming out of the mouth of the dragon and out of the mouth of the beast and out of the mouth of the false prophet, three unclean spirits like frogs; for they are spirits of demons, performing signs, which go out to the kings of the whole world, to gather them together for the war of the great day of God, the Almighty. ... And they gathered them together to the place which in Hebrew is called Har-Magedon. (Revelation 16:12-16)

The sixth bowl judgment involves the drying up of the Euphrates River to prepare the way for the "kings of the east," the Asian invasion of 200 million men.

Since 1990, it is now technologically possible to dry up the Euphrates River. The water flow can be diverted at will.[109] We know that the River Euphrates will be dried up toward the end of the Tribulation Period. This can happen through a human act or through a supernatural act. God parted the Red Sea to provide an escape from Egypt for the Israelites. In the sixth bowl, the Euphrates River is dried up to provide a passageway for the final battle of Armageddon.

In Revelation 9, the sixth trumpet judgment, we saw the release of the four fallen angels (demons) who were bound at the Euphrates River. They mobilized 200 million men from the east for the invasion of Israel. Phase two of this operation is found in Revelation 16 under the sixth bowl judgment, to prepare the way by drying up the Euphrates.

Almost in the same breath, we see a release of supernatural demonic activity (Revelation 16:13-14): "… for they are spirits of demons, performing signs, which go out to the kings of the whole world, to gather them together …" (v. 14).

In the time remaining in the Great Tribulation, sorcery is at an all time high. In reference to the world religion (mystery Babylon), Revelation 18:23 says, "… all the nations were deceived by your sorcery." God reveals Satan's use of sorcery, drugs, and the occult. Hal Lindsey calls it "a world stoned out of its gourd."[110] This is the New Age movement at its zenith. It is not as subtle as it may appear today.

The demons in Revelation 16:14 go out to the "kings of the world" and "perform signs" to bring them together for the final battle. This is the battle at Armageddon.

SEVENTH BOWL: "IT IS DONE" – LIGHTNING, THUNDER, EARTHQUAKE, HAIL

"Then the seventh angel poured out his bowl upon the air, and a loud voice came out of the temple from the throne, saying, 'It is done.'" (Revelation 16:17)

The seventh bowl is characterized by lightning, thunder, hail, and a great earthquake (v. 18). The magnitude of this earthquake is beyond imagination. "The great city was split into three parts, and the cities of the nations fell. Babylon the great was remembered before God, to give her the cup of the wine of His fierce wrath. And every island fled away, and the mountains were not found. And huge hailstones, about one hundred pounds each, came down from heaven upon men; and men blasphemed God because of the plague of the hail, because its plague was extremely severe" (Revelation 16:19-21).

The Lord will literally be stoning people to death. The law requires that a blasphemer be stoned to death (Leviticus 24:16). God will be enforcing the law in a very big way.

ANTICHRIST AND FALSE PROPHET: AN ALIEN CONNECTION?

This chapter discussed the possibility of the Antichrist having an alien connection. Remember, the world is moving toward the New Age belief in monism, which is a disregard of a dualistic system (good and evil). It is an "all is one" belief system. Add ETs and UFOs to a monistic belief system, and it will produce a worldview fertile for demonic deception in the latter times. Once the Rapture has occurred, it is possible that belief in ETs and UFOs will mushroom.

Demonic activity may be disguised through the belief in aliens. There is a growing belief that aliens are our creators. The scientific community, led by NASA and various scientific academies, is continually looking for confirmation of life on other planets. Millions of people look to the skies for our space brothers to save us from our advancing planetary predicament.[111]

There is a "prevailing view that our highly evolved ancestors with incredibly advanced technology have prepared the world to receive them as our technological saviors ... the stage is set for the worship and reverence of alien entities ..."[112]

ARMAGEDDON: THE FINAL CONFLICT

The final battle of Armageddon is the culmination of a world war, possibly World War III. This battle is a result of demon spirits that will draw the kings of the whole world together for the final battle (Revelation 16:14).

The Bible describes four destructive spheres of power in the last days: the northern powers, which includes Russia; the kings of the East, Asia; the revived Roman Empire, probably under the name European Union, led by the Antichrist; and the kings of the South, Pan-Arab power.[113]

This final battle will produce a blood bath that cannot be rivaled. Revelation 14:20 states, "And the wine press was trodden outside the city, and blood came out from the wine press, up to the horses' bridles, for a distance of two hundred miles."

"Armageddon" is a translation from the Greek *Harmagedon,* which is the transliteration of the Hebrew words for "Mount (*har*) of Megiddo." "That mountain is near the city of Megiddo and the plain of Esdraelon, the scene of many Old Testament battles."[114] The final battle of Armageddon in Revelation 16 is portrayed from God's point of view. In Revelation 19, we see the final battle from man's point of view.[115]

HEAVEN'S INVASION

And I saw (heaven opened, and behold, a white horse, and He who sat on it is called Faithful and True, and in righteousness He judges and wages war. His eyes are a flame of fire, and on His head are many diadems; and He has a name written on Him which no one knows except Himself. He is clothed with a robe dipped in blood, and His name is called The Word of God. And the armies which are in heaven, clothed in fine linen, white and clean, were following Him on white horses. From His mouth comes a sharp sword, so that with it He may strike down the nations, and He will rule them with a rod of iron; and He treads the wine press of the fierce wrath of God, the Almighty. And on His robe and on His thigh He has a name written, "KING OF KINGS, AND LORD OF LORDS." (Revelation 19:11-16)

Jesus came the first time two thousand years ago and suffered a cruel death on a wooden cross. He shed His blood to pay the ultimate sacrifice for man's sins. The first time He came as a lamb with a love beyond our understanding, but He will return as the Lion of Judah.

When Jesus Christ returns, He cuts through all dimensions of space and time. The infinite Lord of the universe, Jesus of Nazareth, comes back in glory. It will be beautiful to those that have turned to Him and terrifying to those who have hardened their hearts.

SECOND COMING:
(From *Mere Christianity* by C.S. Lewis)

God is going to invade alright: but what is the good of saying you are on His side then, when you see the whole natural universe melting away like a dream, and something else—something it never entered your head to conceive—comes crashing in; something so beautiful to some of us, and so terrible to others, that none of us will have any choice left? For this time it will be God without disguise; something so overwhelming that it will strike either irresistible love or irresistible horror into every creature. It will be too late then to choose your side when it has become impossible to stand up. That will not be the time for choosing; it will be the time when we discover which side we have really chosen, whether we realized it before or not. Now today, this moment is our chance to choose the right side. God is holding back, to give us that chance. It will not last forever. We must take it or leave it.[116]

THE FINAL ACT

It is a terrifying thing to fall into the hands of the living God.
— Hebrews 10:31

This will be the fate of everyone who rejects Jesus Christ. The following is a quote by Chuck Swindoll:

If our greatest need had been information,
God would have sent us an educator.

If our greatest need had been technology,
God would have sent us a scientist.

If our greatest need had been money,
God would have sent us an economist.

If our greatest need had been pleasure,
God would have sent us a treasure.

But our greatest need was forgiveness,
so God sent us a Savior!

C.S. Lewis, a professor at Cambridge University and once an agnostic, discussed man's options concerning Jesus' identity. To accept Jesus as a great moral teacher, but not accept His claim to be God, is really foolish, according to Lewis. For Jesus to be a mere man and to make the statements He made, He would have to be a "lunatic" or the "devil of Hell." Jesus "was and is the Son of God, or else a madman, or something worse."[117]

Concerning Jesus, C.S. Lewis proposes that we have only one of three choices:

1. **Jesus was a liar.**
2. **Jesus was a lunatic.**
3. **Jesus is Lord.**

There are no other alternatives. Jesus stands at the door of your heart and knocks (Revelation 3:20). His gift of salvation is free (Ephesians 2:8-9). If you would like to ask Jesus into your heart, pray the following suggested prayer (or use your own words):

Lord Jesus, I need you. Thank you for dying on the cross for my sins. I open the door of my life and receive You as my Savior and Lord. Thank you for forgiving my sins. Make me the kind of person you want me to be.

If you prayed this prayer and it was the desire of your heart, you are saved. You will spend eternity in heaven with Jesus. He promised it. You are a child of God (John 1:12). If you ask Jesus into your life prior to the Rapture, I'll meet you at the Rapture. If you pray this prayer after the Rapture, I'll meet you at the Second Coming.

The final words of Jesus in the Gospel of Matthew, "... and lo, I am with you always, even to the end of the age" (Matthew 28:20). He will never leave you and never forsake you. *Maranatha!

*Come, Lord Jesus.

NOTES:

Appendix A

New Age Apostasy

"For the time will come when they will not endure sound doctrine;
but wanting to have their ears tickled, they will accumulate for
themselves teachers in accordance to their own desires."
— 2 Timothy 4:3

DEPARTURE FROM THE FAITH

How popular is the New Age Movement, and what does it encompass? Take note of the religion section of a bookstore. You might find one shelf devoted to Bibles or biblical literature compared to eight or more shelves devoted to New Age books—psychology, philosophy, and self-help.

The New Age Movement is very broad and includes many other areas, such as parapsychology, astrology, psychic phenomena, extrasensory perception (ESP), UFOs, and the occult, to name a few. Some of the common beliefs of New Agers include: a universal force, a god within all men, reincarnation, and a "belief that Jesus and the Christ consciousness are two separate entities and that Christ is an office rather than a man."[1]

New Age philosophy is so accepted and widespread that it influences the vast majority of the population. People are influenced without even being aware of it. Today, even highly educated people follow occult practices. Thirty years ago, it would only have been those with little or no education. Our nation is not moving closer to the God of our forefathers, but to the "god of this world."

As we have stated earlier, our belief system is built on one of only two foundations or kingdoms—the kingdom of Jesus Christ or the kingdom of Satan. There is not a third foundation. One end of the New Age spectrum is witchcraft and paganism. This is obviously built on Satan's kingdom. The other end of the New Age spectrum is still demonic, but it is much more subtle.

The Eastern culture has always been open to various forms of the occult. Now the West is also mushrooming in occult practices. The generation that grew up in the sixties has been exposed to a distorted and anti-biblical worldview. This anti-biblical worldview has permeated Christian churches to such an extent that pagans have targeted them for conversion.[2] For example, a group called the Temple of Understanding, associated with the Gaia Institute and the United Nations Global Committee of Parliamentarians on Population Development, "is behind a new push to inundate Christian churches with nature worshipping propaganda."[3]

NEW AGE CLOAKS OCCULT

One end of the New Age spectrum is very subtle and easily disguises the occult. *Occult*, by definition, means "secretive or hidden from view." It hides under the cloak of "New Age Enlightenment."

The West has picked up Eastern occult practices due to an increasing dissatisfaction with life. Science and established religion have not provided answers, especially for those growing up during and after the 1960s. "Instead of turning to Christ and His church, they are filling their spiritual world with old-fashioned occultism dressed in the modern garb of parapsychology ... Eastern mysticism and numerous cults marching under the banner of the new age movement."[4]

The New Age Movement uses the appeal that people have the potential to be like God. This is the same appeal Satan used in the Garden of Eden. "The new pitch is the oldest lie of Satan; 'you will be like God' " (Genesis 3:5).[5] The great appeal of Satan's kingdom is to become like God or to become God. The emphasis is always self-centered, toward pride or pleasure. The appeal is one of self-deification. This is the prominent theme in New Age literature. It is also the prominent theme in cults.

DO ALL ROADS LEAD TO ROME?

The modern-day teaching that there are many paths to God and salvation is a lie straight from hell. A central belief of the New Age movement is that all religions are various expressions of the same God from different perspectives, from different prophets, and at different times in history. This position stresses that no one religion is more accurate or correct than any other since each person defines his own truth.[6]

The New Age Movement attempts to water down Christianity. It dilutes it, reinterprets it, or denies it. Let's look at what the Bible says for a more clear understanding.

God commanded Adam and Eve not to eat the fruit of one tree in the Garden of Eden. They could eat of any other tree except this one. If they ate of it, they would die. This is a physical death and a spiritual death that would result from sin (disobeying God). "The serpent said to the woman, 'You surely will not die! For God knows that in the day you eat from it your eyes will be opened, and you will be like God, knowing good and evil" (Genesis 3:4-6). Let's examine each point of this dialogue.

1. **"You surely shall not die."** Satan is saying, "Don't believe God. He lied to you."
2. **"The day you eat from it ... you will be like God ..."** He appealed to Eve's pride, a desire to be like God. He lied to Eve and tempted her with the belief that she would be exalted, equal to God.
3. **"Knowing good and evil."** This is true. Eve now had the knowledge of good and evil.

Note that Satan inserted one true statement with two false statements. He still operates in the same fashion. The gospel of John says of Satan, "... for he is a liar and the father of lies" (John 8:44). "... Satan disguises himself as an angel of light" (2 Corinthians 11:14). He lies and disguises himself. **He gives enough truth so you will believe the lies that are mixed in with it.** A perfect modern-day example of this can be seen in the popular novel and movie, *The DaVinci Code*. Dan Brown, the author, combines actual historical facts with lies and fiction. The lies and facts are interwoven within the novel to lead the reader, or the audience watching the movie, to doubt God's Word, i.e., to deny the divinity of Christ and to undermine the credibility of the New Testament.

Universalism is another lie. It promotes the belief that there are many paths to God. While this may be a "politically correct" theology in our day, it is the neopaganism of the New Age. People who buy into universalism are risking where they will spend eternity on a gamble that the Bible is wrong.[7] Jesus said, " … I am the way, and the truth, and the life; no one comes to the Father but through Me" (John 14:6).

It is important to determine our source of authority. What is our standard, or reference point, to distinguish truth from error? "The Unitarian Universalist movement holds that personal experience, conscience, and reason should be the final authorities in religion. The Unitarian Universalist Church claims that, in the end, religious authority lies not in a book, or person, or institution, but in the self."[8]

Thus, the Universalist position that "religious authority lies not in a book … but in the self" is erroneous. It does not provide any reliable road to the truth. Truth gained through personal experience with self as the reference point may be quite different than someone else's truth. This truth is subjective, rather than an objective reality.

Truth does exist as an objective reality, grounded in history, and revealed in the Bible. This reality consists of biblical revelation and was historically revealed in the person of Jesus Christ. "For by Him all things were created, both in the heavens and on earth, visible and invisible, whether thrones or dominions or rulers or authorities—all things have been created through Him and for Him. He is before all things, and in Him all things hold together" (Colossians 1:16-17). This is a reality regardless of one's personal experience or human reasoning.

True Christianity is not a man-made religion, but it involves a personal relationship with Jesus Christ. God loved you so much that He sent His Son to pay the price for your sins through His death on a cross. The only thing He requires is that you believe in Him (John 3:16); then ask Him into your life and accept His forgiveness of your sins (Revelation 3:20). You can do that right now by a prayer using your own words. God knows your heart. Salvation is a gift and cannot be earned (Ephesians 2:8-9), but it must be accepted (Revelation 3:20; Romans 10:9).

THE GOSPEL ACCORDING TO THE NEW AGE

When we look at the New Age Movement and literature, it is important to stay grounded in God's Word as our reference point. Any reference point originating from self or personal experience will throw us off track.

Remember that Satan's mode of operation involves lying, distorting, or reinterpreting. The New Age gospel is an example of Satan interpreting and distorting God's Word.

According to Redfield, author of *The Celestine Prophecy*, "All the things you took for granted now need new definition, especially the nature of God and your relationship to God."[9] Redfield's book helps provide those new definitions, according to his view.

The opening page of *The Celestine Prophecy* quotes Daniel 12:3-4. "Those who have insight will shine brightly like the brightness of the expanse of heaven, and those who lead the many to righteousness, like the stars forever and ever. But for you, Daniel, conceal these words and seal up the book until the end of time; many will go back and forth, and knowledge will increase."

This book quotes God's Word, yet, has nothing to do with God's Word or the correct interpretation of the prophecy given to Daniel by God. From a biblical perspective, this book is a clear example of distorting God's Word.

A number of sources within New Age literature attempt to create their own gospel and then attempt to use the Bible to back their beliefs. Barbara Hubbard, author of *The Revelation*, "helps us" redefine what God really meant by some of the names and terms in the Bible. She states, "These words, 'Virgin Mary,' 'Jesus,' 'the elect,' 'Israel,' the 'New Jerusalem,' must be reinterpreted now. They do not relate to doctrines, ideologies, institutions, powers, or principalities. They relate to human potentials in every person on Earth."[10]

Again, we come to the question of authority. What authority gives Hubbard the right to redefine these biblical terms? Her answer is in the preface of *The Revelation*. "This book, and the larger *Book of Co-Creation* from which it comes, was inspired by my direct experience of Christ in 1980 ... I experienced the Christ as a living presence guiding us through the great transition to universal life. He seemed to me to be our potential self."[11]

Her authority is based on her personal experience with "the Christ" whom she defined as our "potential self." She relies on her own experience, in which she is her own reference point.

What does God's Word say about her definition of His terms? "But know this first of all, that no prophecy of Scripture is a matter of one's own interpretation" (2 Peter 1:20).

Scripture is our authority, not voices or visions. If a person's experience confirms God's Word, it is valid. If the experience contradicts or redefines God's Word, it is not from God. God does not contradict Himself. "... any kingdom divided against itself is laid waste ..." (Matthew 12:25).

What does the New Age gospel proclaim about man's basic nature? Hubbard's personal experience provides the answer in a quote allegedly from Jesus. She states that Jesus told her, "I, Jesus, have come to inform you that humanity is innocent of the conscious intent to reject God. You have been infected by a disease of a higher being other than your own ... This awareness of your innocence is essential for your salvation."[12]

Once again we look to Scripture. Can Hubbard's quote, attributed to Jesus, be validated by God's Word? The answer is an emphatic, "No." Genesis 8:21 says, "... for the intent of man's heart is evil from his youth ..." Romans 3:23 says, "[F]or all have sinned and fall short of the glory of God."

Once again, the Bible contradicts the New Age gospel. This gospel, the New Age, has a supernatural power and purpose that serves as its driving force. As shown, it is contrary to God's Word and is fueled by the demonic world, Satan's kingdom.

In the coming Tribulation Period, during a horrible time of judgment (Matthew 24:21-22), a man will come to power who will rule the world. He will be the epitome of evil, empowered by Satan, and will deceive many people (2 Thessalonians 2:4-10).

What makes the New Age gospel so attractive to so many people when we already have the Gospel of Jesus Christ? One explanation is that the acceptance of the Biblical Gospel means acceptance of personal accountability to our Creator. Most of mankind refuses to acknowledge or accept that accountability.[13]

The alternative gospel of the New Age requires no accountability. This is more appealing and is in line with what the Bible predicts. "For the time will come when they will not endure sound doctrine; but wanting to have their ears tickled, they will accumulate for themselves teachers in accordance to their own desires" (2 Timothy 4:3). Sadly, many people are looking for knowledge and power in all the wrong places.

Remember, there are two foundations and two kingdoms. One is God's kingdom and is built on a rock. The other is Satan's kingdom and is built on sand. If Satan deceives you into believing a lie, he controls that area of your life.[14]

PROPHECY ACCORDING TO THE NEW AGE

Our focus has been on biblical prophecy, the reliability of the Bible, and how to discern a belief system that is a counterfeit of God's truth as revealed in His Word. God's Word establishes that there are two supernatural kingdoms. One is God's kingdom that is built on a rock foundation—Jesus Christ and God's Word. The other is Satan's kingdom that is built on a foundation of lies without substance. Satan, the father of lies, attacks God's truth in every area. Satan disguises himself as an angel of light (2 Corinthians 11:14).

In New Age literature, Jesus is never called Messiah or Savior. Rather, He is referred to as a great man, one whom we all have the potential to be, a Christ. Jesus Christ is removed and a New Age Christ, or none at all, is substituted.[15]

Numerous New Age authors predict a "rapture" event when large numbers of people disappear. Some New Age writers describe this disappearance as space ships removing people like "Beam me up, Scotty" in the *Star Trek* series. Others talk in terms of "vibrations" accelerating until people disappear. In *The Revelation*, Hubbard states, "Those vehicles which you have called UFOs are moving in ultra high frequencies, and they slow down to 'appear' and quicken to 'disappear.' You shall do the same, and shall be taken up in the fullness of time in those vehicles in your quickened condition."[16]

Going back to our reference point—the Bible—we can assess this New Age prediction. The Bible refers to a "Rapture" event. The actual words used are "caught up." In Latin the word for "caught up" is *rapturo*, from which comes the word "rapture." This is when Jesus Christ removes His true followers from this planet to be with Him. The Bible described this event in the following way.

"For the Lord Himself will descend from heaven with a shout, with the voice of the archangel, and with the trumpet of God, and the dead in Christ shall rise first. Then we who are alive and remain will be caught up together with them in the clouds to meet the Lord in the air, and so we shall always be with the Lord" (1 Thessalonians 4:16-17).

This great disappearance, commonly referred to as the Rapture, will happen, but it will not be the result of vibration levels or UFOs.

Satan is preparing an unbelieving world for this event, so people left behind, who will live during the Tribulation Period, can somehow explain it away. Once again, he is distorting God's Word through the New Age prophets, so the people left behind (after the Rapture) will believe a lie.

ONE WORLD GOVERNMENT,
ONE WORLD RELIGION, ONE TRIGGER

The stage is set for a one world government and a one world religion. Both are symbolized by the image of the harlot, "Babylon the Great," riding on a beast. The harlot represents the false religion, and the beast represents the Revived Roman Empire and the Antichrist. He is identified with a one world government (Revelation 17:3, 11-12).

The groundwork has been laid by the knowledge explosion, high tech communication systems, the "Babel reversal" (communication across languages), and, finally, the manipulation of the media.

We have also seen how the stage is set for a one world false religion. We have explored the New Age movement—its scope, acceptance, and popularity. We have reviewed the movement away from the one true God and His Word through universalism and the increase in the occult. We have seen how the New Age distorts God's Word to form a New Age gospel and its own predictions of the future to deceive large populations. Ancient paganism has re-emerged and has become acceptable in many different forms. With the stage set to activate both a world government and a world religion, the next step requires a catalyst or a cataclysmic event. The current status could be compared to the completion of the electrical wiring in a large building. Nothing is left undone. In order to activate the power within the building, a switch has to be thrown.

The catalyst, or trigger mechanism, could be a number of possible events. One possibility is a nuclear incident caused by terrorism. This is a very real possibility. Many experts say the question is not, "*Will* a terrorist set off a nuclear device or employ a weapon of mass destruction (WMD)," but "*When* will it happen?" Another possibility is a UFO threat. In Geneva in 1985, world leaders Ronald Reagan and Mikhail Gorbachev discussed ways to end the cold war. According to several sources, Reagan stated, "If suddenly there was a threat to this world from other species from another planet, we'd forget all the little local differences that we have between our countries, and we would find out once and for all that we are really all human beings on this earth together."[17]

This is a very possible reality. Whitley Streiber, a well-known author and expert in the area of the UFO phenomenon, believes that one unde-niable UFO sighting would have a major global impact. "… [A] global, ecumenical religion that generates 'beliefs so broad in their scope and deep in their impact' could be built around a UFO motif. All that is need-ed, according to Streiber is 'a single undeniable sighting.' "[18]

The goals of the New Age movement involve creating world peace through a one world spiritual system and a one world governmental system with a leader of their choosing. Their covert goals are to destroy all systems based on the Bible in the beginning of the Age of Aquarius, A.D. 2000.[19]

We are currently in the early stages of the Age of Aquarius. It is easy to observe the deterioration of Bible-based systems.

Appendix B

The UFO Grand Deception

The March 2000 cover of *Life* magazine featured the subject, *UFOs —Why do we believe?* The article on page 48, "The Search for Extraterrestrial Life," contained the following statement:

> Meanwhile, according to a *Life* poll, 30 percent of us think aliens have already landed. The number of Americans who say they have been abducted is "staggering," says one St. Louis psychiatrist. Harvard Medical School's John Mack has treated hundreds and has a new book out. There are 300 UFO organizations, 38 UFO magazines. China reportedly has 40,000 ufologists.

THE MEXICO FLAP

Mexico City became the site of one of the best-documented reports of UFO sightings in recorded history. The event occurred on January 1, 1993, at 2:00 p.m. On this date, thousands of people sighted a UFO during the daytime. Reports swamped radio stations; television stations broadcast the sighting. Traffic was snarled as people left their cars to view the shiny metal disc in the sky.[1]

Even though it was publicized, documented, and witnessed by thousands, it was not reported in the U.S. news. There were also numerous videotapes of the incident. Since the early 1990s, many UFO sightings have occurred over Mexico. The sightings have been by pilots, citizens, and government authorities. "Although the sightings have been thoroughly covered in the Mexican press, ... the majority of the populace has become desensitized to their presence and ... view the sightings as 'routine.' While opinions vary, many of the witnesses believe that the Mexican flap represents the fulfillment of ancient Mayan or biblical prophesies."[2] A "flap" is a large number of sightings in a short period of time.

THE ISRAEL FLAP

Since 1996, there have been hundreds of reports in Israel of sightings of UFOs. According to *UFO Reality*, UFOs began to appear in 1996 in Israel, Iran, and Australia. Mass eyewitness reports came in, including intervention by police and the army. "The succession of reports is so staggering that it is already impossible to keep track of the hundreds of thousands of eyewitness reports that pour in each day."[3]

One well-documented sighting occurred in 1996 in Israel. A group of fifty people watched a UFO at 2:30 a.m. One official described the event, "... like a giant tent full of lights, light up the sky above two residential districts. The UFO passed just over our heads at a height of not more than 100 to 200 meters. The event lasted close to ten minutes. Suddenly, without any advance warning, it disappeared."[4] Israel is well known for its UFO sightings. "Israel is recognized as an international UFO hot spot —with an unsurpassed quantity and quality of evidence."[5]

ROSWELL INCIDENT

This is one of the best-known UFO events in history and is also believed by many to be one of the biggest cover-ups in history. The following will briefly review the incident at Roswell, New Mexico.

In July 1947, Mac Brazel, a local New Mexico rancher, went to check his sheep after an intense thunderstorm the previous night. He discovered a lot of debris, including a crashed disk and a shallow gouge several hundred feet long. He took the debris to authorities at Roswell Army Air Field.

On July 8, 1947, Colonel William Blanchard, Commander of the 509th Bomb Group, issued an official press release about the "crashed disk." It appeared in many major U.S. newspapers.

Hours later, a second press release was issued by General George

Ramey, Commander of the Eighth Air Force at Fort Worth Army Air Field in Texas. This rescinded the first press release, claiming that Colonel Blanchard made a mistake, and described the debris and crashed disk as a "weather balloon and its radar reflector." This was followed by fifty years of cover up.

There was too much evidence to continue the cover up. In 1994, Steven Schiff, United States Congressman from New Mexico, told the press that he was stonewalled by the Defense Department regarding the 1947 Roswell event. Congressman Schiff, planning to do a further investigation, said the Defense Department's refusal to respond was astounding and was another government cover-up.[6]

Since the Freedom of Information Act, further attempts were made to obtain UFO documents. The government claims they cannot be released or do not exist. Government agencies have continued to hide behind national security. "… UFOs appear to involve the highest categories of security classifications available."[7]

THE UFO WORLDVIEW

Our beliefs determine our behavior and attitudes. We have discussed historical worldviews from the viewpoints of philosophy, psychology, and religion, including New Age and occult beliefs. This brings us to belief in UFOs and extraterrestrials.

Worldviews have changed over the last fifty to 100 years in areas such as philosophy and the New Age movement, and people have increasingly accepted the reality of UFOs. For example, Missler and Eastman in their book, *Alien Encounters*, state, "… we have been conditioned by an unparalleled media fixation with UFOs and extraterrestrials. Now more than 75 percent of Americans believe extraterrestrials exist and have been visiting us for millennia."

There is a sufficient amount of evidence to support the existence of UFOs and actual alien encounters. Despite this preponderance of evidence, the government and military have taken extreme measures to cover up the UFO phenomenon.

The general belief in UFOs and ETs is becoming so prevalent that people tend to accept the whole UFO and ET phenomena. What does this belief mean, and how does it affect you and me personally?

Missler and Eastman provide an answer. If UFOs and ETs are real, this "will lead to the biggest challenge ever faced by mankind. If these things are not real, they bear evidence of a gigantic delusion—one that is being orchestrated with a political end in sight ... what lies behind these strange events will soon affect every living person on this planet."[8]

SCIENCE AND THE NEW AGE PROPHETS STRUGGLE WITH THE ORIGIN OF LIFE

Some scientists have a problem dealing with the origin of life. They reject the creationist view. After all, it could not be proven scientifically. They also have a problem with the chance-probability explanation.

There is now a third explanation of the origin of life. Sir Fredrick Hoyle, a prominent astronomer, researched the spontaneous generation theory. In 1981, Hoyle expressed the following view:

> The likelihood of the formation of life from inanimate matter is one to a number with 40 thousand naughts (zeros) after it. It is enough to bury Darwin and the whole theory of evolution. ... [I]f the beginnings of life were not random they must therefore have been the product of purposeful intelligence.[9]

Hoyle was among a small number of prominent scientists who believed that life was delivered from outer space either by aliens or a comet, infected with bacteria. He did not accept the chance-probability theory or a miraculous cause for the origin of life.[10] Francis Crick, a brilliant molecular biologist, agreed with Hoyle.

Combine the beliefs of some scientists who reject the chance-probability theories and the supernatural with the belief in UFOs. The result is the Church of ET, which Missler and Eastman describe as the result of the UFO movement of the 1960s and 1970s. The theme of these UFO Churches is identical to those of Eric Von Daniken (author of *Chariots of the Gods*) and Zecharia Sitchin, an expert in Semitic languages. Life on earth was delivered and created by ETs. Humans are their children, and the ETs are returning to help us evolve into the next stage of our evolutionary process.[11]

There are numerous reports of alien abductions or encounters. People claim to have been abducted by aliens, physically examined, and have undergone surgical procedures. They have experienced amnesia, but under hypnosis they have total recall of the procedures. Many abductees have very similar experiences as recalled under hypnotic regression.

Whether UFOs and ETs are real or not is only part of a mounting problem. What mankind believes is extremely powerful. "... in today's world it is not so important whether UFOs exist as whether we believe they exist. And one in three Americans actually expects that we will be contacted by aliens within the next century." [12]

Some astronomers believe in the possibility of alien contact, and they believe the world should prepare for such an event. Ian Crawford is an astronomer in the department of physics and astronomy at University College, London. "He believes that the cosmic perspective provided by the exploration of the universe argues for the political unification of our world. He explains, '... and if we do ever meet other intelligent species out there among the stars, would it not be best for humanity to speak with a united voice?' " (*Scientific American*, July 2000, "Where Are They?" Ian Crawford). This leads us to the biblical viewpoint for the origin of "other intelligent species." The following statement represents a biblical viewpoint as well as interbreeding accounts given by abductees.

> In ancient times the ETs were referred to as gods. In our day they are referred to as Aliens or ETs. What appears to be a common denominator, both in ancient times and in the biblical account in Genesis 6, is an interbreeding of some form of ET and human beings.
>
> There seems to be a relationship between the interbreeding accounts and the reports given by abductees who have undergone physical exams by aliens. The abductees report entering the craft and being in a white room like an operating room. Then, they typically "report contact with the same gray-skinned aliens who methodically perform head to toe examinations with special attention to the genital area. In hundreds of cases, women report being probed with long metallic devices in the abdominal or genital area." [13]

WHERE DO UFOS AND ALIENS COME FROM?

While there is considerable evidence for the existence of UFOs and ETs, their origin is very controversial even among experienced UFO investigators. The common view is the "extraterrestrial hypothesis

(ETH)." This is the belief that extraterrestrials come from another star system. However, in recent years, a number of prominent UFO researchers have challenged this hypothesis as a result of well-documented accounts of UFOs defying the laws of physics.[14]

There have been UFO reports of encounters where the UFO materialized and dematerialized within our three dimensional space. Some observers have suggested UFOs might exist in a parallel universe, one orthogonal (at right angles) to our own.[15] Cosmologists Andrei Linde and Alex Vilenkin have "shown how certain mathematical assumptions lead, at least in theory, to the creation of a multiverse" (*Scientific American*, December 1999, "Exploring Our Universe and Others," Martin Rees).

The next question to explore in this discussion of UFOs, universe, multiverse, and aliens is, where does science end and religion or the supernatural begin? John Mack, a psychiatrist with more than forty years of training, believes that the dualistic view of religion and science is breaking down. Mack views the phenomenon of UFO abduction "as a merging of science and religion, the appearance of a new paradigm of thought—one in which the lines separating faith and science, religion, philosophy, the material world, and the spirit world are blurred. The result ... is a merging and unification of science, religion, philosophy, and the spiritual realm."[16] This loss of dualism in science and religion leads to a merging of these areas, including the spiritual realm, which moves us toward the New Age religion.

SCIENCE IN THE NEW AGE — HOW MANY DIMENSIONS?

Science has taken on a whole new meaning in modern times, especially in the area of physics. Out of the quantum theory and the theory of relativity, the new physics has emerged.[17]

Remember, we live in a three dimensional world. For illustration purposes, a two-dimensional world is a drawing on a flat piece of paper. When you add a third dimension, we have depth. It is the difference between a square and a cube. Our three-dimensional world includes length, width, and height. Our fourth dimension, time, is temporal.

Once we go beyond our three-dimensional existence, we move into hyperspace. These dimensions are beyond our reality and may be more in line with a multiverse, parallel universe, or the supernatural.

William Alnor, in *UFOs in the New Age*, describes the concept of a multiverse. Alnor refers to Albrecht and Alexander's work in the Spiritual Counterfeits Project 1977 *Journal on UFOs*. They describe how UFOs could be the work of beings from another dimension, and they describe and draw a two-dimensional world, "Flatland." Someone living in a two-dimensional world would have a distorted view of objects from a three-dimensional world (height, depth, width). Albrecht and Alexander take this a step further by asking the question, how would we, living in a three-dimensional world, view objects from the fourth dimension or beyond?[18]

In other words, a being in hyperspace or in a dimension beyond our three-dimensional existence would have capabilities and rules of their own geometry beyond our understanding. "Imagine a universe of only two dimensions: a flat plane. This imaginary universe is inhabited only by two-dimensional beings—we'll call them Mr. and Mrs. Flat. They can only conceive of two dimensions since that is all they are capable of experiencing directly."[19] **Any intrusion by us on their two-dimensional existence would give them a distorted view of a three-dimensional being.** In other words, if you stick a pencil through a piece of paper with a picture of Mr. and Mrs. Flat on it, all they would see is a circle where the pencil goes through the paper (two dimensional or flat view).

We have only dealt with a two- and three-dimensional existence and touched on the fourth dimension. We now know from particle physics that we live in a universe of at least ten dimensions.[20]

NEW PHYSICS: QUANTUM WHAT?

The quantum theory is extremely difficult and technical; an explanation will not be attempted here. This section looks at some of the possible implications and interpretations of the "New Physics" and how it applies to a New Age philosophy.

According to physicist Paul Davies, "[U]ncertainty is the fundamental ingredient of the quantum theory. It leads directly to the consequences of unpredictability ... The quantum factor apparently breaks the chain by allowing effects to occur that have no cause,"[21] (at least no known explainable ones).

This breaking of cause-effect relationships is a conclusion reached when the rules of physics, as currently understood, do not answer man's questions in a way that makes sense to him. By definition the word "effect" has the following meaning: "something that is produced by an agency or cause; result; consequence" (*Random House Webster's College Dictionary*).

Let's consider one of the ramifications of breaking cause-effect relationships. If one cannot scientifically draw a conclusion in any particular area based on a cause-effect relationship, one must reason that something either does not exist, exists without a cause, or exists for no apparent reason. We can only know it (whatever "it" may be) by our experience. As we have already seen, we cannot rely on experience alone to confirm a reality. In the preceding section on dimensions, we saw how a being in hyperspace (beyond our three dimensional existence) could easily deceive us through our five senses. An example of this is the materializing and dematerializing of UFOs.

When experience alone becomes man's criteria for determining reality, he is a candidate for demonic deception. Disregarding cause-effect relationships helps lay the groundwork for such a deception to take place.

Some people have drawn erroneous conclusions about quantum theory because of its complexity and their inability to understand it. For example, they erroneously believe that full account must be taken of quantum theory in the search to understand God and existence. An example of this can be seen in the following statement: "[M]any modern writers are finding close parallels between the concepts used in the quantum theory and those of Oriental mysticism, such as Zen. But whatever one's religious persuasions, the quantum factor cannot be ignored."[22]

The content of this statement suggests that man, through science, can potentially gain the knowledge necessary to understand God and existence. This also opens the door to mysticism or experience. It is interesting to note that when science, which is based on logic and cause-effect relationships, runs into an unknown, they become "religious." We are beginning to see the line between science and religion become very blurred.

Quantum theory forms one of the pillars of the "new physics and provides the most convincing scientific evidence yet that consciousness plays an essential role in the nature of physical reality."[23] By connecting consciousness to physical reality, we have a paradigm shift. Consciousness, or the perception of the observer, becomes more relevant than the external world. As stated by Paul Davies, in his book, *God and the New Physics*, "[T]his mosaic of self-reference is the essential feature of consciousness."

What we now have is an emphasis on the importance of consciousness as opposed to an external reality. **This leads directly into the evolution of consciousness, which is a dominant theme in the New Age movement.** What is also of interest is Davies' emphasis on "self-reference" as the "essential feature of consciousness."

When a scientist uses self as a reference point and applies science to understand infinite truths, he will inevitably run aground. He is attempting to reason his way into the infinite, an impossible task. Let's look at the attempt of one scientist to reason his way to the infinite.

> A God who is in time is, therefore, in some sense caught up in the operation of the physical universe. Indeed, it is quite likely that time will cease to exist at some stage in the future. ... In that case God's own position is obviously insecure. ... There is thus a grave and fundamental difficulty in reconciling all the traditional attributes of God. Modern physics—drives a wedge between God's omnipotence and the existence of his personality.[24]

This is an example of man trying through reason to understand God. The following quote from the Bible is God's answer to the preceding statement. "'For My thoughts are not your thoughts, nor are your ways My ways,' declares the Lord. 'For as the heavens are higher than the earth, so are My ways higher than your ways and My thoughts than your thoughts' " (Isaiah 55:8-9). Notice the emphasis in these two verses. It compares God's thoughts, which are infinite, to man's thoughts, which are finite. One is higher than the other. **This barrier between finite and infinite thinking cannot be crossed while in a temporal body.** Attempting to cross that line is an attempt to become like God or to bring Him down to our level.

Ultimately, using self as a reference point, can lead to the New Age concept of One Universal Mind. An example of this is found in the following statement.

> We could describe this state of affairs by saying that nature is a product of its own technology, and the universe is a mind: a self-observing as well as self-organizing system. Our own minds could then be viewed as localized "islands" of consciousness in a sea of mind, an idea that is reminiscent of the oriental conception of mysticism ...[25]

This section is not an argument against physics or quantum theory. It merely shows what happens when a scientist reaches conclusions using himself as a reference point. He also has "an exaggerated trust in the efficacy of the methods of natural science applied to all areas of investigation." This is the definition of "scientism" as quoted from *Miriam Webster's Collegiate Dictionary*, tenth edition. In other words, "scientism" is putting too much trust in the methods of science and applying them to all other areas of investigation.

Paul Davis' conclusions from his understanding of physics contrasts with another view. Hugh Ross, a minister with a Ph.D. in astronomy, discusses science's limitations and his conclusions in his book, *Beyond the Cosmos*. He states, "[I]n 1931 Australian mathematician Kurt Godel established that mathematical 'truths' exist for which we can develop no absolutely rigorous proofs. No set of axioms can be proven totally consistent. No set of axioms, then, is provably complete."[26] Ross goes on to say that "perfect insight into the physics of the cosmos will always remain beyond our capability."[27] Note that he recognizes the limitations of science and man; yet, he is a brilliant scientist. His book, *Beyond the Cosmos*, covers recent discoveries in astrophysics and what it reveals about God.

Ross' reference point is God and His Word. He states: "[T]he limits on our abilities to know truth and visualize truth merely remind us that we are the creatures, not the Creator. But the limits do not stop us from seeking to gain a clearer picture of Who He is through studying both His inspired Word and His creative work."[28]

ALIENS! WHO ARE THEY? WHAT ARE THEY SAYING?

Considering the fact that aliens and UFOs appear to exist but do not fit into the extraterrestrial hypothesis, i.e., from another star system, what options are left? We have described the inter-dimensional possibility, which means that they have the capacity to move out of a higher dimension into our three-dimensional world at will. Previously, we described this in terms of "flatland," a two-dimensional existence touched by a three-dimensional object.

We have also discussed the duality of the universe. There are two kingdoms and two foundations. There is God's kingdom and Satan's kingdom. We can therefore conclude that these ETs or aliens fit into one of these two kingdoms.

The Bible never discusses UFOs or aliens, but it does describe fallen angels and demons. The New Age literature reviewed so far concerning aliens and abductees has left out the message and gospel of Jesus Christ.

The "messages" that the "contactees" (humans on earth) receive from the "space brothers" (ETs) are distortions of God's Word concerning prophecy, if it is mentioned at all. Alnor suggests that the extraterrestrial beings give messages to humans that could lead the world into a delusion. "[I[n each of their biblical parallels concerning the end times, they have carefully excised Jesus Christ from the picture and have substituted a new age Christ, or none at all."[29]

In every way, the messages and the UFO religious movement reject traditional Judeo-Christian ideas about God, morality, and even reality itself, in favor of a new world order and an occult-based spirituality.[30] This UFO religious movement is included under the New Age umbrella.

A popular New Age UFO writer, Brad Steiger, has collected messages from the "space brothers" for years and included them in a book called, *The Fellowship*, a new type of bible. He wants the ideas to replace traditional Christianity in favor of a new world occultic faith.[31]

The new world occultic faith is really old-fashion paganism presented with a New Age disguise. As mentioned in the prior section, the UFO occult movement tends to talk in pagan terms, especially when it concerns prophecy. Contactees receive messages regarding the need for Mother Earth to be cleansed. "According to hundreds of contactees, earth changes are part of a cleansing that could be catastrophic if our space brothers didn't intervene, but they will. The ETs, we are told, have a plan to salvage our planet and prevent Earth Mother from destroying the majority of life as she cleanses herself."[32]

UFO abductees are rarely, if ever, practicing Christians. Los Angeles Christian journalist, Stuart Goldman, made the following statement based on a lengthy investigation of Whitley Strieber, author of best sellers *Communion* and *Transformation*. In an unpublished manuscript, Goldman examined the background of UFO abductees. Almost all "have some background in New Age or occultic beliefs. Interestingly, studies show that there are very few practicing Christians or Jews amongst UFO contactees. What could this mean? Are the aliens racist? Or does this, rather, indicate something about the belief systems of the abductees themselves?"[33]

The deception involved in the New Age movement is extremely powerful and is very subtle. It is seductive and deceptive enough to draw in born-again believers in Jesus Christ, especially if they have moved away from God's Word (the true standard or reference point). Christians increasingly tend to combine their faith with New Age beliefs.[34]

The following surveys were reviewed in *Jubilee* magazine, Spring 2000. According to a 1999 Gallup poll, 39% of Americans describe themselves as born-again, evangelical Christians, 25% say they are fundamentalist, while 15% say they are evangelical. Of those self-described born-again, evangelical Christians:

20% believe in reincarnation;
26% believe in astrology;
16% have visited a fortune teller; and
33% are pro-choice.

A survey of born-again Christians by the Barna Research Group (www.Barna.org), found that:

45% believe that if people are good enough, they can earn a place in heaven;
34% believe that Jesus committed sins like other people;
35% do not believe that Jesus was physically resurrected from the dead; and
45% believe that Satan is not a living being, but is a symbol of evil.

Clearly, some New Age beliefs affect most people to some degree. The UFO movement is prominent within the New Age Movement and has grown in momentum.

Christians are referred to collectively as the "Bride of Christ" (2 Corinthians 11:2). The Bible considers it spiritual adultery when a Christian becomes involved in a false religious belief system, such as the New Age Movement, the occult, witchcraft, astology, etc.[35]

THE UFO / RAPTURE CONNECTION

The Rapture will happen instantly; it will be a signless event. The Rapture will not be preceded by any particular sign. It will be an event that happens in two stages. One Bible reference concerning the Rapture is as follows:

> For the Lord Himself will descend from heaven with a shout, with the voice of the archangel and with the trumpet of God, and the dead in Christ will rise first. Then we who are alive and remain will be caught up together with them in the clouds to meet the Lord in the air, and so we shall always be with the Lord. (1 Thessalonians 4:16-17)

The "dead in Christ will rise first." This refers to Christians who have died previously. It is a resurrection of their bodies to unite with their souls. Immediately following this event, the Christians "who are alive and remain will be caught up together with them in the clouds to meet the Lord in the air."

In other words, if you are a true believer in Jesus Christ and you are alive at the time of the Rapture, you will bypass death. You will be instantly changed. You will have a glorified body as Jesus had after His resurrection.

Another Bible reference concerning the Rapture is found in 1 Corinthians. It says:

> Behold, I tell you a mystery; we will not all sleep, but we will all be changed, in a moment, in the twinkling of an eye, at the last trumpet; for the trumpet will sound, and the dead will be raised imperishable, and we will be changed." (1 Corinthians 15:51-52)

Four points from this reference explain the Rapture:

1. "Behold, I tell you a mystery." A mystery is a secret in the mind of God, as revealed through Paul. This word is used when referring to the Church Age in Ephesians 3:1-7; Romans 16:25-27; and Colossians 1:26-29.
2. "We will not all sleep." We will not all die. "Sleep" here is referring to the believer's death.
3. "But we will all be changed." The Christian's body is transformed into a glorified body.
4. "In the twinkling of an eye." It happens instantly in a fraction of a second.

From these references we can conclude the following: the "dead in Christ" are resurrected first; there is a generation of Christians who will not die; it is a mystery; Christians who are alive will have their bodies transformed; this generation of believers will go to be with Jesus Christ; and it will happen instantaneously.

THE "NEW AGE RAPTURE"

Previously, we reviewed media deception. More and more, as man becomes oriented toward a world that is ruled by Satan, he moves farther away from God's truths as set forth in His Word.

He actually goes through a desensitization process, much the same way a cold-blooded animal can be slowly boiled to death. He becomes like his environment, until it is too late.

As God permits, the world is temporarily under Satan's control, and he has power over it (1 John 5:19). As Satan deceives mankind through the media, culture, and literature, mankind is set up to believe a lie. The ones who hear the gospel and, yet, do not receive it (harden themselves toward God), God in turn sends a "deluding influence so that they will believe what is false" (2 Thessalonians 2:11).

Let's look at what form this delusion may take. We have looked at the UFO cover-up by the government for national security reasons. We have also looked at Chapter 13, "Enemy Attack and UFO Potential," in the Federal Emergency Management Agency (FEMA) 1992 training manual, *The Fire Officer's Guide to Disaster Control*.

In order for a counterfeit gospel to stand up in the last days, it would have to provide an alternative explanation for the events that will occur as a fulfillment of Bible prophecy.[36] The Star Trek mentality and "beam me up, Scotty," merely laid the groundwork for UFOs and alien encounters to provide a delusion for the remaining unbelievers after the Rapture occurs.

Second Thessalonians 2:3-10 discusses the apostasy (falling away from the truth) that is currently present, the activity of the Antichrist, and the removal of the "restrainer" (Holy Spirit who indwells every believer). This occurs by way of the Rapture of the True Church of Jesus Christ. In verse 11 of the same chapter it states, "For this reason God will send upon them a deluding influence so that they might believe what is false."

In *The Celestine Prophecy*, James Redfield states that everyone at some point "will vibrate highly enough so that we can walk into heaven in our same form."[37] It is true that a rapture of our bodies will take place, but it does not include everyone. It will only include the true believers in Jesus Christ.

Many New Age prophets believe in a disappearance or rapture by way of UFOs. Barbara Hubbard, a New Age author, makes the following statement. "Those vehicles which you have called UFOs are moving in ultra-high frequencies. They slow down to 'appear,' and 'quicken to disappear.' You shall do the same, and shall be taken up in the fullness of time in those vehicles, in your quickened condition."[38] Of course to make this trip we have to be an ascended being, which requires a quickened being, that is a quickened human, according to Hubbard. The definitions are vague.

When Christians disappear, what will the New Agers think? Will they think the wicked have been removed as some of their "prophecies" imply? Will they think the Christians were beamed aboard a spaceship? Or will they believe a different lie?

When the world is falling apart following the Rapture, will they look for salvation in a spaceship or in the God who formed the universe?[39] Or, will they look for a man, the Antichrist, who will later claim to be God (2 Thessalonians 2:4)?

It is interesting to note that many New Age prophets make predictions according to messages they receive from spirits or guides. Ruth Montgomery, a well-known New Age writer, claims to have guides that speak through her.

She speaks of the earth going through an axis shift, which will have catastrophic effects. The guides tell her that most people will remain on the planet to ride out the shift, but some will be temporarily removed. She quotes her guides as saying the following: "Now as to those being rescued," they write, "it will be a massive undertaking, but the space aliens, as you call them, will indeed be on hand to lift off some chosen earthlings who will remain in earth orbit until that planet settles back into proper rotation."[40]

There will be a removal of people from the earth, but they are the true believers in Jesus Christ. They will meet the Lord at the Rapture (1 Thessalonians 4:16-17). They will not go into "orbit" for a temporary period of time.

According to Frank Stranges, Ph.D., author of *Stranger at the Pentagon*, there are certain events that will transpire in the last days. Stranges claims that he received this message directly from an alien in human form from another planet. His first three predictions are as follows:

1. Millions will vanish from the face of the earth.
2. Children will be reported missing (remember the prediction that the space brothers will take our youngsters first), loved ones gone, graves opened.
3. Distress of nations, such as never before transpired on this planet.[41]

These predictions are very close to Bible prophecy with two critical differences. Stranges never specifies what group disappears in the vanishings. There is no reference to the disappearance of true believers in Jesus Christ. The other difference is the reference to the space brothers. There is no biblical confirmation of "space brothers."

According to some New Age literature, ETs are concerned that "Mother Earth" will destroy a majority of life as she attempts to "cleanse herself." In order to prevent this from happening, ETs have a plan to "remove, that is, evacuate the millions of people who are 'out of vibration' with Earth Mother! ... When the global situation reaches a crisis point on Earth, they will evacuate these people in a 'twinkling of an eye,' then transfer them to larger ships for re-education and initiation into higher levels of consciousness!"[42]

In this consciousness evolution we have what one New Age author refers to as the "quantum instant." In Hubbard's words, "[T]hose of you who happen to be alive at the time of the actual quantum instant will be changed while still alive. You will not have to undergo physical death or the reconstitution process."[43] She identifies the people who bypass death as the saints. This is true. When the word "saint" is used in the Bible, it refers to true believers in Christ. The author identifies saints as people who follow Jesus' example. Salvation is not following Jesus' example; it is believing that he died for your sins (John 3:16) and accepting Him into your heart (Revelation 3:20).

Satan is a master counterfeiter and disguises himself as an angel of light. This is characteristic of the New Age Movement. Truth and lies are intermingled. It is next to impossible to separate the lies from the truth without using God and His Word as your reference point. The New Age Movement is very deceptive. Christians are often deceived by it. The best choice is to stay away from it.

Missler and Eastman, Christian writers, conducted extensive research concerning messages from aliens. In *Alien Encounters*, they summarize alien messages:

In the last several decades, dozens of contactees have delivered messages from alien entities, which state that Earth changes are not the wrath of God; they are the birth pangs of our Earth Mother who is trying to expel the "dark forces" from her surface so she can evolve to a higher dimension of existence.[44]

We could continue to quote New Age prophets at length about a rapture-type event. However, the difference between a New Age rapture and the Rapture referred to in God's Word is clear.

Some people propose that the biblical Rapture and the coming alien evacuation (New Age rapture) are one and the same. They propose that the apostle Paul and Jesus were both describing a coming evacuation by extraterrestrials.[45]

The distinction between the two events is very clear. **The prediction of an alien evacuation may set the stage so the people who remain will "believe a lie"** (2 Thessalonians 2:10-11 KJV).

If you do not know Jesus Christ as your Lord and Savior, there is still time. You can use your own words or say the following prayer:

> Lord Jesus, forgive me for my sins and come into my heart. Make me the kind of person you want me to be. Thank you for dying on the cross for my sins. Thank you for forgiving my sins and giving me eternal life.

If you say this prayer and it expresses the desire of your heart, Christ will come into your life as He promised. Revelation 3:20 says, "Behold, I stand at the door and knock; if anyone hears My voice and opens the door, I will come in to him, and will dine with him, and he with Me."

If you prayed this prayer and it expressed your heart, you are now a born-again Christian and will meet Jesus at the Rapture. If you are left behind after the Rapture, you can still be saved, but you will have to endure a horrible Tribulation Period. This Tribulation Period is God's judgment on the earth. According to Jesus, "… there will be a great tribulation, such as has not occurred since the beginning of the world until now, nor ever will" (Matthew 24:21). You will not want to go through this Tribulation Period. Today is the day of salvation.

Appendix C

Tribulation Judgments:
Seals, Trumpets, and Bowls

SEVEN SEAL JUDGMENTS
SEALS 1–4 REPRESENT THE FOUR HORSEMEN

1. **White horse / Conqueror**
   (Antichrist in power; first half of Tribulation Period—three and one-half years peace; Revelation 6:1-2.)
2. **Red horse / War**
   (Antichrist; begins second half of Tribulation Period—"The Great Tribulation," represents war; Revelation 6:3-4.)
3. **Black horse / Famine**
   (Starvation/poverty; Revelation 6:5-6.)
4. **Pale Horse / Death and Hades**
   (Kills one-fourth of population, i.e., by weapons, starvation, and disease; Revelation 6:7-8.)
5. **Saints Martyred; they cry out under altar in heaven.**
   (Antichrist killing believers; Revelation 6:9-11.)
6. **Great Earthquake: sun-black, moon-red, sky-split, stars-fall.**
   "… every mountain and island were moved. … and they said to mountains and to the rocks, 'Fall on us and hide us from … the wrath of the Lamb' " (Revelation 6:12-17).
   Angels seal 144,000 believers—Foreheads of Jewish Believers; 12,000 from each of the 12 tribes (Revelation 7:2-4). What about

non-Jews? A great multitude, from every tribe and nation, (such a great number that no one could count) in white robes, standing before the throne of God and praising God (salvation to our God who sits on the throne, and to the Lamb). These are the ones who come out of the Great Tribulation and have washed their robes and made them white in the blood of the Lamb (Jesus Christ) (Revelation 7:14).

7. **Silence in heaven for thirty minutes; Earthquake, Thunder, Lightning; begin trumpet Judgments**

   Revelation 6:9-15 (fifth and sixth seal judgments); Revelation 8:1-5 (seventh seal); Revelation 8:7-12 (first-fourth trumpets); Revelation 9 (fifth-sixth trumpet); Revelation 11:15-19 (seventh trumpet); Revelation 11:2-6 (two witnesses of God prophesy for 1,260 days; fire comes out of their mouths); Revelation 11:5 (if anyone tries to harm them, they must be killed); Revelation 11:7 (the Beast will kill them); Revelation 11:11 (then three and one-half days later they come alive again by the breath of God); Revelation 11:13 (a great earthquake will kill 7,000 people). Revelation 11:14-17 (seventh seal).

SEVEN TRUMPET JUDGMENTS

1. **Hail-fire-blood:** Destroys One-third of Earth, One-third Trees and All Grass (Revelation 8:7).
2. **Seas Struck:** One-third Becomes Blood; One-third Sea Creatures Die; One-third of Ships Destroyed (Revelation 8:8-9).
3. **Wormwood (star, meteorite) Falls and Poisons Water:** One-third of Rivers & Springs; many die from bitter waters (Revelation 8:10-11).
4. **Darkness: Heavens Struck:** One-third of Sun, Moon, and Stars do not Shine (Revelation 8:12).
5. **Demonized Locusts from Bottomless Pit:** Torments unbelievers for five months (Revelation 9:1-11).
6. **Four Angels Released:** 200 Million Horsemen Kill: One-third of People with fire, smoke, and brimstone; mighty angel with little book (Revelation 9:13-21).
7. **Kingdom of God and Jesus Christ proclaimed / Bowl Judgments Are Opened**

SEVEN BOWL JUDGMENTS

1. **Malignant Sores on Unbelievers:** those with mark of beast and who worship image of beast (Revelation 16:2).
2. **All the Sea Turns to Blood: All Sea Creatures Die** (Revelation 16:3).
3. **All Rivers/Springs turn to Blood** (Revelation 16:4).
4. **Men Scorched with Fire and Heat** (Sun) (Revelation 16:8-9).
5. **Darkness and Pain** (gnaw tongues); (Revelation 16:10-11).
6. **Euphrates River Dries Up:** Demon spirits gather kings of world to battle (Revelation 16:12-14).
7. **Final bowl:** Thunder, Lightning, Great Earthquake, Islands Disappear and Mountains Flatten; Hail of 100 pounds each (Revelation 16:17-21).

SEQUENCE OF EVENTS FOLLOWING THE TRIBULATION PERIOD

1. **Then Christ Returns** on a white horse with the armies of heaven (Revelation 19:11-12).
2. **Satan is bound for 1,000 years**, and then released for a short time at the end of 1,000 years (Revelation 20:1-3, 7).
3. **Saints from the Tribulation Period reign with Christ for 1,000 years** (Revelation 20:4).
4. **The final battle occurs** (Revelation 20:8-9).
5. **The devil is cast into the lake of fire where the beast and the false prophet** are and will be tormented day and night forever (Revelation 20:10).
6. **Great White Throne Judgment:** unbelievers judged (Revelation 20:11-15).
7. **New Heaven and a New Earth:** New Jerusalem comes down out of heaven. No more death, sorrow, crying, or pain (Revelation 21: 1-4).

Jesus states: "I am the Alpha and the Omega, the first and the last, the beginning and the end" (Revelation 22:13).

Come soon, Lord Jesus!

Appendix D

For the Reader's Consideration

This book was written to answer some very critical questions about life, truth, meaning, and one's source of authority. One of the primary purposes of this book was to guide the reader in answering the following questions:

1. What is truth?
2. Where do I find it?
3. How do I know that my source of truth is reliable?
4. When I know the truth, what does it mean to me?
5. What are my choices once I know the truth?
6. What is the outcome of my choices?

When answering the above questions, the reader may want to consider the following "what if" questions:

1. **What if:** the Bible was shown to be the Word of God and does contain ultimate truth?
2. **What if:** the Bible says that Jesus is the Way, the Truth, and the Life, and no one comes to the Father [God] but through Him?
3. **What if:** the Bible says that man is a sinner and cannot be saved by his own good works?
4. **What if:** the Bible says that Jesus paid the penalty for my sins by dying on the cross?

5. **What if:** the Bible said I could be saved from eternal judgment by taking the following steps?
   A. Believe Jesus died for my sins and was resurrected (John 3:16; 1 Corinthians 15:14).
   B. Ask Him in prayer to come into my life (Revelation 3:20).

Would I do it?

The following are a few of the points covered in this book. Points 1 through 5 cover the foundation for our biblical source of authority. Points 6 through 13 cover a few of the reasons to believe that the Rapture is right at the door.

FOUNDATIONS FOR BIBLICAL AUTHORITY

1. The Bible is God's Word as established by historical fulfillment of prophecy (see Chapter Three).
2. Jesus fulfills 333 Old Testament prophecies as the Messiah (see Chapter Three).
3. The miraculous rebirth of the nation Israel in 1948. It had not been a sovereign nation for over 2,500 years, but the Old Testament prophesied it in Ezekiel 37:11-14 (see Chapter One).
4. The literal prophetic fulfillment of the Seventy Weeks of Daniel 9:24-27 (see Chapter Three, Chart 7).
5. Jesus prophesied the destruction of Jerusalem because they rejected Him as their Messiah (Luke 19:41-44). This was fulfilled when the Romans, under Titus, overthrew Jerusalem in A.D. 70.

REASONS TO BELIEVE THE RAPTURE IS NEAR

6. The exponential increase in the signs preceding the Second Coming of Christ, as shown in the increase in earthquakes (refer to Chapter One, Chart 2), and the exponential increase in knowledge in reference to Daniel's prophecy (Daniel 12:4) and general knowledge (refer to Chapter Four, Chart 8).
7. The prediction of the nearness of the end times from the secular (non-biblical) scientist's viewpoint (refer to Chapter One).
8. Evidence of the movement toward a one world system that includes

the three pillars of: government, economics, and religion (refer to Chapters Four, Five, and Six), which will characterize the development of the one world system as it has currently developed as we approach the Rapture, prior to the Tribulation Period.

9. The parable of the fig tree. Within one generation of the establishment of Israel as a nation (1948), Jesus will return at the Second Coming (refer to Chapters One and Seven).

10. A counterfeit rapture proposed by the New Age authors to deceive the people who are left behind when the biblical Rapture happens (see Chapter Seven and Appendix B: The UFO Grand Deception).

11. Political treaties, high-tech communication networks, religious developments, and the New Age Movement have laid the groundwork for a one-world system (see Chapters Four, Five, Six, and Eight).

12. The movement toward rebuilding of the Jewish temple (see Chapter Eight).

13. Certain events must take place in the Last Generation prior to the Second Coming of Christ, including the rebirth of Israel as a nation, revival of the old Roman Empire (modern Europe or the EU), and the formation of a worldwide government through peace. These events have already happened or are in the process of happening. All of these events mentioned in this book would make our generation (starting with the birth of Israel, 1948) the Last Generation.

ENDNOTES

Internet links listed here were active at the time of research. Sites on the Internet are often changed and updated. We apologize if resource links are no longer active.

Chapter One

1. Hal Lindsey, *Planet Earth: The Final Chapter*, Western Front Ltd., 1998, p. 125
2. Josh McDowell, *Evidence That Demands a Verdict*, Here's Life Publishers, 1972, Campus Crusade for Life, p. 315
3. J. Douglas Pentecost, *Things to Come*, Zondervan, 1974, p. 317
4. Hal Lindsey, *Planet Earth: The Final Chapter*, Western Front Ltd., 1998, p. 81
5. Ibid, p. 82
6. Christine Simmons, *Prophecy*, Southwestern Topographies, 1976, p. 15
7. Chuck Missler & Mark Eastman, *Alien Encounters*, Koinonia House, 1997, p. 274
8. For Development in Europe, see briefing package, Iron mixed with Clay, Koinonia House, Missler and Eastman
9. Simmons, p. 14
10. Lindsey, *Planet Earth: The Final Chapter*, p. 69
11. Ibid, p. 96
12. Ibid, p. 97 (These nine points are found in Matthew 24:4-7; Luke 21:25, 26)
13. These signs of the end times are found in: Matthew 24:4-7; Luke 21:8-26; Mark 13:6-25; Daniel 12:4; 2 Thessalonians 2:3; 1 Timothy 4:1-3; Revelations 9:21; and 2 Timothy 4:3
14. Missler and Eastman, p. 182
15. Ibid, p. 183
16. www.earthquake.usgs.gov/
17. Ibid.
18. Missler and Eastman, p. 171
19. Global Warming: A Natural Cycle by Melinda Zosh, May 29, 2008, Accessed at: www.academia.org/global-warming-a-natural-cycle/
20. Ibid.
21. Ibid.
22. Ibid.
23. Ibid.
24. Capital Weather Gang, "Do Solar Storms Threaten Life As We Know It?" by Steve Tracton, April 6, 2009. Accessed at: voices.washingtonpost.com/capitalweathergang/2009/04/do_solar_storms_threaten_civil.html
25. Ibid.
26. Ibid.
27. Harvard University Gazette, 1998, "Brightening Sun is Warming Earth" by William Cromie. Accessed at: www.news.harvard.edu/gazette/1997/11.06/BrighteningSuni.html
28. Graham Hancock, *Fingerprints of the Gods*, Crown Publishers, New York, N.Y., 1995, p. 484
29. Ibid.
30. Ibid.
31. Ibid, p. 485
32. Ibid.
33. Missler and Eastman, p. 172
34. Lindsey, *Planet Earth: The Final Chapter*, p. 105
35. Ibid.

36. Ibid, pp. 105-106
37. Missler and Eastman, p. 173
38. Billy Graham, *Approaching Hoofbeats: The Four Horsemen of the Apocalypse*, World Books, Inc., 1983, p. 135
39. Sourcebook of Criminal Justice Statistics Online (www.albany.edu/sourcebook/pdf/t31062004.pdf)
40. Lindsey, *Apocalypse Code*, p. 177 [Since this book was written in 1997, the approximate time period was inserted by author]
41. Adapted from: Sourcebook of Criminal Justice Statistics Online (www.albany. edu/sourcebook/pdf/t31062004.pdf) and Table 1 – Crime in the United States 2005 (www.fbi.gov/ucr/05cius/data/table_01.html)
42. Global Report on Crime and Justice, United Nations Office for Drug Control and Crime Prevention
43. Chip Ingram, "What We Must Learn From the Killings at Columbine High," Living on the Edge, P.O. Box 2370, Santa Cruz, California (Radio Broadcast), 1999
44. Lindsey, *Apocalypse Code*, p. 178
45. Ibid, p. 295
46. International Christian Concern, Global Persecution Update: Pakistan, August 9, 1998 (www.persecution.org)
47. International Christian Concern, Top Ten Priority Watch List of Countries Where Christians are Persecuted, Oct 22, 1998 (www.persecution.org)
48. Nina Shea, *In the Lions Den: A Shocking Account of the Persecution and Martyrdom of Christians Today and How We Should Respond*, Broadman and Holman, 1997, p. 1
49. Lindsey, *Apocalypse Code*, p. 299
50. Ibid, p. 137
51. Ibid, p. 137
52. Peter and Paul Lalonde, *2000 AD*, Thomas Nelson, 1997, p. 34
53. Lindsey, *Apocalypse Code*, p. 10 (quotation from Dr. George Wald, Nobel prize-winning scientist, Harvard University)
54. SCP Newsletter, Fall 2001, Vol. 26:1, p. 6
55. Martin Rees, *Our Final Hour*, Published by Basic Books, A member of the Perseus Book Group, New York, N.Y. 2003, p. 28
56. Ibid, p. 32
57. Bulletin of the Atomic Scientists, Doomsday Clock, History, June 27, 2005 (www.thebulletin.org/doomsday-clock)
58. Ibid, Current Time

Chapter Two

1. *Time* magazine (July 4, 2005), Suicide Bomber, pp. 23, 24, 29
2. *Dallas Morning News*, Friday, July 8, 2005, p. 1A
3. Ravi Zacharius, *Deliver Us From Evil*, Word Publishing, 1997, p. 219
4. Ibid, p. 217
5. Ibid, p. 224

6. Ibid.
7. Hal Lindsey, *Satan is Alive and Well on Planet Earth*, Zondervan, 1972, p. 85
8. Brad Scott, *Streams of Confusion*, Crossway Books, 1999, p. 289 (adapted from table 2 of the appendix).
9. Desmond Morris, *The Naked Ape*, McGraw Hill, 1969
10. Lindsey, *Satan is Alive and Well on Planet Earth*, p. 91
11. Charles Colson, *How Now Shall We Live?*, Tyndale House Publishers, 1999, p. 148
12. Ibid, p. 149
13. Ibid, p. 186
14. Ibid, p. 149
15. Tal Brooke, *One World*, End Run Publishing, 2000, p. 183
16. Ibid.
17. Brad Scott, *Streams of Confusion*, p. 244
18. Tal Brooke, p. 150
19. Ibid, p. 30
20. Brad Scott, p. 249
21. Ibid, p. 249 (quoting Barna Research 1996)
22. Ibid, p. 251
23. J. Budziszewski, *How to Stay Christian in College*, NavPress, 1999, (quoting from Christianity and Liberalism), p. 41
24. Bishop Spong, *Why Christianity Must Change or Die*, p. 19
25. Ibid, pp. 186-197
26. Brad Scott, p. 262
27. Ravi Zacharius, p. 115
28. Francis Schaeffer, *The God Who Is There*, InterVarsity Press, 1968, p. 93
29. Charles Colson, p. 148
30. Frank Minirth and Paul Meier, *Counseling and the Nature of Man*, Baker Book House, 1982, p. 10
31. Viktor Frankl, *Man's Search for Meaning*, Pocket Books, Simon and Schuster, 1963, p. 154
32. Minirth and Meier, p. 13
33. Victor E. Frankl, p. 153
34. Lindsey, p. 53
35. Neil T. Anderson, *The Bondage Breaker*, Harvest House Publishers, 1990, p. 53
36. Ibid, p. 83
37. Ibid, p. 99
38. Minirth and Meier, pp. 10-11
39. Hal Lindsey, *Faith for Earth's Final Hour*, Oracle House Publishing, Murrieta, 2003, p. 33
40. Ibid, p. 31
41. Ibid, p. 31
42. Ibid, p. 32
43. Missler and Eastman, *Alien Encounters*, Koinonia House, 1997, p. 149
44. Schaeffer, p. 17
45. Proverbs 14:12 NASB
46. Minirth and Meier, p. 10
47. Missler and Eastman, p. 153
48. Schaeffer, p. 62
49. Ibid, p. 61
50. Alcoholics Anonymous, Alcoholics Anonymous World Services, 1976, p. 53

Chapter Three

1. *Dallas Morning News*, October 15, 1999, Morning Briefcase, Forward Thinking, p. 2D
2. Ibid.
3. Christine Simmons, *Prophecy*, Southwestern Topographies, 1976, pp. 1-2
4. Brad Scott, *Streams of Confusion*, Crossway Books, 1999, p. 275
5. Charles Colson, *How Now Shall We Live*, Tyndale House Publishers, 1999, p. 174
6. John Shelby Spong, *Why Christianity Must Change or Die,* Harper Collins Publishers, 1998, p. 63 (Thesis was advanced from Bultman's major works.)
7. Josh McDowell, *More Than A Carpenter*, Tyndale House Publishers, 1977, p. 43
8. Lee Strobel, *The Case For Christ*, Zondervan, 1998, p. 265
9. Spong, p. 60
10. Ibid, p. 63
11. Ibid, p. 11
12. *Christianity Today*, October 23, 2000, The Transcendental Al Gore, p. 100
13. Brad Scott, p. 287
14. C. S. Lewis, *Mere Christianity*, Macmillan, 1947, p. 62
15. Josh McDowell, p. 42
16. See the following resources: *The Dead Sea Scrolls* (DVD) by Randall Price; *Biblical Archaeology* (DVD) by Price; *Searching the Original Bible* (DVD) by Price; *Digging for the Truth* (DVD or CD Audio) by Price. Also, go to www.worldofthebible.com. for further resources
17. Josh McDowell, p. 47
18. Josh McDowell, *More Than A Carpenter*, p. 49
19. Cited by an editorial comment by Randall Price, Ph.D., President of World of the Bible Ministries, Inc.
20. Ibid.
21. Josh McDowell, *Evidence that Demands a Verdict*, Here's Life Publishers, 1972, pp. 42-43
22. Ibid.
23. Grant Jeffrey, *Signature of God*, p. 114
24. Spong, p. 14
25. Lee Strobel, *The Case for Christ*, Zondervan, 1998, p. 84 (quotation was a footnote from Gary Habermas, *The Historical Jesus*, Joplin, Missouri: College Press, 1996, pp. 196-197)
26. Ibid, p. 84
27. Ibid, p. 85 (Partial quote from Paul Maier)
28. Josh McDowell, *More Than a Carpenter*, p. 37
29. Ibid, p. 38
30. Ibid, p. 38
31. Ibid, p. 50
32. Josh McDowell, *Evidence that Demands a Verdict*, Here's Life Publishers, 1972, Campus Crusade for Christ, p. 16
33. *Denton Record Chronicle*, December 3, 1999, *A Scientist Eyes Noah's Flood*, Religion, p. 1B
34. Josh McDowell, *Evidence that Demands a Verdict*, p. 22
35. Hal Lindsey, *Apocalypse Code*, Western Front Ltd., 1997, p. 48
36. Ibid, p. 64
37. McDowell, *Evidence that Demands a Verdict*, p. 269
38. Chuck Missler and Mark Eastman, *Alien Encounters*, Koinonia House, 1997, p. 225
39. McDowell, *Evidence that Demands a Verdict*, p. 274-302 (These pages give all of the

specific historical fulfillments and details that surround each prophecy.)

40. Lindsey, Apocalypse Code, p. 55

41. Lindsey, *Apocalypse Code*, p. 57

42. Ibid, p. 57

43. Ibid, p. 61

44. Ibid, p. 61

45. Simmons, p. 8

46. McDowell, *Evidence that Demands a Verdict*, p. 170

47. Ibid, p. 170

48. Simmons, pp. 8-9

49. Hal Lindsey, *Planet Earth: The Final Chapter*, Western Front Ltd., 1998, p. 78

50. Missler and Eastman, pp. 227-228

51. Daniel 9:24

52. J. Dwight Pentecost, *Things to Come*, Zondervan, 1974, p. 241

53. McDowell, *Evidence that Demands a Verdict*, p. 172 [Genesis 7:11 makes reference to the second month, seventeenth day. Genesis 8:4 makes reference to the seventh month, seventeenth day. This is a span of five months. Genesis 7:24 and Genesis 8:3 lay out a 150-day span. The time span is five months, which equals 150 days. Each month represents 30 days and one year (30 x 12) equals a 360-day year (the Jewish year)] [brackets by author]

54. Pentecost, *Things to Come*, p. 244

55. Ibid, p. 244

56. McDowell, *Evidence that Demands a Verdict*, p. 173

57. Ibid, p. 173 (quoting Harold Hoehner, *Chronogological Aspects of the Life of Christ*, Zondervan, 1977, p. 138)

58. For other charts of Daniel's seventy weeks, see: McDowell, *Evidence that Demands a Verdict*, p. 174; Walvoord and Zuck, *The Bible Knowledge Commentary, Old Testament*, p. 1363; and Missler and Eastman, p. 232

59. Missler and Eastman, p. 234

60. John Walvoord, *Major Bible Prophecies*, Zondervan, 1991, p. 207

61. Fred John Meldau, *Messiah in Both Testaments*, Christian Victory Publishing, 1956, p. 5

62. Ibid, p. 5

63. Ibid, p. 8

64. Jim Simmons, The Last Hour: Prophecy, World views and UFOs, Fairway Press, 2001, p. 37

Chapter Four

1. John F. Walvoord and Roy B. Zuck, *The Bible Knowledge Commentary, Old Testament*, SP Publications, 1983, p. 1326

2. Ibid.

3. Ibid, p. 1324

4. Ibid, p. 1123

5. Ibid, p. 1323

6. Ibid, p. 1332

7. Ibid, p. 1333

8. Daniel 2:42; 7:24 and Revelation 13:1

9. Walvoord and Zuck, *The Bible Knowledge Commentary, Old Testament*, pp. 1335-1336

10. Ibid, p. 1336

11. Eric Nelson, *The Complete Idiot's Guide to the Roman Empire*, Alpha Books, Indianapolis, Indiana, 2002, p. 257
12. Walvoord and Zuck, *The Bible Knowledge Commentary, Old Testament*, p. 1354
13. Art Bell and Whitley Streiber, *The Coming Global SuperStorm*, Pocket Books, a division of Simon and Schuster Inc., 2000, p. 33
14. Ibid.
15. Eric Nelson, *Pagan Work Criticizing Book of Daniel*, p. 236-237, 299
16. Ibid, pp. 236-237
17. Ibid, Ch. 4, p. 289
18. http://www.wfm.org/site/index.php/articles/9
19. *Universal Declaration of Human Rights*, Article 29, p. 253
20. International Intelligence Briefing by Hal Lindsey, July 27, 2005
21. Alan Franklin, *EU, The Final Empire*, Hearthstone Publishing, Oklahoma City, OK, 2002, p. 51
22. International Intelligence Briefing by Hal Lindsey, July 27, 2005
23. Ibid.
24. http://en.wikipedia.org/wiki/NATO
25. International Intelligence Briefing by Hal Lindsey, July 25, 2005
26. Hal Lindsey, Planet Earth: The Final Chapter, Western Front Ltd., 1998, p. 96
27. Ibid, p. 96
28. Ray Kurzweil, "The Law of Accelerating Returns," 2001 (www.kurzweilai.net/articles/art0134.html)
29. Ibid, Ch. 4, p. 289
30. Ibid.
31. Ibid, p. 4
32. Ibid, p. 165
33. Ibid, p. 168
34. *Time* magazine, December 6, 1999, p. 1 (Agilent Technologies Innovating the HP Way)
35. Walvoord and Zuck, *OT*, p. 1372. Also, see comments on Revelation 12:15 from *The Bible Knowledge Commentary, New Testament*, pp. 959-960
36. http://en.wikipedia.org/wiki/NATO
37. http: www.fulfilledprophecy.com/2010.html, "What Herb Thinks: Overview."
38. Ibid.
39. *Javier Solana, Europe's Uber Fuhrer?* By Jack Kinsella
40. http://fulfilledprophecy.com/rec666_ch_11.html
41. *Javier Solana, Europe's Uber Fuhrer?* By Jack Kinsella
42. http://fulfilledprophecy.com/rec666_ch_11.html
43. International Intelligence Briefing by Hal Lindsey, July 27, 2005 (television broadcast)
44. Ibid.
45. Alan Franklin, *EU, The Final Empire*, p. 17
46. www.prepare-ye-the-way.com/gat 1.html
47. Prophecy in the News, *South American Nations Announce Their Move Toward "Union,"* Volume 28, Number 7, July 2008, p. 16.
48. Ibid.
49. http://www.gulfnews.com/opinion/columns/world/10204638.html
50. http://en.wikipedia.org/wiki/Constitutive_Treaty
51. Prophecy in the News, *The Late Great USA*, by Bob Ulrich, Volume 27, Number 9, September 2007, p. 17 [NOTE: Endnotes 47-53 in Chapter Four also refer to: *The Late Great USA: The Coming Merger with Mexico and Canada*, by John Corsi]

52. Ibid. [Also see #47]
53. Personal Update, *The Deliberate Destruction of America*, by Chuck Missler, Volume 17, No. 9, September 2007, p. 5. [Also see #47]
54. Last Days Chronicles (Hal Lindsey website ministries), *From the Arctic to the Caribbean*, by Jack Kinsella, Volume 8, Number 9, September 2007, p. 5 [Also see #47]
55. Prophecy in the News, *The Late Great USA*, by Bob Ulrich, Vol. 27, No. 9, September 2007, p. 17 [Also see #47]
56. Last Days Chronicles (Hal Lindsey website ministries), *From the Arctic to the Caribbean*, by Jack Kinsella, Vol. 8, Number 9, September 2007, p. 5 [Also see #47]

Chapter Five

1. Chuck Missler, *Europa Rising*, A DVD Presentation, Koinonia House, Coeur d'Alene, Idaho, 2003
2. Ibid.
3. Jack Kinsella, *Javier Solana, Europe's Uber Fuhrer?* 12-10-04
4. Chuck Missler, *Europa Rising*, A DVD Presentation
5. http://clintonnazarene.org/articles/eurodollar.html
6. Alan Franklin, *EU: Final World Empire*, Hearthstone Publishing, Oklahoma City, Oklahoma, 2002, p. 16
7. Chuck Missler, *Europa Rising*; Euro-Indicators, News Release, November 2006, "Euro area external trade surplus 3.1 bn euro" accessed at:/ http://ec.europa. eu/eurostat/
8. Ibid.
9. Ibid; Wikipedia, United Nations, "Membership" accessed at: http://en.wikipedia.org/wiki/United_Nations#Financing
10. Hal Lindsey, *Planet Earth: The Final Chapter*, Western Front, Ltd., 1998, p. 105
11. Ibid.
12. Chuck Missler, *Europa Rising*; Quaker Council For European Affairs, "The EU's Relationship with the United Nations" accessed at: http://www.quaker.org/qcea/briefings/peacebuilding/pbuilding/pbuildbriefing4.htm#3
13. Hal Lindsey, *Planet Earth: The Final Chapter*, p. 85
14. Alan Franklin, *EU: Final World Empire*, p. 116
15. Ibid.
16. Ibid.
17. http://www.fulfilledprophecy.com/2010.html. "What Herb Thinks: Overview"
18. Ibid.
19. Ibid.
20. Ibid.
21. Alan Franklin, *EU: Final World Empire*, p. 47
22. http://www.ianpaisley.org
23. Ibid.
24. Chuck Missler, *Europa Rising*
25. Ibid.
26. International Intelligence Briefing by Hal Lindsey, July 27, 2005
27. Alan Franklin, *EU: Final World Empire*, p. 12
28. Ibid.
29. Ibid.

30. Ibid, p. 15
31. Ibid.
32. Ibid, pp. 15-16
33. Ibid.
34. Alan Franklin, *EU: Final World Empire*, p. 30
35. Ibid.
36. Ibid.
37. Tal Brooke, *One World*, End Run Publishing, Berkeley, California, 1989 & 2000, p. 223
38. Ibid.
39. Ibid.
40. Ibid.
41. Ibid.
42. Alan Franklin, *EU: Final World Empire*, p. 33
43. Ibid.
44. Tal Brooke, *One World*, pp. 223-224
45. Ibid.
46. *The Writings of George Washington*, published by the US Government Printing Office, 1941, Vol. 20, p. 518
47. Tal Brooke, *One World*, p. 224
48. Ibid, p. 225
49. www.eurockwell.com/yates14.html. "From Carroll Quigley to the U.N. Millennium Summit: Thoughts on the New World Order" by Steven Yates, 9/11/00
50. Tal Brooke, One World, p. 225
51. Ibid, p. 225
52. Carroll Quigley, *Tragedy and Hope: A History of The World in Our Time*, The Macmillan Co., N.Y., 1966, p. 324
53. Ibid.
54. www.eurockwell.com/yates14.html. "From Carroll Quigley to the UN Millennium Summit: Thoughts on the New World Order" by Steven Yates, 9/11/00
55. Tal Brooke, *One World*, p. 229
56. Carroll Quigley, *Tragedy and Hope*, pp. 326-327
57. Tal Brooke, *One World*, p. 226
58. Carroll Quigley, *Tragedy and Hope*, p. 56
59. Tal Brooke, *One World*, p. 243
60. Carroll Quigley, *Tragedy and Hope*, p. 950
61. Ibid, p. 132
62. Tal Brooke, *One World*, p. 234
63. Ibid, p. 236
64. Ibid, p. 235
65. Ibid, p. 236
66. Ibid.
67. http://www.conspiracyarchive.com/NOW/Council Foreign _Relations.html
68. Ibid.
69. Ibid.
70. Tal Brooke, *One World*, p. 240
71. Ibid, p. 254
72. Ibid, p. 245
73. Ibid, p. 246

74. Ibid.
75. Ibid.
76. Ibid, p. 247
77. Ibid, p. 248
78. Ibid, p. 249
79. Ibid, p. 252
80. Ibid.
81. Ibid.
82. Ibid.
83. Ibid, pp. 252-253
84. Ibid, p. 253
85. Ibid.
86. Ibid.
87. Ibid, pp. 253-254
88. Ibid, p. 254
89. Ibid, p. 251
90. Ibid, p. 252
91. Genesis 9:1
92. Genesis 10:32
93. Genesis 11:4
94. Genesis 10:10
95. John Walvoord and Roy Zuck, *OT*, p. 43
96. Genesis 11:4
97. Genesis 11:1
98. Alan Franklin, *EU: Final World Empire*, p. 46
99. Ibid, p. 51
100. Ibid, p. 32
101. Ibid.
102. Genesis 11:4
103. 2 Thessalonians 2:4
104. Eric Nelson, p. 4
105. Ibid, p. 5
106. 2 Thessalonians 2:4
107. Eric Nelson, *The Complete Idiot's Guide to The Roman Empire*, p. 5
108. Revelation 13:15
109. Hal Lindsey, *Planet Earth: The Final Chapter*, p. 19
110. Alan Franklin, *EU: Final World Empire*, p. 45
111. Ibid, p. 46
112. Ibid.
113. Ibid, p. 38

Chapter Six

1. Ron J. Bigalke Jr., General Editor, *One World: Economy, Government & Religion In The Last Days*, 21st Century Press Publications, 2005, pp. 337-393
2. Ibid, *"Nations Role in World Religion"* by Arno Froese, p. 383
3. Ron J. Bigalke, Jr., *"Religion of the Future"* by Roger Oakland, p. 347

4. Ibid.
5. Romans 10:17
6. Exodus 7:8-12
7. Chuck Missler and Mark Eastman, *Alien Encounters*, Koinonia House, 1997, p. 323
8. Matthew 7:13-14
9. John F. Walvoord and Roy B. Zuck, *The Bible Knowledge Commentary, New Testament*, SP Publications, 1983, pp. 957-958
10. Genesis 37:10
11. Alan Franklin, *EU: The Final World Empire*, Hearthstone Publishing, Oklahoma City, Oklahoma 2002, p. 38
12. John F. Walvoord and Roy B. Zuck, N.T., p. 970
13. Ibid, p. 972
14. Revelation 17:18
15. Ibid, 13:11-13
16. C.S. Lewis, *Prelandra*, Simon and Schuster, 1944, p. 122
17. Genesis 10:9-10
18. Dr. Joe Koevering, God's News Behind the News, *The Pope, The Prophecy, and The Promise*, 2005, p. 49
19. Dr. H.A. Ironsides, *"Lectures on the Revelation,"* p. 298
20. Ibid.
21. Walvoord and Zuck, N.T., p. 970
22. Alexander Hislop, *The Two Babylons*, S.W. Partridge & Co., London, 1903, p. 20
23. Ibid, pp. 58-59
24. Ibid.
25. Ibid, p. 59
26. Ibid, p. 22
27. Walvoord and Zuck, N.T., p. 970
28. Joe Van Koevering, p. 49
29. Hislop, p. 19
30. Ibid.
31. Ibid, p. 19 from Jamblichus, *On the Mysteries*, sect. viii, chap. iii
32. Ibid, p. 20
33. Ibid, p. 20-21
34. Walvoord and Zuck, N.T., p. 971
35. Ibid.
36. Ibid.
37. Ibid.
38. Koevering, p. 50
39. Ibid, p. 50
40. Ibid, p. 31
41. Ibid, p. 28
42. Ibid, p. 27-28
43. Ibid, p. 28
44. Dr. David Reagan, Lamplighter magazine, *"The Legacy of Pope John Paul II,"* Vol. XXVI, July/August, 2005, No. 4, pp. 7-8
45. Ibid.
46. Gary Kau, Hope for the World (Newsletter), *"A Man or a God?"* Spring, 2005, p. 1
47. Joe Van Koevering, p. 33

48. Ibid.
49. Pope John Paul II, *"Crossing the Threshold of Hope"*
50. Ibid.
51. Joe Van Koevering, p. 33
52. Ibid, p. 34
53. Malachi Martin, *The Keys of This Blood*, Simon & Schuster Publishers, 1990, pp. 626-627
54. Joe Van Koevering, p. 34
55. Ibid, p. 36
56. Ibid.
57. Ibid, p. 37
58. Catholic Catechism, paragraph 411
59. Joe Van Koevering, p. 28
60. Ibid, p. 30
61. Ibid.
62. William T. James, *Foreshocks of Antichrist*, quoting from the Associated Press, p. 111
63. Ibid, p. 111
64. Ibid, pp. 111-112
65. Joe Van Koevering, p. 55
66. Cardinal Joseph Ratzinger, *Roman Catholic Church Congregation for the Doctrine of the Faith* (CDF), 1984
67. Nicole Winfield, *"New Pope Vows to Continue Church Reforms,"* Associated Press, April 20, 2005
68. Joe Van Koevering, p. 18
69. Nicole Winfield, *"New Pope Lays Out Vision in First Mass,"* Associated Press, April 20, 2005
70. Angela Doland, *"New Pope Inspired by Anti-War Pontiff,"* Associated Press, April 20, 2005
71. Nicole Winfield, *"New Pope Lays Out Vision in First Mass,"* Associated Press, April 20, 2005
72. *"Pope Seeks 'Bridges of Friendship' with Muslims,"* Associated Press, April 25, 2005
73. Joe Van Koevering, p. 25
74. Cardinal Joseph Ratzinger, *Roman Catholic Church Congregation for the Doctrine of the Faith (CDF)*, 1984
75. Joe Van Koevering, pp. 55-56
76. *"Queen of Rome,"* www.understandingthetimes.org, p. 3
77. Ibid, quoting from Joe Van Koevering's book, *The Pope, The Prophecy, and The Promise*, p. 57
78. Joe Van Koevering, p. 66
79. *"Queen of Rome,"* www.understandingthetimes.org, p. 11
80. *The Tablet*, February 29, 1994, p. 5
81. Ibid.
82. Joe Van Koevering, p. 63
83. Bishop Fulton J. Sheen, *"Mary and the Muslims," The World's First Love*, Garden City Books, 1952
84. Joe Van Koevering, p. 64
85. John Hogue, *The Last Pope: The Decline and Fall of the Church of Rome*, Boston, Massachusetts, Element Books, 2000, Book Cover
86. Ibid.
87. Ibid.
88. Joe Van Koevering, pp. 72-73
89. Ibid, p. 79
90. John Hogue, p. 355
91. Ibid, p. 371

92. Joe Van Koevering, p. 74 (Quote within from John Hogue, *The Last Pope: The Decline and Fall of the Church of Rome*, Boston, Massachusetts, Element Books, 2000, Back Cover)
93. Ibid, (Hogue's book), p. 343
94. Ibid.
95. Joe Van Koevering, p. 75
96. Ibid.
97. Ibid, p. 76
98. John Hogue, p. 349
99. Hal Lindsey, *International Intelligence Briefing*, April 9, 2006
100. Ibid.
101. Ibid.
102. Ibid.
103. Ibid.
104. Ibid.
105. Ibid.
106. Ibid.
107. Ibid.
108. Ibid.

Chapter Seven

1. H. Wayne House and Randall Price, *Charts of Bible Prophecy*, H. Wayne House and World of the Bible Ministries, Inc., Zondervan, Grand Rapids, Michigan, 2003, p. 98 (adapted in part)
2. *Prophecy in the News* magazine, "He Calls It... Osama's Revenge" By Gary Stearman, p. 4, Oklahoma City, Oklahoma, Volume 25, Number 9, September 2005 (quoting from "Osama's Revenge... The Next 911" by Paul L.Williams, p. 41)
3. Ibid,.
4. Ibid, p. 46
5. Ibid, p. 3
6. Ibid, p. 3
7. *Forbes* magazine, "The Invisible Bankers" by Michael Freedman, Volume 176, Number 8, October 17, 2005, p. 95
8. Ibid.
9. *Prophecy in the News* magazine, "He Calls It... Osama's Revenge" by Stearman, Oklahoma City, Oklahoma, Volume 25, Number 9, Sept., 2005, p. 4
10. Ibid, p. 4, quote within, p. 33
11. International Prophecy Conference, March 1, 2006, "Islam and Prophecy" presented by Randall Price
12. Ibid.
13. Ibid.
14. Hal Lindsey, *The Everlasting Hatred*, Oracle House Publishing, Murrieta, CA, 2002, p. 145
15. *Prophecy in the News* magazine, Vol. 25, Number 9, September 2005, p. 14
16. Ibid, p. 14 (quoting from "Osama's Revenge ... The Next 911" by Paul L. Williams, p. 174)
17. Adapted from: International Prophecy Conference, 2006, "Islam and Prophecy," by

Randall Price, March 1, 2006, and World of the Bible Ministries Newsletter, "The Second Coming of Islam," by Randall Price, Volume 8, No. 1, Summer, 2006, p. 3

18. International Prophecy Conference, 2006, Comments by Perry Stone (on Panel of Speakers), March 4, 2006

19. John Hagee, *Jerusalem Countdown*, Front Line Publishing Co., Lake Macy, Florida, 2006, p. 7

20. Ibid, p. 8 and "Diplomats: Iran still refuses cameras," Associated Press, by George Jahn, accessed at http://www.iranfocus.com/modules/news/article.php?storyid=10361 on March 4, 2007

21. Associated Press, "Israel Shares Intel With US on Iran Nukes," Fox News.com, accessed at http://www.foxnews.com/story/0,2933,153342,00.html on September 15, 2005

22. Ibid.

23. John Hagee, *Jerusalem Countdown*, pp. 8-9 (quote within from William M. Arkin, "Secret Plan Outlines the Unthinkable," *Los Angeles Times*, March 9, 2002, accessed at http://www.commondreams.org/cgi-bin/print.cgi?file=/views0210309-04.htm on September 30, 2005)

24. Ibid.

25. John Hagee, p. 11

26. John Hagee, p. 12 (quoting from, "Multinuclear Middle East — Iran, the Bomb, and Israel," Strategic Dialogue Center Conference, Netanya College, Israel, April 17, 2005)

27. Hal Lindsey Report, July 30, 2006

28. John Hagee, p. 6

29. *Prophecy in the News* magazine, "Russia Built Iran's New Nuclear Power Plant" by J.R. Church, p. 28, Oklahoma City, Oklahoma, Vol. 24, No. 12, December 2004

30. Hal Lindsey, *Planet Earth: The Final Chapter*, Western Front Ltd., 1998, p. 178

31. Ibid.

32. Ibid, p. 179

33. Adapted from Hal Lindsey, *Planet Earth: The Final Chapter*, p. 179

34. Safari Haeri, "Iran on Course for a Showdown," accessed at http://www.atimes.com/atimes/Middle_East/GJ28Ak03.html/on October 28, 2005

35. Ibid.

36. John Hagee, p. 17

37. Ibid, p. 18

38. *Prophecy in the News* magazine, "Russia Built Iran's New Nuclear Power Plant" by J.R. Church, p. 28, Oklahoma City, Oklahoma, Vol. 24, No. 12, December 2004

39. International Prophecy Conference, 2006, Presentation by Chuck Missler, March 3, 2006

40. John Hagee, p. 4

41. Ibid, p. 4 (quoting Ahmed Rashid, "I've Sold Nuclear Weapons to Libya, Iran, and North Korea," Telegraph .co.uk, on August 16, 2005, as viewed at: http://www.telegraph.co.uk/news/main.jhtml?xnal=/news/2004/02/03/wpak03.xml)

42. John Hagee, p. 26

43. Ibid, pp. 27-28

44. "Iran Plans to Knock Out U.S. With 1 Nuclear Bomb," from Joseph Farah's *G2 Bulletin, WorldNet Daily*, April 25, 2005 accessed at http://worldnetdaily.com/news/article.asp?Article_ID=43956 on September 30, 2005

45. John Hagee, p. 28, adapted from the Senate Judiciary Subcommittee on Terrorism Technology and Homeland Security, chaired by Senator Kyle of Arizona, March, 2005

46. John Hagee, p. 28

47. Ibid, p. 29, (quoting from "Iran Plans to Knock Out US With 1 Nuclear Bomb")

48. *UFO* magazine, "UFO Secrets: India's Military; Joint Russian/Iranian Study" by Guy Malone, p. 21, Vol. 20, No.1, February/March 2005
49. Ibid.
50. Ibid.
51. Ibid.
52. Ibid.
53. Ibid.
54. John Hagee, p. 10 (quoting Felix Frish, "How to Attack Reactors in Iran," Ma'ariv, April 19, 2005)
55. http://www.thefirearmsforum.com/showtheend.php?p=198405#post198405
56. Random House Webster's College Dictionary, Random House, Inc., New York, 1992
57. International Prophecy Conference 2006, "Damascus and Gaza" presentation by Perry Stone, March 4, 2006
58. Ibid.
59. Ibid.
60. Joe Van Koevering, sermon on "Lebanon and Hezbollah," August 5, 2006
61. Personal Update, News Journal of Koinonia House, "Magog Revisited" by Chuck Missler, p. 6, August 2006
62. Ibid, p. 7
63. Ibid, p. 8
64. World of the Bible News and Views, "The Second Coming of Islam" by Randall Price, Vol. 8, No. 1, p. 1, Summer 2006
65. Personal Update, "Magog Revisited" by Chuck Missler, p. 6, August 2006
66. Ibid, p. 9
67. Hal Lindsey Report, July 30, 2006
68. Ryan Mauro, "Paul Williams Details American Hiroshima," *WorldNet Daily*, September 3, 2005, accessed at http://www.worldnetdaily.com/news/article. asp?ARTICLE_ID=46127 on September 30, 2005
69. Ibid.
70. Ibid. John Hagee, p. 27
71. Ibid.
72. John Hagee, p. 27
73. John Hagee, p.27 (quote within: William M. Arkin, "Secret Plan Outlines the Unthinkable")
74. William M. Alnor, *UFOs in the New Age*, Baker Book House, 1993, p. 73 (quoting Douglas Curran, *In Advance of Landing: Folk Concepts of Outer Space*, New York: Aberville Press, 1985, p. 4)
75. Chuck Missler and Mark Eastman, *Alien Encounters*, Koinonia House, 1997, p. 9 (quoting Gallup Polls done in 1991 and 1996)
76. Missler and Eastman, p. 9 (quoting George M. Eberhart, *UFOs and the Extraterrestrial Contact Movement: A Bibliography*, Vol. 2, Scarecrow Press, London, 1986)
77. Timothy Good, *Above Top Secret*, William Marrow Co., 1998, p. 384
78. Missler and Eastman, p. 28
79. Ibid, p. 28
80. Ibid, p. 57
81. I.D.E. Thomas, *The Omega Conspiracy*, Hearthstone Publishing Ltd., Oklahoma City, Oklahoma, 1986, p. 38
82. *UFO Conspiracy*, A DVD Presentation by I.D.E. Thomas and Dave Hunt
83. Missler and Eastman, p. 66

84. Ibid, p. 32
85. Ibid, p. 67
86. William M. Alnor, *UFOs in the New Age*, p. 16 (referencing Tara Gravel, "Interview with David Jacobs, Ph.D.," Temple University Journalism Paper, December 6, 1990)
87. Missler and Eastman, p. 35
88. Ibid, p. 38
89. Ibid, p. 37
90. I.D.E. Thomas, *The Omega Conspiracy*, p. 93
91. Missler and Eastman, p. 50
92. I.D.E. Thomas, *The Omega Conspiracy*, p. 84
93. Missler and Eastman, p. 52
94. Ibid, p. 67
95. Jacques Vallee, *Dimensions*, Ballantine Books, New York, New York, 1988, pp. 252-253
96. Missler, p. 86
97. Ibid, p. 80

Chapter Eight

1. John F. Walvoord and Roy Zuck, *O.T.*, p. 127
2. Christine Simmons, *Prophecy*, Southwestern Typographies, 1978, p. 16
3. John Walvoord, *Major Bible Prophecies*, Zondervan, 1991, p. 314
4. Ibid, p. 313
5. Ibid, p. 314
6. Chuck Missler and Mark Eastman, *Alien Encounters*, Coeur d' Alene, ID: Koinonia House, 1997, p. 234
7. J. Dwight Pentecost, *Things to Come*, Zondervan, 1974, p. 137
8. Tim LaHaye and Jerry Jenkins, *Are We Living in the End Times?*, Tyndale House, 1999, p. 116
9. Hal Lindsey, *Planet Earth: The Final Chapter*, Western Front Ltd., 1998, p. 150
10. Ibid, p. 77
11. Hal Lindsey, *Apocalypse Code*, Western Front Ltd., 1997, p. 137
12. Lindsey, *Planet Earth: The Final Chapter*, p. 200 (quoted from Lindsey, *Apocalypse Code*, 1997)
13. Lindsey, *Apocalypse Code*, p. 154
14. Pentecost, p. 215
15. Lindsey, *Planet Earth: The Final Chapter*, p. 155
16. LaHaye and Jenkins, pp. 275-276
17. Lindsey, *Planet Earth: The Final Chapter*, p. 158
18. Missler and Eastman, p. 285
19. Ibid, p. 285
20. John Walvoord, *The Revelation of Jesus Christ*, Moody Press, 1966, p. 178
21. LaHaye and Jenkins, p. 304
22. Ibid, p. 311
23. Lindsey, *Planet Earth: The Final Chapter*, p. 159
24. Ibid, p. 101
25. Walvoord and Zuck, *N.T.*, 1983, p. 947
26. Lindsey, *Planet Earth: The Final Chapter*, p. 172
27. Ibid, (as quoted from Daniel 8:25, literal translation from the Hebrew Masoretic text)
28. Walvoord, *Major Bible Prophecies*, p. 351
29. Lindsey, *Planet Earth: The Final Chapter*, p. 160
30. LaHaye and Jenkins, p. 122

31. Thomas Ice & Timothy Demy, *The Truth About the Last Days' Temple*, Harvest House, 1997, p.29
32. Modern Attempts to Revive the Sanhedrin. Assessed at:
    http://en.wikipedia.org/Modern_attempts_to_revive_the_Sanhedrin#_note-15
33. Irvin Baxter, "Religion and Politics," End Times Ministry, Radio Broadcast, Garland, Texas, October 18, 2006
34. Walvoord and Zuck, *N.T.*, p. 959
35. Missler and Eastman, p. 321
36. William M. Alnor, *UFOs in the New Age*, Grand Rapids, MI: Baker Book House, 1992, p. 34
37. Ibid, p. 205
38. John Mack, *Abductions*, Ballantine Books, 1994, p. 411
39. Missler and Eastman, p. 259
40. Ibid, p. 259
41. Ibid, p. 260
42. Ibid, p. 261
43. Ibid, p. 275
44. Ibid, p. 276
45. Walvoord and Zuck, N.T., p. 948
46. Joel Rosenberg, *Epicenter*, Tyndale House Publishers, Inc., Illinois, 2006, pp. 53-54
47. Ibid, p. 60; (quoting *The Great Treasure Hunt,* by James Spillman and son, Steven Spillman. See *Breaking the Treasure Code: The Hunt for Israel's Oil*, True Potential Publishing, Medford, Oregon, 2005; original copyright 1981), pp. 3-4
48. Rosenberg, p. 57
49. Ibid, pp. 57-58
50. William A. Orme Jr., "Gas Deposits off Israel and Gaza Opening Vision of Joint Ventures," *New York Times*, September 15, 2000
51. Rosenberg, pp. 5-6 (quoting William A. Orme Jr., "Arafat Hails Big Gas Find off the Coast of Gaza Strip," *New York Times*, September 28, 2000)
52. Rosenberg, p. 63; Philip Mandelker, personal interview with Joel Rosenberg
53. Rosenberg, p. 60
54. Ibid, p. 56 (quoting Ross Dunn, "Israel Geologist Drills for Oil Based on Biblical Guidance," VOA/Israel Fax, November 20, 2002)
55. Rosenberg, p. 57; (quote within: "Oil Traces Found East of Kfar Sava," Haaretz, Sep. 12, 2003)
56. Associated Press, "Israel Oil Company Claims Oil Find Valued at $6 Billion," May 4, 2004
57. Rosenberg, p. 58; (quoting "Moses' Oily Blessing," *The Economist*, June 18, 2005)
58. Rosenberg, p. 59
59. Ibid, p. 61-62
60. Ibid, p. 62
61. Conde Nast Portfolio, "Drilling for God" by Gabriel Sherman, October 2007, p. 98
62. Ibid.
63. Rosenberg, p. 62
64. Ibid, p. 62
65. Ibid, p. 63
66. Ibid, p. 64
67. Ibid.
68. Walvoord, *Major Bible Prophecies*, pp. 329-330
69. Lindsey, *Planet Earth: The Final Chapter*, p. 180
70. Simmons, *Prophecy*, pp. 161-162.
71. Lindsey, *Planet Earth: The Final Chapter*, p. 180

72. *Dallas Morning News*, January 1, 2000, p. 1A

73. Ibid, p. 29A

74. Lindsey, *Planet Earth: The Final Chapter*, p. 213

75. Ibid, p. 227

76. Simmons, pp. 94-95

77. Ibid, p. 95

78. Pentecost, *Things to Come*, p. 360

79. Lindsey, *Planet Earth: The Final Chapter*, p. 200

80. Simmons, p. 104

81. Lindsey, *Planet Earth: The Final Chapter*, p. 208

82. Ibid, p. 226

83. Walvoord and Zuck, *N.T. New Testament*, p. 952

84. Lindsey, *Planet Earth: The Final Chapter*, p. 234

85. Simmons, p. 110

86. Lindsey, *Planet Earth: The Final Chapter*, p. 240

87. Walvoord and Zuck, *N.T.*, p. 953

88. Simmons, p. 113

89. Lalonde, *2000 AD*, p. 174

90. Irvin Baxter, End Time Ministries, Broadcast, October 30, 2006

91. Greg Jacobson, "Technology Revolution Underway," Chain Drug Review, October 22, 2001

92. Gary Kau, Hope for the World Update, "The Total Information Society," Spring 2005, p. 5

93. US General Accounting Office, Technology Assessment: Using Biometrics for Border Security (GAO-03-174, November, 2002 p. 4)

94. Gary Kau, Hope for the World Update, "The Total Information Society," Spring 2005, p. 5.

95. Ibid, p. 5.

96. Ibid.

97. Accessed at: http://www.tarrantcounty.com/esheriff/cwp/view.asp?a=792&q=437447&esheriffNav=|

98. Walvoord and Zuck, *N.T.*, p. 963

99. Pentecost, *Things to Come*, p. 337

100. Ibid.

101. Lindsey, *Planet Earth: The Final Chapter*, p. 220

102. Ibid, p. 244

103. Ibid, p. 246

104. Walvoord and Zuck, *N.T.*, p. 953

105. Simmons, p. 144

106. Tim LaHaye and Jerry Jenkins, *Are We Living in the End Times?*, Wheaton, Illinois: Tyndale House Publishers, 1999, pp. 207-208

107. Simmons, p. 149

108. Ibid, pp. 208-209

109. Accessed at: http://www.endtime.cour/special page. asp? Page ID=20

110. Lindsey, *Planet Earth: The Final Chapter*, p. 261

111. Missler and Eastman, p. 261

112. Ibid, p. 261

113. Lindsey, *Planet Earth: The Final Chapter*, p. 279

114. Walvoord and Zuck, *N.T.*, p. 968

115. Simmons, p. 152

116. C.S. Lewis, *Mere Christianity*, Macmillan, 1947, p. 66

117. C.S. Lewis, *Mere Christianity*, Macmillan, 1947, p. 56

Appendix A

1. Chuck Missler and Mark Eastman, *Alien Encounters*, Koinonia House, 1997, p. 145
2. Hal Lindsey, *Apocalypse Code*, Western Front Ltd., 1997, p. 209
3. IBID
4. Neil T. Anderson, *The Bondage Breaker*, Harvest House Publishers, 1990, p. 32
5. IBID, p. 122
6. Missler and Eastman, p. 149
7. IBID, p. 323
8. *Denton Record Chronicle*, Friday, October 22, 1999, "Denton Unitarian Church Lands Fifty Years Milestone," p. 1B
9. James Redfield, *The Celestine Prophecy*, Warner Books, 1993, p. 24
10. Barbara Hubbard, *The Revelation*, Nataraj Publishing, 1995, p. 192
11. IBID, p. 15
12. IBID, p. 187
13. Peter and Paul Lalonde, *2000 AD*, Thomas Nelson, 1997, p. 53
14. Neil T. Anderson, p. 80
15. William M. Alnor, *UFOs in the New Age*, Baker Book House, 1992, pp. 53-54
16. Hubbard, p. 271
17. Lalonde, p. 154
18. Missler and Eastman, p. 302
19. IBID, p. 145

Appendix B

1. Missler and Eastman, p. 12 (sources include: Brit Elders, Connecting *Link* magazine, Issue 27, Spring 1995, p. 92; La Presna, January 2, 1992; and Voyagers of the Sixth Sun, produced by Genesis III)
2. Missler and Eastman, p. 14
3. Missler and Eastman, p. 15 (quoting *UFO Reality* February/March, 1997, Issue 6, p. 10)
4. Missler and Eastman, p. 15 (quoting *UFO Reality* February/March, 1997, Issue 6, p. 11)
5. *The Plain Dealer* newspaper, March 31, 1996. Plain Dealer Publishing Co., p. 1F
6. Missler and Eastman, pp. 55-56
7. IBID, p. 56. As obtained from Lawrence Fawcett and Barry J. Greenwood, *Clear Intent: The Government Coverup of the UFO Experience*, Prentice Hall, 1984
8. Missler and Eastman, p. 32
9. Nature, November 12, 1981; 294: 105
10. Missler and Eastman, p. 129
11. IBID, p. 134
12. Peter and Paul Lalonde, *2000 AD*, Thomas Nelson, 1997, p. 75
13. Missler and Eastman, pp. 106-107 and Jim Simmons, *The Last Hour: Prophecy, World views, and UFOs*, Fairway Press, Lima, Ohio, 2001, p. 138
14. Missler and Eastman, p. 52

15. IBID, p. 95
16. IBID, pp. 119-120
17. Paul Davies, *God and the New Physics*, Simon and Schuster, 1983, p. 119
18. William M. Alnor, *UFOs in the New Age*, Baker Book House, 1993, p. 237 (quoting Mark Albrecht and Brooks Alexander, "UFOs: Is Science Fiction Coming True?" SCP Journal 1, 1977, pp. 21-22)
19. Missler and Eastman, p. 86 (quoting Edwin A. Abbott, 1836-1926, a distinguished clergyman, who wrote *Flatland* in 1884, an allegorical approach to dimensionality).
20. Missler and Eastman, p. 86
21. Paul Davies, *God and the New Physics*, Simon and Schuster, 1983, p. 102
22. IBID, p. 101
23. IBID, p. 100
24. IBID, pp. 133-134
25. IBID, p. 210
26. Hugh Ross, Ph.D., *Beyond the Cosmos*, Nav Press, 1999, p. 51
27. IBID, p. 51
28. IBID, p. 52
29. Alnor, pp. 53-54
30. IBID, p. 14
31. IBID, p. 15
32. Missler and Eastman, p. 187
33. Alnor, p. 42-43 (quoting Stuart Goldman, unpublished manuscript on Whitney Streiber on file, cited in Alnor, "UFO Cults...")
34. Lalonde, p. 67
35. Bible references declaring the occult wrong: Deut. 18:10-11; Isaiah 47:9-13; Lev. 19:31; Isaiah 8:19; and 2 Cor. 11:14-15. These references include: witchcraft, astrology, mediums-channeling, and white magic. Also, the Book of Hosea is about Israel's spiritual adultery through idolatry.
36. Lalonde, p. 54
37. James Redfield, *The Celestine Prophecy*, Warner Books, 1993, p. 242
38. Barbara Hubbard, *The Revelation*, Nataraj Publishing, 1995, p. 271
39. Alnor, p. 55
40. Ruth Montgomery, *Ruth Montgomery: Herald of the New Age*, Doubleday, 1986, p. 269
41. Frank Stranges, *Stranger at the Pentagon*, Inner Light Publications, 1991, p. 125
42. Missler and Eastman, p. 187
43. Hubbard, p. 197
44. Missler and Eastman, p. 256
45. IBID, p. 199

www.ingramcontent.com/pod-product-compliance
Lightning Source LLC
Chambersburg PA
CBHW062200270326
41930CB00009B/1595